YEARNING
TO BELONG

Advance Praise for Yearning to Belong

This book presents — for the first time in a single volume — fascinating historical and ethnographic details of five hybrid ethnic minorities in Peninsula Malaysia. Written with sensitivity and insight towards both minorities and the larger communities, this book is an outstanding contribution to inter-ethnic understanding, to ethnic studies in general, and minority studies in particular. For Malaysian Studies enthusiasts this is a must read.

Professor Shamsul A.B.
Founding Director, Institute of Ethnic Studies,
Universiti Kebangsaan Malaysia, and
Member, International Advisory Board,
ISEAS–Yusof Ishak Institute, Singapore

Once I started reading this book I didn't want to stop! It's a lovely book. Pillai's skills of story-telling and clarity of expression make the book accessible to a broad popular audience, while the facts and insights from interviews and local documents are an original contribution to scholarship. The five case-studies also make this publication distinctive.

Charles Hirschman
Boeing International Professor of Sociology, University of Washington, and
Fulbright Visiting Professor, University of Malaya, 2012–13

For decades — beginning long before Independence in 1957 — governments and academic analysts have tended to configure Malaya/Malaysia in terms of a simplistic race paradigm: Malay/Chinese/Indian. This very readable book reaches beyond that paradigm, demonstrating how it has distorted reality. In one perceptive and sensitive chapter after another Pillai discloses the ethnic complexity of Malaysia, and in doing so makes the country all the more interesting to the general reader as well as the professional sociologist.

Anthony Milner
Tun Hussein Onn Chair, ISIS Malaysia (2014–15);
Co-editor, Transforming Malaysia: Dominant and
Competing Paradigms (ISEAS, 2014);
Basham Professor of Asian History, The Australian National University

This is a work that came from the heart and that is why it carries the colour and warmth of its birth place. Relying on history and narratives, Patrick Pillai paints a beautiful picture of the many cultural streams that contributed to Malaysia's dazzling diversity. But his work is not just a nostalgic yearning for a more harmonious society as in the past. There is a powerful message for greater understanding of our unacknowledged commonalities and more tolerance and acceptance of our differences.

Professor Dr Shad Saleem Faruqi
Emeritus Professor of Law, UiTM (Malaysia)

The **ISEAS–Yusof Ishak Institute** (formerly Institute of Southeast Asian Studies) was established as an autonomous organization in 1968. It is a regional centre dedicated to the study of socio-political, security and economic trends and developments in Southeast Asia and its wider geostrategic and economic environment. The Institute's research programmes are the Regional Economic Studies (RES, including ASEAN and APEC), Regional Strategic and Political Studies (RSPS), and Regional Social and Cultural Studies (RSCS).

ISEAS Publishing, an established academic press, has issued more than 2,000 books and journals. It is the largest scholarly publisher of research about Southeast Asia from within the region. ISEAS Publishing works with many other academic and trade publishers and distributors to disseminate important research and analyses from and about Southeast Asia to the rest of the world.

YEARNING TO BELONG

Malaysia's Indian Muslims, Chitties,
Portuguese Eurasians, Peranakan Chinese
and Baweanese

PATRICK PILLAI

ISEAS YUSOF ISHAK
INSTITUTE

First published in Singapore in 2015 by
ISEAS Publishing
30 Heng Mui Keng Terrace
Singapore 119614

E-mail: publish@iseas.edu.sg
Website: <http://bookshop.iseas.edu.sg>

The responsibility for facts and opinions in this publication rests exclusively with the author and his interpretations do not necessarily reflect the views or the policy of the publisher or its supporters.

ISEAS Library Cataloguing-in-Publication Data

Pillai, Patrick.
    Yearning to Belong : Malaysia's Indian Muslims, Chitties, Portuguese Eurasians, Peranakan Chinese and Baweanese.
    1. Ethnology—Malaysia.
    2. Ethnicity—Malaysia.
    3. Malaysia—Social life and customs.
    4. Indians (Asian people)—Malaysia—Religion.
    5. Indians (Asian people)—Malaysia—Ethnic identity.
    6. Portuguese—Malaysia—Ethnic identity.
    7. Chinese—Malaysia—Ethnic identity.
    8. Chinese—Malaysia.
    9. Boyanese (Indonesian people)—Malaysia—Cultural assimilation.
    I. Title.
DS595 P65   2015

ISBN 978-981-4519-67-0 (soft cover)
ISBN 978-981-4519-68-7 (e-book, PDF)

Photo credits:
Cover photographs are from the author's collection.

Typeset by Superskill Graphics Pte Ltd
Printed in Singapore by Markono Print Media Pte Ltd

For K K

CONTENTS

LIST OF FIGURES AND TABLES

FOREWORD

This book presents — for the first time in a single volume — fascinating historical and ethnographic details of five hybrid ethnic minorities in Peninsula Malaysia. They comprise Penang's Indian Muslims, Malacca's Chitties and Portuguese Eurasians, Trengganu's Peranakan Chinese, and the Baweanese, who are of Indonesian origin. The Baweanese chapter, in particular, stands out as a significant contribution to the literature on Peranakan-types in the Malay world.

Combining the acuity of a scholar with the skills of a journalist, Patrick Pillai leads us on an intriguing journey, tracing how migration histories, occupations and residential locations facilitated interaction and acculturation.

His aim is to highlight Malaysia's rich diversity, and to discover how the experiences of these Peranakan-type communities can provide useful lessons in cultural intermingling, sharing and ethnic harmony. He finds that working, living and schooling together are essential prerequisites, as is proficiency in Malay, which bridges and bonds diverse ethnic groups.

However his fieldwork indicates that acculturation is a necessary but insufficient prerequisite to fostering inter-ethnic harmony; a sense of belonging is equally vital. Such inclusiveness, he argues, is best achieved through multi-ethnic politics and policies consonant with affirmative action. He concludes with a plea for inter-cultural dialogue to cultivate greater understanding, empathy and trust between diverse ethnic and religious groups.

Written with sensitivity and insight towards both minorities and the larger communities, this book is an outstanding contribution to inter-ethnic understanding, to ethnic studies in general, and minority studies in particular. For Malaysian Studies enthusiasts this is a must read.

Shamsul A.B.
Distinguished Professor and Founding Director,
Institute of Ethnic Studies, Universiti Kebangsaan Malaysia
and
Member, International Advisory Board,
ISEAS–Yusof Ishak Institute, Singapore

PREFACE

WHY I WROTE THIS BOOK

This book is inspired by my childhood experiences in the diverse cultural milieu of old Malacca. I grew up in Bandar Hilir, near the seaside fronting the Straits which gave birth to its great cosmopolitan port. My neighbours and playmates included Peranakan Chinese, Portuguese and Dutch Eurasians. We spoke Malay, and our playground was the breezy seaside *padang* (field) near the town centre. A tourist would have had a hard time figuring us out; there were Malay-looking boys with *vibhuti* on their foreheads, Indians buying Malay-style cakes from a Chinese, and Portuguese Eurasian, Peranakan Chinese and Peranakan Indian mothers in Malay-style *kebaya* and *kerongsang*. Yet we were doing just what Malaccans had done for centuries in this multi-ethnic port-city — revelling in its rich hybrid culture which had seeped through porous ethnic borders.

I had multiple identities. I was Malayan, Malay-speaking, Malaccan, Ceylonese Tamil and Catholic. When firecrackers exploded non-stop one night in 1963 I realized I had also became Malaysian. But there were no contradictions between the many worlds I inhabited. My religious values were universal and perennial, but my cultural boundaries were permeable. For me this was so natural that I simply never thought about it.

However I soon came to realize that my Malacca childhood had insulated me from the harsh realities of my own country. During two careers spanning thirty years, first as a journalist and later as a migration researcher, I travelled to various parts of the country and met Malaysians of many ethnic backgrounds. While I was impressed by high economic growth, I was distressed by the way ethnic ideology and politics was engendering a hardening of cultural boundaries, particularly between Malays, Chinese and Indians. Worse, there was a lack of creative and concerted attempts to counter these divisive trends by highlighting our shared histories and cultures, common universal spiritual values and our interlinked future.

The gap between economic growth and ethnic harmony is particularly high in Malaysia. This is despite the fact that affirmative action via the New Economic Policy (NEP), the main thrust of Malaysian nation-building since 1970, has in many ways made Malaysia a model multi-ethnic developing society. Professor Donald Snodgrass, a development economist who helped formulate the NEP, once told me that "we (at Harvard) have not come across a single developing multi-ethnic society on the entire planet which has survived and thrived after independence as Malaysia has done" (Personal communication). Even today Malaysia remains the only post-colonial multi-ethnic country which has successfully transformed a wide swathe of its once poverty-stricken indigenous majority from rural-agricultural to urban-industrial and created a broad middle class within one generation.

However in multi-ethnic societies, growth and inter-ethnic wealth redistribution alone are no guarantees of ethnic harmony; people can still be driven apart by ethnic and religious-based politics. As a bulwark against such divisive forces, Malaysia needs to build strong bridges of understanding, appreciation and empathy between people of varied cultures and faiths. Knowledge of our shared histories, rich diversity and overlapping identities can imbue a sense of solidarity to counter the primal pull of ethnic politics. This book is a modest contribution to that goal.

My main motivation in writing this book was to trace the process through which long-settled ethnic minorities acculturated without being assimilated. I was curious about how and why the so-called "hard" cultural boundaries we see today were "soft" in the past, at least among the ethnic minorities of my Malacca childhood. I learnt that this was related to their heterogeneity, mixed ancestry, and cultural sharing — features shared by the three main ethnic groups — but also to their smaller numbers and longer periods of interaction and intermingling. In the process of researching this book however, I also discovered something unexpected — that some among these minorities are deeply anxious about their identity and their future, and pine for a State-recognized indigenous *bumiputera* identity. The implications of this trend for ethnic relations are also discussed in this book.

METHODOLOGY AND LIMITATIONS

This work is based on both primary and secondary research. In addition to consulting academic publications and local history accounts, I conducted fieldwork over three years (2008–11), covering five communities selected on the basis of their long settlement, culturally hybrid character and geographical spread. This encompassed Penang (Indian Muslims), Malacca (Chitties/Peranakan Indians and Portuguese Eurasians), Terengganu (Peranakan Chinese) and Selangor (Baweanese). For the Baweanese chapter, the historical background and life histories are based on my PhD (Pillai 2005), updated with fieldwork for this book in 2010 and 2011.

I talked directly to people on the ground. I met and spoke to community leaders, local historians and ordinary people using structured and unstructured interviews and informal conversations, some of which led to the writing of concise life histories. Pseudonyms were used in cases where informants and respondents requested privacy. I also drew from "participant observation" in major cultural and religious events and visits to homes.

No quantitative surveys were carried out. The views in this book represent those of the people I spoke to and are an indication of the experiences and perceptions of a cross-section in each community, often the less skilled and less mobile segments still living in traditional ethnic spaces. In any case conceptions of ethnicity and identity are fluid and flexible, and vary over time, place and situations, especially in a society where "race" is the dominating discourse.

There are other limitations. Each community is so rich and complex that it is impossible to fully cover all issues thoroughly in a single chapter; there are many PhD's waiting to be written on each group. Chapter contents also vary according to information access. The Peranakan Chinese of Malacca and Penang were left out because there are several publications on them. The same applies to the Peninsular Malaysia's Orang Asli. It must also be emphasized that this book covers five groups in Peninsular Malaysia only. Regretfully, Sabah and Sarawak, which have a large number of highly diverse ethnic minorities, have been excluded; the groups there are far more diverse and complex and demand specialist knowledge which is beyond the scope of this book.

SOME TERMS AND DEFINITIONS

An "ethnic group" shares a collective history and identity, with their own culture, beliefs and language; membership is acquired through birth, marriage or other socially sanctioned routes. "Race" is a socially constructed category, a scientifically discredited term once used to describe biologically distinct groups with unchangeable natures. "Ethnic group" is thus not synonymous with "race". (David and Julia Jary 1995, pp. 205, 540).

The term "Malay" is constitutionally defined as a person who is Muslim, speaks Malay, and practises Malay customs.[1] *Bumiputera*, a political term of Sanskrit origin meaning "sons of the soil", was introduced after the formation of Malaysia in 1963 to encompass Malays and other indigenous communities in the Peninsular Malaysia, Sabah and Sarawak. Thus all Malay-Muslims are *bumiputera* but not all *bumiputera* are Malay-Muslims, especially in Sabah and Sarawak, where many are Christians. Three of the five ethnic minorities discussed in this book — Indian Muslims, Baweanese and Portuguese Eurasians — have acquired full or partial *bumiputera* status from the government. The Peranakan Indians have begun articulating requests for similar recognition, but not the Peranakan Chinese of Terengganu.

"Acculturation" and "assimilation" demand clarification since both terms are often poorly defined and used loosely and interchangeably. In fact they are specific terms with particular meanings. Acculturation refers to cultural change in the direction of another ethnic group, while assimilation is the adoption of the ethnic identity of another group, thus losing one's original identity. Acculturation can be mutual while assimilation is a one way process (Tan 1984, p. 190). In acculturation contact may have distinct results such as the borrowing of certain traits by one culture from another, or the relative fusion of separate cultures (*The Columbia Electronic Encyclopaedia*, 6th ed. 2007).

Assimilation has also been defined as the process whereby individuals or groups of differing ethnic heritage are absorbed into the dominant culture of a society. The process of assimilating involves taking on the traits of the dominant culture to such a degree that the assimilating group becomes socially indistinguishable from other members of the society. As such, assimilation is the most extreme form of acculturation (Encyclopaedia Britannica 2011).

The term "Peranakan" is a Malay word which means "local-born people" and often refers to an ethnic minority living in a Malay environment (Tan 2002, p. 148). The Peranakan Chinese for example, may be loosely defined as Malay-speaking Chinese who show a significantly high level of acculturation but no sign of eventual assimilation.[2] Fieldwork for this book indicates that the degree of acculturation also varies with the length of stay in Malaysia, occupation, residential location, education and class. Long stays, common occupations and shared residential locations and schools tend to increase the degree of interethnic interaction and are a prerequisite — though not a cause — of acculturation.

Hybridity refers to "dynamic mixed cultures" (Cohen and Kennedy 2000, p. 377), a common feature of archipelagic Southeast Asia and the Caribbean, where maritime cultures have long fostered inter-ethnic interaction, and where mixed ancestry and heterogeneity is the norm rather than the exception. In contrast to colonial racial ideology, hybridity in Southeast Asia is not therefore seen in negative terms. In fact hybridity is also defined by some scholars as a form of liminal or in-between space which is an antidote to colonial essentialism; the hybrid has the ability to transverse several cultures and to "translate, negotiate and mediate affinity and difference" (Meredith 1998, p. 3, in discussing Bhabha 1994, 1996).

Discussion of the immigration history of various ethnic groups is done merely for purposes of analysis and understanding, and is not meant to demean them or question their background or loyalty. The forefathers of most minorities originated from immigrant groups, but their descendants were born and have lived in Malaysia; they are full-fledged Malaysians and Malaysia is their home.

Some pre-war names have been retained, especially historical and geographical place-names. To ensure simplicity no honorifics have been used; no disrespect is intended towards anyone.

MALAYSIA'S POPULATION AND ETHNIC COMPOSITION

In 2013 Malaysia had 27 million citizens comprising Malays (55 per cent), Other *bumiputeras* (13 per cent), Chinese (24 per cent), Indians (7 per cent) and Others (1 per cent). In Peninsular Malaysia, Malays are predominant, comprising 66 per cent of citizens. Sabah and Sarawak, each with 2.5 million citizens, are far more diverse, with Kadazan-Dusun being the single largest group in Sabah, and Ibans being the single largest community in Sarawak. Malaysia employs 2.5 million documented non-citizens, a million of whom live in Sabah (Department of Statistics 2014). Islam is the most widely professed religion in Malaysia (61.3 per cent), followed by Buddhism (19.8 per cent), Christianity (9.2 per cent) and Hinduism (6.3 per cent) (Population and Housing Census, Department of Statistics 2010).

Notes

1. A fourth but little-known prerequisite of being Malay is that the person must have local Malaysian/Singapore "roots" or patriality. According to Article 160(2) of the Malaysian Constitution, to be recognized as a Malay the person should also be — before Merdeka Day (31 August 1957) — born in the Federation or Singapore, or have a parent born in the Federation or Singapore, or is on that day domiciled in the Federation or Singapore, or is the issue of such a person. [I am grateful to Emeritus Professor Shad Saleem Faruqi of UiTm for pointing this out (Interview, Monday, 18 May 2015).]
2. According to Tan, the preconditions for the emergence of Peranakans include inter-ethnic interaction, Malay fluency and a "religious barrier" (Tan 1984, pp. 192, 195–99), since conversion to Islam is a legal prerequisite to marrying a Malay-Muslim in Malaysia, and eventually leads to assimilation.

ACKNOWLEDGEMENTS

I used to wonder why the acknowledgements sections of many books were so long. Now I know why. Researching and writing a book is both an individual and shared effort, involving debts to many people. In my case many wonderful souls helped and nourished me along the journey. During fieldwork for this book many ordinary people whom I met at community events and random home visits were very generous with their time. Community leaders, some of whom requested anonymity, also provided insights and introduced me to a range of useful contacts and informants. Virtually everyone was delighted to help, indicating perhaps how proud Malaysians are about their diversity. Below is a list of just some of the many people who assisted me.

For insights about the Indian Muslim community, I wish to thank Abdur-Razzaq Lubis, Asraf Fazal, A.V.M Haja, Dr Mohamed Iqbal, Fatimah Hassan, Fidha Ulla, Haja Mohideen, Himanshu Bhatt, Ibrahim Vengai, Khoo Salmah Nasution, Mydin Sultan, Najmudeen Kader, SM Mohamed Idris, Professor Yousof Ghulam-Sarwar and the late Meera Nagore.

For help in understanding the Peranakan Indians of Malacca, I am grateful to Madam Meenachi, K. Narayanasamy, Nadarajan Raja, K. Arunasalam Pillay, S.K. Pillay, Sithambaram Pillay, Amu Pillay, K. Shanmugan Rajan and his family, and many other villagers, including several families who had me over for coffee and cakes.

For assistance with the Portuguese Eurasian community I wish to particularly thank Michael Barneji, Martin Carvalho, Percy D'Cruz, Peter Gomez, Joseph Sta Maria, Dr Margaret Sarkissian, Michael Singho, Philomena Singho, Horace Sta Maria and Sara Sta Maria.

My understanding of the Peranakan-type Chinese in Terengganu was enriched by Chia Ban Hock, Koo Ong Jin, Lua Yik Hor and their families,

Tan Teng Hong, Professor Tan Chee Beng, Tan Teng Liang, Madam Wee Kwee Siew, Madam Wee Kim Beng and a number of Kampung Tirok and Kuala Terengganu residents.

My knowledge of the Baweanese community deepened because many Indonesian immigrants willingly shared their life-histories. Accounts from five of them — Alim, Azmi, Baharuddin, Dzulfilki, Hamzah and Lokman — are used in this book. (Pseudonyms have been used for all Indonesian respondents.) Alim has not only been a rich source of information and insights for more than a decade, but also arranged for a group interview/ discussion with a group of community leaders in Gombak in late 2011. I would also like to thank the Kampung Sungei Kayu Ara community leaders, survey participants, and other immigrants who were interviewed. My PhD supervisor Professor K.S. Jomo expertly guided me on a multi-disciplinary topic, while my co-supervisors Dr Chan Kok Eng and Richard Dorall provided crucial guidance and encouragement, especially in the early stages. The feedback from examiners Professor Lee Boon Thong, Professor Graeme Hugo and Dr Diana Wong are also gratefully acknowledged. I am also thankful to the University of Malaya for permission to publish parts of my thesis.

I thank the ISEAS–Yusof Ishak Institute in Singapore for a Visiting Fellowship which supported this project, and especially the then Director Mr K. Kesavapany for his trust and patience. The well-stocked ISEAS library was indispensable, as was feedback from the institute's outstanding Malaysian, regional and international scholars. I am particularly grateful to ISEAS International Advisory Board member and Founder-Director of Malaysia's Institute of Ethnic Studies, Professor A.B. Shamsul, for his encouragement, suggestions, and for writing the foreword to this book. I also enjoyed many stimulating discussions with Dr Lee Hock Guan and Dr Johan Saravanamuttu of ISEAS. A special thanks to Rahilah Yusuf of ISEAS Publishing for taking the book through to publication.

In Malaysia I had valuable feedback on the book drafts from Abdur-Razzaq Lubis, Khoo Salmah Nasution, Professor Charles Hirschman, Dr Sumit Mandal, Philip Mathews, Lim Siang Jin, Shahriman Lockman and a good friend, the late Philip Lim Chin Guan. I am very grateful to all of them.

This book is also inspired by the writings of the Malaysian academic Dr Farish Noor who has passionately argued about the need to highlight Malaysia's diversity, and by the work of the prolific Professor Chandra

Muzaffar of 1Malaysia Foundation, who has for many years championed the need for inter-ethnic and inter-religious dialogue based on universal values, a clearer appreciation of Malaysia's history, and mutual empathy.

In addition, I owe a debt of gratitude to two towering Malaysians who are no longer with us. One is Dr Noordin Sopiee who was Chairman of Malaysia's Institute of Strategic and International Studies (ISIS). He recruited me, first a journalist with the *New Straits Times* and later as a researcher at ISIS, where he facilitated the completion of my doctorate. Dr Noordin was a sincere and fervent advocate of "Bangsa Malaysia" (Malaysian nationality) outlined in Malaysia's "Vision 2020" ideal of a mature, developed society. The other is Professor Syed Hussein Alatas, a committed intellectual and deeply caring Malaysian whom I first met as a journalist in 1988. He constantly urged me to research, write and find my voice.

Finally, I must thank my family and friends for their support over the years. My deepest appreciation to Janet Pillai in Penang, Dr Kamala Lingam in Malacca, and Joseph Gomez, Dr Dennis Hew, Dr Mely Caballero-Anthony, Edmund Rajendra and Suzanne Xavier in Singapore for hospitality during outstation work trips. I am also beholden to Professor Kosaku Yoshino, Anis Taufik, Su Wan Fern, Victor Vasu, Latifah Abdullah, Chak Choy Sim, Dr Anwar Fazal and the late Malathy Malapermal — who drew the maps — for their friendships and assistance. A special thanks to Dr Kenneth James, Daniel Chan, Mohd Souffi Mohd Radzi and Professor Shad Saleem Faruqi for reviewing the final drafts. I am also grateful to Professor Shad for permission to publish, as an appendix, his recent paper on ethnic harmony. Last but not least I thank my family, particularly my wife Carmel, and my children Anand and Kristine, whose constant love and support saw this work through to completion.

While I have received inspiration and assistance from many people, I take full responsibility for the contents of this book. The views here do not reflect those of any persons or institutions mentioned above; rather it presents my own findings and views based on primary fieldwork, secondary research, and my three decades of experience as a Malaysian journalist and policy researcher.

INTRODUCTION

ABOUT THIS BOOK

Malaysia is among the most ethnically diverse and culturally rich nations on earth. Yet much of its cultural wealth lies buried beneath the rubric of its main Malay, Chinese and Indian "race" categories; the dazzling diversity within and outside these groups remains largely unexplored. In this book I uncover some of this fascinating diversity through the stories of five ethnic minorities: the Tamil Muslims of Penang, the Portuguese Eurasians and Chitty of Malacca, the Peranakan Chinese of Terengganu and the Baweanese of Selangor.

The book outlines their shared histories and overlapping identities by examining their migration patterns, occupations, locations, religious traditions and — where relevant — their built-heritage, language, cuisine, dress and music. To what extent have they maintained their identities, or been transformed by inter-ethnic interaction, acculturation and assimilation? How are they affected by social change, inter-marriage and out-migration? How do they harness their multiple identities? What of their futures? What lessons do these hybrid groups offer for inter-ethnic relations and nation-building today? These are some questions this book attempts to answer.

This publication will interest not only laymen, but also scholars, students and visitors interested in culture, ethnicity, heritage and migration in Malaysia and the region. There is little published, discussed and debated about these groups, which by virtue of their smaller numbers and relatively weaker political and economic power are overshadowed by larger communities. While there have been articles, chapters, and in recent years some books on individual groups, there are very few publications introducing a range of ethnic minorities in one volume, allowing for an analysis of common issues.

Most previous work comprises historical monographs or specialized cultural, anthropological and migration studies. There are also a few journal publications, seminar papers and magazine and newspaper articles on their language, music, culture, and performing arts. This book draws on these works to provide a historical and cultural backdrop, but relies on original fieldwork including interviews, personal profiles and local histories from community leaders and ordinary people to link broader historical and cultural trends to experiences and perceptions at group and individual level. In other words, it attempts to give voice to people, and to discuss their past and future as they understand and experience it.

The historical backdrop on Penang's Indian Muslims is drawn from monographs by the Penang-based historian and heritage expert Salmah Khoo (2001a, 2001b, 2009) and scholars Narayanan (2006), Fujimoto (1989), Shankar (2001) and Amrith (2009). The academic Ghulam-Sarwar's thoughtful paper (2001) reminds us of the cultural impact of South Asia on the Peninsula, while research by the once Penang-based anthropologist Judith Nagata (1974, 2006) throws light on their local history, composition and identity dilemmas. A coffee-table book on the Jawi Peranakan by Halimah and Zainab (2004) provides useful information on prominent Malays with Jawi Peranakan roots.

Not much has been published on Malacca's Peranakan Indians. Australian anthropologist David Mearns book (1995) — based on his doctoral thesis — analyses their religion and social identity, while Singaporean historian S. Dhoraisingam's coffee-table publication (2006) and articles traces the community's origins, culture and religious rituals. K. Narinasamy's sociology undergraduate thesis, completed in the 1960s and published as a book chapter in 1983, is also informative.

There are relatively more publications on the Malacca Portuguese Eurasians. A lucid summary of their complex cultural origins is found in anthropologist Margaret Sarkissian's outstanding book (2000) on their performing tradition, while broader historical accounts are provided by Goh (2002), Muzzi (2002) and Thomaz (2000). Reflective insider accounts of the community's struggle to preserve their land and culture are found in booklets and seminar papers by cultural activists Gerard Fernandis (1995, 2000, 2003), Bernard Sta Maria (1979, 1982) (both now deceased) and his brother, community leader Joseph Sta Maria (1994, 1995, 2011). In addition there are journal articles and seminar papers on their culture, including family heritage, music, language and performing arts.

Unlike the Peranakan Chinese of Penang, Malacca and Singapore, very little is known and published on the Peranakan Chinese of Terengganu. American anthropologist Sharon Carstens has written about Chinese identities in Kelantan (1986, 2005), but the only available published work on Terengganu is a small ethnographic study of the Peranakan community in Kampung Tirok in Terengganu by Malaysian anthropologist Tan Chee Beng (2002). For this book, in addition to interviews, local histories have also been culled from publications of the Hokkein Association of Terengganu (2005), the Sam Poh Kong Temple Committee, and Wong and Liew (undated).

This book also recalls the story of the entry, settlement and assimilation of the Baweanese, a small, virtually unknown Indonesian ethnic group with a long history of immigration into Singapore and the Peninsula. There are no publications about them apart from some early work on their migration patterns by the Dutch scholar Vredenbregt (1964), and two journal articles on their history and migration to Singapore and Malaysia by Baginda and Haji Fadzal (1967). A 1996 Harvard doctoral thesis by Singaporean anthropologist Mariam Ali provides a cultural interpretation of emigration from Bawean by explaining macro-level links between religious institutions, emigration networks and identity. In contrast this book examines the factors facilitating their immigration, acculturation and assimilation, based on the author's own PhD fieldwork (Pillai 2005) and follow-up research on the community in 2010 and 2011 in Malaysia.

This publication differs from previous specialized works in that it takes a multi-disciplinary approach, tracing how the cultural history of these groups — including their early migration, shared occupations, neighbourhoods, and interaction and inter-marriage — facilitated acculturation and assimilation. By relating their cultural history to conceptions of personal and group identity this work also contributes to a theoretical understanding of the complex dynamics of diversity and hybridity in a multi-ethnic society. Of particularly interest is the process through which hybrid groups attempt to harness their multiple identities, including an indigenous *bumiputera* identity, to gain cultural recognition and economic opportunity. In addition to examining factors facilitating immigration, acculturation and — where relevant — assimilation, the book discusses the cultural manifestations of acculturation as expressed in religion, language, cuisine, dress, architecture and the performing arts. The book concludes by discussing why and how these groups seek alternative ethnic routes, and its implications for ethnic relations.

DISCERNING DIVERSITY:
WHAT THEIR STORIES TELL US

These communities have at least three important lessons for Malaysians: they remind us of our long history of diversity, shared histories and cultures, and the need to overcome our fear of acculturation. At the same time their struggles to assert their social identities and be part of the national narrative underline the urgency of replacing "race"-based politics and policies with new approaches prioritizing universal human values and social justice.

These hybrid communities remind us that diversity has been a constant throughout the country's history. For centuries, long before colonialism sparked mass immigration, the Peninsula's strategic location and trade and resource networks resulted in cosmopolitan ports which became nodes for small but influential numbers of merchants and missionaries, sojourners and settlers of Indian, Middle-Eastern, Indonesian, and Chinese descent. Long settlement and sustained inter-ethnic interaction fostered acculturation, creating many hybrid groups.

Even today Malaysia's ethnic and cultural diversity continues to enrich, enliven and energize its spiritual, cultural and economic life, as it has for centuries. Embracing this diversity, divergence and difference demands a sympathetic understanding of the history, culture, anxieties and aspirations of its various groups. This book strives towards such understanding.

More importantly, the shared histories of these groups offer valuable lessons on how inter-ethnic harmony can be fostered today. Their past recalls a pre-colonial era when the colonial concept of "race" was non-existent and when trade, common occupations, shared spaces and schools led to organic and spontaneous intermingling between immigrant and indigenous groups. Most of these groups acculturated freely, absorbing elements of language, cuisine, dress, music, performing arts, architecture and even worship practices from each other, without being assimilated and without losing their own identities, particularly their religious values.

Today the hybrid heritage resulting from such cross-cultural fertilization remains, but the consciousness of its shared elements has been virtually forgotten. For example most Malaysians remain unaware of the Indian sub-continent's immense impact on the daily lives of Malaysians through its influences on concepts of royalty, protocol and customs, literature and language, drama and music. Similarly the Malay language is much more than the language of the Malays and the national language of all

Malaysians. It is the lingua franca of the region, and as a language of trade it has through the centuries absorbed not only Arabic, Sanskrit and Persian but also Portuguese, Tamil and Hokkien words.

Instances of such cross-cultural influence are seen most clearly in the everyday lives of minorities covered in this book. In one village in Terengganu in the Peninsula's east coast, visitors will not easily recognize the Chinese, who live in Malay-style houses, speak the Terengganu Malay dialect, wear the *sarong* and eat Malay food with their fingers. In Malacca a deeply religious Hindu community of Peranakan Indians — many of Malay-Chinese-Indian ancestry — pray in Malay and adopt some Chinese ancestor-worship practices. Interestingly, Malacca's long-settled Peranakan Chinese were the cultural intermediaries in the acculturation of these Peranakan Indians. Equally fascinating is the fact that the thousands of Indian Muslim *Mamak* restaurants that dot the country are powerful cultural mediators, serving hybrid dishes such as *pasembur* and *mamak mee* to a multi-ethnic clientele.

The point being made is that there is far more cross-cultural mingling, sharing and co-dependence among us than we care to recognize, admit or celebrate. This book traces the process of these inter-cultural interactions, their manifestations, and their meanings. The stories of these long-established hybrid groups also raise many questions relevant to ethnic relations in Malaysia.

Is a similar process of spontaneous and harmonious acculturation possible between larger groups today? Is it possible to acculturate without being assimilated? What are the preconditions for such acculturation? Why do Malaysians fear acculturation? What can we do to create conditions which will foster such acculturation, and can this by itself contribute to ethnic harmony? These are some issues discussed in this book. My hope is that by showing how some groups adapted and adjusted to each other without losing their own core values, this book will help more Malaysians embrace one another without fear.

1

"MAMAK" AND MALAYSIAN
The Indian Muslim Quest for Identity

INTRODUCTION

Heritage Heartland: Chulia Street, Penang

To understand the story of the Indian Muslims I travel to George Town, Penang, and head for Chulia Street where Indian Muslim immigrants have lived for generations. The town-bus driver is a middle-aged Penang Indian Muslim who, reflecting Penang's ethnic diversity, speaks to his passengers in Malay, English, Tamil and Hokkien. The area is dominated by jewellers, money-changers, wholesale book traders, restaurants and superb examples of South Indian Muslim architecture, including the Nagore Shrine (1801) and the mid-nineteenth century Noordin Tomb. But the heart and soul of the community is reflected in its beautiful two-century old Kapitan Kling Mosque on nearby Pitt Street.[1]

At the mosque entrance I am greeted by Akbar,[2] a twenty-two-year-old Indian Muslim mosque official who is a preacher by day and trader by night (Interview, 5 April 2008). He offers me respite from the intense heat with a glass of *susu bandung,* a refreshing concoction of rose syrup, milk and crushed ice. Urbane, self-confident and knowledgeable, he reveals that his father is an immigrant Indian Muslim, his mother Malay. "Do you see yourself as Indian Muslim, or Malay?" I ask. He replies immediately, but in a slow, deliberate fashion, as if to obliterate all other definitions, "I...am... a...Muslim." He appears to have solved that ambivalence — that inner tension which is often the lot of members of minorities who inhabit contested ethnic spaces — by defining himself in clear, unambiguous terms — in this case, purely as a Muslim rather than an Indian Muslim or Malay. He takes me on a tour of the mosque and invites me to observe the congregation in prayer. The diversity of its worshippers is striking — young and old, rich and poor, and from every corner of the Indian continent — but they all respond to the imam's call to prayer in harmony, as one community. It is a moving sight. Akbar hands me some reading material as I bid farewell. "Hope you find this interesting", he says, smiling.

As I continue walking down Pitt Street I notice a Chinese man praying to a Hindu deity at a tree-shrine. I pass the Taoist Goddess of Mercy Temple (1801), St George's Church (1818) and the Hindu Mariamman Temple (1833). The world's four major religions are represented on this one street.

Soon I am hungry, and follow my nose. I wander into a tiny Chinese coffeeshop located directly in front of the Hokkien Temple on Armenian Street. Outside the shop an old "*Mamak*" (Indian Muslim) hawker fries noodles over a trusty wok. *Mamak mee* (noodles) is a Penang specialty. Noodles are fried with onions, garlic, chilli, bean sprouts and an egg, garnished with fried crisps and a squeeze of lime. This Chinese dish, first adapted by Indian Muslims to cater to Malay customers, is now enjoyed by all ethnic groups throughout the country, and is a fine example of the hybrid cuisine that has developed in Penang over centuries.

I enjoy a plateful, and after lunch my mind returns to Akbar. His zealousness in trade and religion is part of an Indian link to the region which goes back thousands of years. His immigrant Indian Muslim father was merely following a well-trodden route long taken by Indians before him — first to Kedah and Malacca, and later to Penang. Today Penang has the oldest, largest, most diverse and vibrant Indian Muslim community in the country. Malaysia's Indian Muslims are enumerated as either Malays or Indians, and no accurate statistics are available on their numbers or socio-economic position. However community leaders estimate that Indian Muslims, most of whom are Tamils, comprise about 10 per cent or 200,000 of Malaysia's total Indian population of two million.[3] The community's past impact and current influence on Malaysian society and culture is best appreciated by examining its historical links to the Malay Peninsula.

SHARED HISTORIES: FACTORS FACILITATING ACCULTURATION AND ASSIMILATION

Pre-Colonial Indian Links: Kedah and Malacca

Early Indian influence extended to most of Southeast Asia, as evidenced by the huge temple complexes of Angkor (Cambodia), Pagan (Burma), Borobudur (Java) (Tate 2008, p. 4) and the first-century Bujang Valley civilization in Kedah. Peninsular Malaysia's strategic location amidst international trade routes resulted in cosmopolitan ports which became nodes — first for Hindu, then Buddhist and finally Muslim religious scholarship and influence (Ghulam-Sarwar 2001, pp. 1–2). Scholars have long known that from the third century, the region's main port was located in Kedah, and due to regular visits and settlement by Indian traders, it became the centre of the first Indian community in the Peninsula (Fujimoto 1989, pp. 10–13). However recent digs in Kedah's Bujang Valley have uncovered 1st century Sanskrit Pallava inscriptions and temples, a jetty and an iron smelter (Haslam 2010).[4]

More important than the physical evidence is the cultural impact of India. The sub-continent's influences on the region — including Malaysia — are clearly evident in the daily lives of people through the large number of Sanskrit words in local languages and Indian influences in concepts of royalty and protocol, customs, literature, drama and other art forms (Tate 2008, p. 4).

In the ninth and tenth century, Kedah — then a dependency of Srivijaya — was visited by Muslim traders from the Coromandel Coast in southeastern India. They exchanged Indian textiles and rice for pepper, tin and aromatic woods from the region. These early Indian Muslims had more influence in promoting trade than in disseminating Islam, which became a force after the rise of Malacca in the fifteenth century (Fujimoto 1989, pp. 2–3). Many scholars agree that it is these later Indian Muslim traders and missionaries who brought Islam to the Peninsula via Indonesia and Malacca — thus transforming Malay and, eventually, Malaysian society (Fujimoto 1989, pp. 6–8; Nagata 2006, p. 514). Penang had contact with these traders because it was historically and culturally a part of Kedah from as early as the fourth century (Ghulam-Sarwar 2001, p. 3).

The second Indian community developed in Malacca when its ruler Parameswara became a Muslim in 1414. One of the key factors behind

Malacca's prominence was the active role of Gujarati, Coromandel and Malabar Coast traders who exchanged Indian textiles for regional spices, which they sold to Europeans. The Gujarati were the most influential but the Tamil Muslims comprised the largest group of both traders and settlers (Fujimoto 1989, pp. 9–11). Their political influence hinged on their ability to maintain good relations with Malacca's foreign merchants, "their skilled diplomacy as the intermediary between the Sultan and the traders, and the administration of trade upon which the wealth and security of the Sultan was founded" (Fujimoto 1989, p. 70). The fall of Malacca to the Portuguese in 1511 and the Dutch in 1641 diverted Indian Muslim trade to Aceh, which remained important to the Straits Settlements, especially to Penang (Fujimoto 1989, pp. 17–18) right up to 1786 when Francis Light established a trading post there.

Colonial Immigration: Penang's Indian Muslim Settlers

From as early as the eighteenth century, Penang was the first port of disembarkation for most Indian immigrants boarding ships from the eastern port cities of Calcutta in Bengal and Nagapattinam, located in a Tamil Nadu coastal district with the same name. The immigration streams from India to Penang fed into the specialized labour demands of a growing colonial trading port. Family and friends arrived through a process of chain migration, taking up niche occupations through recommendations or via labour recruiters.

These workers came from family-inherited occupations which also reflected clan, caste and class backgrounds. There were further sub-divisions linked to diverse regional origins (village, town, and district) and religious identities (sects, leaders and spiritual paths). For example, those from Kadayanallur in Tamil Nadu — who formed the single largest group of Indian Muslim immigrants with families — were associated with manual work. Muslims from the Malabar Coast — popularly referred to as *Kakas* — were in petty trading and hawking, while the Chulias — merchants from the Coromandel Coast — were involved in import-export, shipping, and jewellery. In addition, there were northern Indian Muslim merchants from Kashmir, Bengal, Gujarat and Sindh (Nagata 2006, p. 518).

In Penang, as in Malacca earlier, each group — following their regional, language and caste origins — clustered around particular residential enclaves dominated by their own mosque and religious endowment land or *wakaf* (Nagata 2006, pp. 515–16; Ghulam 2001, pp. 6–7). Thus a dazzling diversity of immigrants from the Indian sub-continent was transplanted onto Penang's economic and social fabric.

These mostly Tamil Muslim immigrants into Penang should be distinguished from the thousands of indentured Tamil-Hindu plantation workers who arrived a century later and whose descendants now comprise the majority of the Peninsula's Indians. These plantation workers entered via the Straits Settlements after 1872, and flowed into the Protected Malay States after 1884, when the British legalized Indian immigration to these areas (Andaya 1982, p. 178).

(a) *Early Arrivals: Traders, Money-Lenders, Labourers*

Penang's Tamil immigrants were not homogenous but belonged to at least six highly diverse groups which arrived separately over a century, beginning in 1786 when Francis Light established a trading post in Penang, says local historian N. Meera (Interviews, April–June 2008).[5] It is well known that Tamil settlers, traders and labourers were among the first to arrive when Light founded the settlement (Amrith 2009, p. 549). According to Meera, some Tamil Muslims accompanied Light from India, and within three days of his landing another 150 Tamil Muslim traders arrived on small wooden boats or *tongkangs* from Kedah.[6] To encourage them to settle Light gave them land, says Meera, who has seen one such land grant. "As soon as they got land in the Market Street and Pitt Street area they cleared the jungle, built huts and set up businesses trading in nails, ropes and sails, among other items. For water they dug wells, one of which still exists behind the Light Street Convent."

The second group of immigrants, who were Hindus, comprised Nattukotai Chettiars, a clan of money-lenders who preceded modern banking and played an important role in the rise of colonial capitalism in Southeast Asia. "They came with gold coins from Siam, Phuket, Sri Lanka and Burma, which they used to grant loans to capital-short British traders in Penang," says Meera.

The third group comprised Chulia-Muslim traders who arrived from Aceh, where they were well established. The British welcomed them and trade boomed (Meera 2008). The fourth group comprised labourers. To cope with a labour shortage caused by the boom, from as early as 1794 thousands of Tamil Muslim labourers arrived annually for sojourns lasting months or years. These workers entered under the patronage of Chulia traders, who advanced their passage costs and linked them to employers in Singapore and Penang. By the 1820s, Tamil settlers comprised the largest single group in George Town (Amrith 2009, pp. 550, 556). Roughly three-quarters of the recruited workers in this fourth group came from the village of Nagore, and the descendants of these workers settled in what is now called Little India in George Town, says Meera. The 1801 Nagore Memorial in Chulia Street — the oldest Indian Muslim memorial on the island and a miniature of the original in Nagore — is dedicated to their thirteenth-century Muslim saint Syed Shahul Hamid.

The fifth batch of immigrants arrived between 1790–1873 when Penang was a penal station for India and convicts from penal settlements in the Andamans, Madras, and Calcutta were brought in to alleviate the labour shortage. In 1825 alone a batch of 900 was interned at "Chowrasta Lines", a Penang Road prison where they were trained in construction skills. It has recently been suggested that many of these prisoners were not convicted criminals but anti-colonial political exiles (Khoo 2009, p. 104), a fascinating claim which merits further research. Among them were Malabaris who built Penang's public roads, buildings and elite Muslim homes, and Sufi Muslims who constructed the seventy Muslim shrines of Penang. They lived in Kampung Malabar in the city and intermingled with the Tamils, but they brought their *achi* (brides) and *nanak* (grooms) from Kerala.[7] Others became petty traders in Chowrasta Market. These labourers had a saintly leader and upon his death a tomb and Muslim shrine were built on Dato Koya Road, which is named after him.

The 1833 census recorded about 11,000 settlers of Indian origin among Penang Island's 40,322 population, of which 7,886 were Chulias and 1,322 Bengalese (Newbold 1971, pp. 54–55, 96, quoted in Khoo 2009, p. 104). Most of the Indians were workers; a minority comprised traders. Many of the larger traders descended from inter-marriages between Arab merchants and Tamils from the Coromandel Coast, but in India they had maintained their clan-related occupational specializations after conversion. They included the coastal Marakaryar (who were once sailors, shipbuilders and shipowners), and inland Rawther (horse traders and cavalrymen) and Lebai (religious teachers). The Marakayars (later called Mericans) financed the building of the Kapitan Kling Mosque (1802), while other Indian Muslim merchants sponsored the construction of the Nagore Memorial in Chulia Street.

(b) *Later Arrivals: Kadayanallur Immigrants*

The sixth and largest group — who arrived with their families and to whom many of today's Penang Indian Muslims trace their ancestry — entered after 1882, almost a century after the arrival of the Chulia traders and Tamil workers. They originated from the tiny poverty-stricken village of Kadayanallur in Tirunelveli District, Tamil Nadu. This was a village of handloom weavers hit by massive retrenchments during the Industrial Revolution, when machines replaced handlooms. Unemployment and poverty was worsened by famine, which drove thousands of families to Penang. They were soon followed by some families from Thenkasi, sixteen kilometres from Kadayannallur (Khoo 2001a).

Meera says the Kadayanallur people travelled for one week on a newly-built British train before arriving in Nagapattinam Port. Here they lived in labour camps before undertaking the eleven-day journey on the "Negapat Line", a Dutch ship leased by a British company. Due to miscommunication — possibly linked to profit-hungry labour recruiters — the British were unprepared for the arrival of the first batch of 200 families and they remained destitute for months until they were granted pull-cart licences to transport goods for shipping firms. "Unlike other immigrants who could afford to leave their families behind, our people were so poor that they were forced to bring along their wives and children despite an uncertain future in Penang," recalls Haja Mohideen, 57, a George Town petty trader whose father was part of the Kadayanallur immigrant cohort (Interviews, 7, 8 April 2008) (See interview in Appendix 1.1).

Bereft of a trading background, many Kadayanallur folk merely secured low-paid menial jobs in cargo handling, construction and road sweeping. Others apprenticed as petty traders with business-savvy Malabaris (also called "Kakas")[8] hawking food, including *teh tarik* (pulled tea) and *roti canai* (flatbread). Both food items, highly popular among Malaysians today, were pioneered by the Malabaris, says Meera. Kadayanallur women specialized in making *rempah giling* (grounded spices) and fresh curry paste, popularly enjoyed today in Penang's famous *nasi kandar*. The vendors were usually Tamil males from Ramnath District who carried two baskets, one of rice and another of curry, slung on a *bakau* (mangrove) wood yoke (Khoo 2001a).

As a result of full family formations, the Kadayanallur community comprised three large endogamous groups, each with its own *sheikh* (religious teacher), *tarikat* (spiritual path), and association. For many years these were considered different clans but today there is intermingling and intermarriage between them. In 1929 a group formed by descendants of a *sheikh* organized themselves under the United Muslim Association, which still has its own building and hall on Transfer Road. In the 1930s another group formed the Anjuman Himayathul Association, with a mosque and *madrasah* in Chulia Street. In 1941 a third cluster established the Hidayathul Islam Association on Kedah Road. All three groups set up the Kadayanallur Muslim Association (KMA) in 1945 (Khoo 2001*a*; Najmudeen 2007, pp. 14–21). The KMA is still active and was in the news when Malaysia's ex-Prime Minister Dr Mahathir Mohamad — who has Penang Indian Muslim heritage — addressed them in late 2009 (Bernama, 24 December 2009).

Half a century ago most Kadayanallur Indian Muslims were clustered around the Hutton Lane area — in the vicinity of Transfer, Halfway, Ariffin, Kedah and Argyll Roads — in addition to locations surrounding the present Chowrasta Market. Today only about a quarter of them are still in these areas; the rest are dispersed across the island and the Penang mainland (Interview, Mydin Sultan, 17 June 2008). In 2001 it was estimated that Penang had 20,000 Kadayanallur and 5,000 Tengkasi Tamil Muslims (Khoo 2001*a*).

CULTURE AND IDENTITY: INDIAN MUSLIM IMPACT AND INFLUENCE

Historical Impact on Religion, Leadership, Trade

The impact of the Indian Muslims on Malaysian — particularly Malay — culture is far greater than other ethnic minorities due to their early historical links, their influential economic and political role, and a common religion, which has made cultural assimilation with Malays easier (Ghulam 2001, p. 8). Indian Muslims played an important role in drawing the Peninsula into global trade networks, introducing Islam, pioneering Malay and Tamil publications, establishing mosques and bequeathing religious endowments.

(a) *The Legacy of Islam: Religion and Built Heritage*

The greatest legacy of the Indian Muslims is their introduction of Islam to the Peninsula. Greater geographical proximity, numbers and inter-marriage meant that South Indian Muslims had a greater impact in Islamizing Malay courts compared to Arab, Gujerati and Chinese Muslims (Khoo 2009, p. 98).

Over the centuries Indian Muslims built mosques in almost every town where they settled in Peninsular Malaysia. Today virtually every state capital, district centre and small town in Peninsular Malaysia has a Tamil Muslim mosque. For example, "the Ipoh Indian Muslim mosque is a century-old and even the tiny rural town of Ijok in Selangor has a 120-year-old Tamil Muslim mosque," notes Fidha Ulla, a journalist with the Kuala Lumpur-based Indian Muslim magazine, *Nambikai*[9] (Interview, 17 June 2008).

In Penang each Indian Muslim immigrant group clustered around residential areas dominated by their own religious endowment land or *wakaf*. The *wakaf* have helped preserve much of Penang's Muslim built-heritage, including mosques, cemeteries, mausoleums, "compound houses", bungalows, shophouses and association buildings[10] (Khoo 2009, p. 109). Large numbers of Indian Muslims settled around the city, as reflected in today's rich and diverse examples of South Indian mosques, many built in the 1800s. Almost one third of the sixty-eight mosques in Penang were founded by Indian Muslims (Nagata 2006, p. 516). As mentioned earlier, Penang's Indian Muslim influence is well reflected in its splendid two-century old Kapitan Kling Mosque (1802) in Pitt Street. The street, dominated by Indian Muslims from colonial times, still has a very strong Indian Muslim presence in its religious shrines, jewellers, money-changers, retailers and wholesalers, book traders and restaurants. Shop names like Othman Pillai and Habib Jewels are landmarks here. (Appendix 1.2)

In addition Penang has the greatest concentration of *keramat* (shrines). These are based on certain interpretations of Sufism (Islamic mysticism), which came to the Peninsula from the Middle East via South Asia and Indonesia. Numbering seventy at its peak, today there are about fifteen active shrines, including the Nagore Shrine (Ghulam-Sarwar 2001). "Penang's Indian Muslim mosques and shrines reflect the diversity of South Asian Islam," writes Dr Ghulam-Sarwar. "Together with the surrounding development in Pitt Street and Buckingham Street, it creates the sort of traditional ambience encountered in similar settings with large populations of South Asian Muslims such as Old Delhi, Lahore, Singapore or Rangoon," he observes. The Bengali (1803) and Alimsah (1811) Mosques, the Rawana, Hashim Yahya and Pakistan Mosques, together with those on Prangin and Pahang Road are other examples of the diversity of South Asian Islam. These mosques have also contributed to inter-ethnic interaction by operating as cultural centres, with libraries open to all ethnic and religious groups.

(b) *Political and Intellectual Leadership*

The Tamil Muslims from the Coromandel Coast, like the Arabs from Hadramaut, traded extensively, were influential in commerce and the courts, moved easily between cultures, and helped Muslim missionaries spread Islam to Malacca and the region. Many Indian Muslims rose to high office. Among powerful Indian Muslims during the time of the Melaka Sultanate was Tun Mutahir (1500–10) the Bendahara, a post with functions of the prime minister, treasurer and chief of justice combined. His daughter was consort to the Sultan, and his grandson, Raja Alauddin Syah, later became Sultan.

During British rule, a person of Indian (and Arab) origin who had a great impact on Malay thought was Munshi Abdullah (1796–1854). An intellectual, his book on his travels through the region (1838) and his biography (1840) provide a rare glimpse of the Malay Muslim world of the nineteenth century (Noor 2009).

In the early twentieth century, a gentleman named Mohamad Iskandar, who was a Jawi Peranakan — a locally-born Muslim with Indian blood — moved from Penang to Kedah, where he became the respected headmaster of Alor Star's first English school. He married a Kedah Malay, Wan Tempawan Wan Hanafi, and the youngest of their nine children, Mahathir bin Mohamad, a doctor, rose to become Malaysia's longest-serving and most influential Prime Minister from 1981–2003 (Morais 1982; Wain 2009, pp. 4–5; Mahathir Mohamad 2012, p. 14).

Indian Muslims also played the role of intellectual intermediaries between ethnic groups by publishing the Peninsula's first newspapers, which enjoyed a multi-ethnic readership. In the early nineteenth century, some Straits Settlement-born Indian Muslims and Jawi Peranakan who were exposed to Malay and English print media through urban schools, apprenticed at government and missionary presses. They later owned and ran hand-lithographed presses, publishing religious and secular works in Malay. In the first thirty years of the Malay Press, at least sixteen Malay-language journals — seven in Singapore, five in Penang and four in Perak — were published, mostly by Jawi Peranakan writing as Malays and identifying themselves with Malay interests (Khoo 2009, p. 115).

In 1876 Mohamed Said Mohiddin of the Jawi Peranakan Company edited the first Malay newspaper titled *The Jawi Peranakan*. Published in Singapore and covering the Straits Settlements, the Malay States and the region (National Archives, Malaysia 2012), it appealed to a broad readership including Arabs, Peranakan Chinese, Indians and Malays. The weekly appeared every Monday, carrying general news, government notices, an editorial, *syair* (poetry) and advertisements (Sulaiman 2008). It remained the most successful Malay newspaper until the Second World War, particularly among the educated, and sparked off a host of other Malay publications. In the same year (1876) Mohiddin also pioneered the first Tamil newspaper in the Straits titled *Tankainecan*, illustrating "the extent to which the hybrid Tamil Muslim community stood quite naturally astride the Tamil and Muslim cultural worlds" (Amrith 2009, p. 557).

Penang's first Tamil newspaper *Vittiya Vicarini* (1883) relocated to Nagore with its editor, the Tamil poet Ghulam Kadir Navalar, exemplifying the circulation of the people and ideas across the Bay of Bengal in the nineteenth century (Amrith 2009, p. 557). Another Tamil newspaper, *Singai Varthamani,* a weekly, was published and edited in Singapore in 1875 by a Tamil Muslim, Magudum Sayabu, who also published *Thangai Nesan* in 1878 and *Singai Nesan* in 1887 (Interview, Fidha Ulla, 17 June 2008).

(c) *Trade and Entrepreneurship: A Pivotal Role*

Despite their relatively small numbers, in pre-colonial times Indian Muslim traders played a pivotal role in plugging the Peninsula into global trade networks, subsequently surviving three imperial powers — the Portuguese, Dutch and British. After 1750 they were sidelined by European control of Tamil ports, English expansion into the China trade and Arab re-entry into the Straits of Malacca trade routes. When the Dutch prevented them from trading in Malacca after the early eighteenth century, many Indian Muslims relocated to Kedah (Khoo 2009, p. 99), and later Penang.

With the advent of colonialism Indian Muslim traders lost their monopoly of the Indian Malayan trade but played a supporting role to the British and Chinese. For example the Merican, Rawther and Lebai clans harnessed their centuries-old trading experience to find niches in varied businesses such as supplying provisions, labour, passengers, crew and packing material to British ships in the main ports of Penang, Port Swettenham (now known as Port Klang) and Singapore. Over the years, containerization wiped out much of this trade, but some trading families switched to related businesses such as freight forwarding (Shanker 2001, p. 27).

Over the span of the twentieth century Indian Muslim traders have remained active in shipping and import-export, and as jewellers, money-changers, bakers, pharmacists and petty traders. However various factors have reduced their influence. Growing numbers had to face competition from generally better-organized Chinese firms, State-backed Malay-run companies (Shankar 2001, pp. 16–17, pp. 27–28) and multinationals. In addition some successful early traders bought property and retired to their home districts, especially where the land was fertile. In contrast the poorer Kadayanallur immigrants established deep roots in Malaysia, partly because they had full family formations here, but also because the environments in their home districts in India were too harsh for survival (Mydin Sultan, Interview, 17 June 2008). Though Indian Muslims still have a business presence, the gaps left by these traders were quickly filled by other firms such as Poh Kong Jewellers, Gardenia Bakery and Guardian Pharmacy. Among the older Indian Muslim trading clans, some family-run businesses have managed to modernize and expand locally and overseas. Examples include Barkarth Store, Habib Jewels and Mydin, a large retailer (see Appendix 1.3 for a description of some companies).

Influences on Popular Malaysian Culture

(a) *Spicing up Malaysian food*

It is well known that the infusion of spices and curries in many Malay dishes reflect Indian influences. But what is often taken for granted is the Indian Muslim impact on popular culture manifested in cuisine such as *roti canai, teh tarik, nasi kandar, pasembur* and *mamak mee*. These have virtually become "national" food items incorporating Malay, Chinese and Indian elements enjoyed by all ethnic and religious groups. As one Indian Muslim hawker on Penang's Chulia Street puts it, "Most Malaysians can eat our food — Malays know it's *halal*, Chinese love our curry, and Indians enjoy it, though they avoid beef" (Hawker, Interviews, Chulia Street, 7–8 April 2008).

In addition to hawkers, there are an estimated 8,000 Indian Muslim restaurants catering to both Muslim and non-Muslim Malaysians. Located at strategic locations in all cities and towns, they provide affordable food in a casual ambiance. No other eateries today have as much cultural significance in Malaysia; indeed for Malaysians, the local "*Mamak* shop" or *kedai Mamak* is as ubiquitous a gathering place as the Turkish teahouse for the Turks or the English pub for the British. Unfortunately not many Malaysians are aware of the origins of these food items.

Roti canai is a pan-fried flatbread served with curry or dhal. A version of north India's ubiquitous *paratha*, it is identical to the Singapore *roti prata* and a close descendant of Kerala's *porotta*. The term *roti* means bread in Hindi, Urdu and Malay, and the word *canai* is believed to be linked to either Chennai in India or to north Indian *channa* — boiled chickpeas in spicy gravy, with which it was traditionally served. In Malaysia and Singapore, *roti canai* is often taken for breakfast or supper, washed down with *teh tarik* ("Mellow Yellow Canai" n.d. and Wikipedia 2007).

Teh tarik, literally meaning "pulled tea", is a well-loved drink amongst Malaysians. Sweetened condensed milk is used and the tea is poured from a mug into a glass repetitively. The higher the "pull" the thicker the froth. The pouring also cools the tea (Wikipedia 2009).

Nasi kandar is a popular northern Malaysian dish originating from Penang. A meal of steamed rice served with a variety of curries and side dishes, it can be eaten any time of the day. The term *nasi kandar* originated when *nasi* (rice) hawkers or vendors would *kandar* (balance) a pole on the shoulder with two huge containers kept in rattan baskets. The name has remained and today the sign *nasi kandar* is seen on many *Mamak* restaurants and stalls. The rice is accompanied by side dishes such as fried chicken, curried spleen, cubed beef, fish roe, fried prawns or fried squid. Vegetables are usually brinjal (aubergine), okra (ladies' fingers), or bitter gourd. A mixture of curry sauces is poured on the rice. This is called *banjir* (flooding) and imparts a diverse taste to the rice. Traditionally, *nasi kandar* is served with its side dishes on a single plate. It is said that the practice evolved when relatives carried food baskets for stevedores at Penang Port. Due to requests for supplies from other workers and the Aurvedic practice of food combination, only certain curries and spices could be mixed with rice at any one time. Cooks therefore carried a variety of dishes and curries, and this eventually evolved into *nasi kandar*. However today the Aurvedic practice of food combination is not observed and curries are mixed at random (Interview, A.V.M. Haja, 17 June 2008; Wikipedia n.d.).

Nasi kandar appeals to all ethnic groups. I once had *nasi kandar* for lunch at a spotlessly clean lean-to shed in a side lane next to a Chinese electrical shop in Datuk Keramat Road, Penang. The stall was run by two

Indian Muslim men, one older and one younger, who were supervised by an older woman in a sari (likely newly arrived from India). The food was tasty and the clientele was multi-ethnic. In the half hour I was there, the customers included a middle-aged Malay man in a long-sleeved batik from a government department nearby, a Chinese lady who arrived on a motorbike, and a well-dressed young Indian Muslim man who worked in the hotel industry. As I left, a young Indian Muslim girl (an office worker) dressed in a silk *baju kurung* ordered a take-away "Milo Ice". She spoke in Malay (Fieldwork, Penang, June 2008).

Pasembur is the Malaysian Indian Muslim version of the Indonesian-Malay *rojak* or salad. Ingredients include shredded cucumber, turnip, potatoes, bean curd, bean sprouts, prawn fritters, spicy fried crab and fried squid. It is served with sweet and spicy nutty sauce. The term *pasembur* is unique to northern Peninsular Malaysia. It is especially associated with Penang, where the best *pasembur* is said to be that sold along Gurney Drive. In other parts of Malaysia, the term *rojak Mamak* is commonly used (Wikipedia n.d.).

Mamak mee, referred to as *Kelinga mee* in the north by Penang Hokkiens, is very popular and one of many fine examples of cross-cultural culinary exchange over two centuries of Tamil Muslim and Chinese social interaction. It is generally believed to be a hybrid of Chinese-style friend noodles and *pasembur*. Both have common ingredients like *cucur* (fritters), *tau kwa* (fried bean curd), squid and a potato-based tamarind-flavoured gravy. There are two versions — *mee goreng* (fried noodles) and *mee rebus* (blanched noodles). *Mee goreng* is fried with all its ingredients, including chopped cabbage, onion flakes, sliced chillies and lime. *Mee rebus* is blanched with bean sprouts, and then served with other ingredients and a generous helping of gravy. Fried or boiled eggs and chilli are optional for both dishes ("Indian Mee" n.d.).

(b) *Language: Enriching Bahasa Malaysia*

Indian Muslims have also played an important role in the development of language in the region. The Tamil Muslims were believed to be instrumental in the development of the Jawi script in the Nusantara due to their role as religious scholars and court scribes at a time when literacy was a specialized skill (Van Ronkel 1922, pp. 30–31 in Khoo 2009, p. 100).

Due to centuries of social interaction between the Indian Muslim and Malay communities, the Malay language has been enriched by Tamil and

Malayalam words (Wake 1890, pp. 81–87). Northern Malay in particular is strongly influenced by Tamil accent and words. The Penang Malay dialect has also borrowed from Sanskrit, Tamil, Hindustani and Urdu, in addition to Persian and Arab (Khoo 2001b).

Malay was the lingua franca linking Penang's disparate Indian immigrant groups, including Indian Muslims. However within each group they spoke Tamil and — depending on their descent — Urdu, Benggali or Hindustani. Like Malays who still resort to regional dialects, some Indian Muslims, particularly the Jawi Peranakan, prefer their Penang sub-dialect called "*Loghat Tanjong*" for inter-group communications, but use standard Bahasa Malaysia on professional and formal occasions (Halimah and Zainab 2004, pp. 127–30).

In recent years there has been greater use of Bahasa Malaysia among Indian Muslims due to inter-marriage to Malays and the Malay medium of education. "Many Indian Muslims also grew up in Malay *kampungs,* so the Bahasa Malaysia taught in school was reinforced by socialization with Malay neighbours," explains Fatimah Hassan an Indian Muslim who works as a researcher at the State-run Socio-Economic Research Institute, (Penang Institute) (Interview, 2 June 2008).[11] Many Indian Muslims see little economic value in Tamil compared to Bahasa Malaysia and English, while others fear that being Tamil means being less Muslim, she says. "What some don't realize is that Tamil is a culture and language, not a religion," she adds (Interview, Fatimah Hassan, 2 June 2008).

Most Indian Muslim youth today do not speak Tamil, and it is mainly the older generation which retains the language. "Things have changed so much that there are now requests for Bahasa Malaysia and English rather than Tamil sermons in Indian Muslim mosques," says A.V.M. Haja, a respected lawyer-businessman who is president of the largely Tamil-speaking Masjid India Mosque (1863),[12] the oldest mosque in Kuala Lumpur (Interview, 17 June 2008).

(c) *Malaysian Theatre and Music: The Indian Link*

The Indian Muslim impact is far stronger in Malaysian theatre and music than is realized. It can be seen in *Boria* and *Bangsawan* theatre, both of which developed indigenously in Penang and spread to the Peninsular Malaysia, says Professor Dr Ghulam-Sarwar, a performing arts specialist at the University of Malaya. *Boria*, connected with the story of Saiyidina Ali, Islam's fourth Caliph, reached Penang via the Sepoy[13] Regiment which accompanied the British. Over the years it evolved to suit the local situation. "Today, shorn of its religious qualities and totally transformed in style and function, *Boria* has become a form of secular song and dance genre incorporating in its lyrics praises for dignitaries," he notes (Interview, 21 April 2008).

Bangsawan, the first style of urban theatre in the Peninsula, has an even more amazing evolution from Muslim India. Created in the palace of the Nawab of Oudh, it reached Bombay under the patronage of Parsee merchants and became known as Parsee Theatre. Performers visited Penang in the 1880s to entertain the Sepoys and merchants, and "the Penang merchants liked it so much that they developed their own troupes and the genre eventually acquired the name *Bangsawan*," he explains. Originally inspired by European Renaissance theatre, Parsee — later *Bangsawan* — theatre adopted Western theatre techniques such as painted backdrops, wings and borders and improvised acting. Today *Bangsawan* has a repertoire that includes Indonesian, Thai and Chinese plays and multi-ethnic casts, crew, owners and managers, and has evolved into the "national" theatre of Malaysia.

Bangsawan has impacted Malaysian music tastes too. Hindustani music, first popularized in Penang by Parsee theatre, has continued to fascinate Malay, Chinese and Indian audiences in the Peninsula, thanks to the legendary P. Ramlee (1929–73). An actor, producer, director and singer, the late P. Ramlee was inspired by Indian, including Parsee themes. *Bangsawan* theatre companies are also responsible for the influence of Carnatic and Hindustani styles seen in the use of the flute and *tabla* in the musical repertoire of top local artistes. Another Indian influence is the Qawwali singing style which has evolved into various *zikir* styles, including the Kelantanese *Dikir Barat*. Like *Boria*, this has transformed into non-religious entertainment and become popularized in Malaysia and Singapore (Interview, Ghulam-Sarwar, 21 April 2008).

STATE-DEFINED CATEGORIES: DIVISIONS AND DILEMMAS

Colonial and Post-colonial Categories

Like other sojourners and settlers from the Malay Archipelago, the Middle East and China, there was a rich diversity among the Indian immigrants who landed on the Peninsula's shores. This diversity appears to have been recognized, experienced and enjoyed by the communities as evidenced by varied sub-ethnic organizations, places of worship and cuisine. This was particularly so in Penang, where other than Tamils, there was a sprinkling of Muslims of Malabari, Punjabi, Pathan, Sindhi, Gujarati and Bengali origins. In addition the 1881 Census recognized the Jawi Peranakan (Nagata 2006, p. 517). However, for administrative convenience and control, the British eventually compressed the highly heterogeneous Indian communities — like the once disparate Malay and Chinese groups — into monolithic, homogenous categories.

Today there are three groups with Indian Muslim lineage categorized by the State according to their ethnic and nationality status. They comprise "Malay Muslim" citizens who make up the majority, in addition to "Indian Muslim" permanent residents (PRs) and "Indian Muslim" citizens (Shanker 2001; Mohamed Iqbal, Interview, 17 June 2008). In terms of their State-recognized identity, those in the last two groups are in an anomalous State and social position because they share the religion of the Malay-majority but the "race" of the Indian minority. Though not all Indian Muslims seek to change their ethnic status, some who have applied claim they have been rejected by the State despite meeting the Constitutional definition of "Malay".

Malay Muslim Citizens: Acculturated and Assimilated

The cultural-based legal definition of "Malay" in the Federal Constitution has since 1957 gradually allowed most Indian Muslims to enter the fold of the Malay with ease. The majority of Indian Muslims today are "Malay Muslim" citizens officially recognized by the State as Malays since they fit into the Constitutional definition of Malay by being Muslim, speaking Malay and practising Malay customs. Some apply directly to the Registration Department to change their own or their children's ethnic status to Malay to overcome their ambiguous identity and to gain from opportunities offered by affirmative action policies related to the special position of the Malays under the Constitution (Stark 2006, p. 387). Most however, eventually become recognized as Malays through acculturation, intermarriage and assimilation. Malay Muslim citizens are classified in their state-issued identity card computer database as Muslim by religion, and their official identity is most clearly evidenced by the Malay Muslim patronymic "bin" and "binti" attached to their names.

"Malay Muslim citizens" with Indian lineage include a minority which is registered as Malay but remains culturally Indian Muslim. Most comprise children of endogamous marriages whose Indian Muslim parents have managed to register them as Malays. The researcher Fatimah Hassan explains:

> These younger Malaysian-born Indian Muslims ensure their children are registered in their birth certificate and identity card (IC) as "Malay Muslim" so that there is no problem from the start. The parents also make sure their children have the Malay patronymic "bin" and "binti" and not "anak" or "son/daughter of", which is usually used in the ICs of Indians.
> (Interview, 2 June 2008)

The majority have intermarried and assimilated with Malays over several generations, and include descendants of Jawi Peranakan. Legally they do not face any problem being categorized as Malays since they not only fit into the constitution's cultural definition of Malay, but have Malay ancestry and therefore do not face any administrative problems in registering their children as Malays. The only trace of their Indian Muslim ancestry is sometimes noticeable in surnames like Mohideen, Mydin or Merican.

The Jawi Peranakan are important in helping us understand the issue of identity. Since most of the early Tamil migrants to Penang were single males, many took Malay wives. Their offspring were known as Jawi Peranakan. The word Jawi is a term of Arabic origin referring to Southeast Asian Muslims, while Peranakan refers to those locally born but non-indigenous (Nagata 2006, pp. 519–20).[14] Despite interethnic marriages in the early years, the Jawi Peranakan remained a "separate and self-perpetuating category" and a new hybrid ethnic group "exhibiting Indian and Malay characteristics and yet belonging …to neither" (Nagata 2006, pp. 519–20). To overcome their minority status and loss of urban land and trade to Chinese they harnessed English education, moved into prestigious jobs as journalists, teachers and civil servants, and took up leadership roles in the Malay community. This helped them to identify with and be accepted by the Malays (Fujimoto 1989, pp. 14–17).

From once derogatory terms used to refer to self-proclaimed "Malays" of Indian ancestry, the terms Jawi Peranakan — and even Mamak — are now acquiring positive connotations, especially among some Malay elite. "Not all stereotypes about us are negative," explains lawyer A.V.M.

Haja. "Some Malays are proud to claim they have *Mamak* blood, in the same way that they often like to be identified with Arabs. This is because most Malays are civil servants while Indian Muslims — like Arabs — are associated with merchants," he says (Interview, 17 June 2008). A growing number of the newly educated Malay middle class are today confident enough to openly admit their Indian roots, especially if the State already recognizes them as Malay Muslim citizens. Such self-descriptions were uncommon in the past (Interviews, A.V.M Haja, 17 June 2008, and Puan Merican, January 2010, Kuala Lumpur).[15]

Politically too it has now become acceptable for Malay elites to highlight their Indian ancestry. The prime example of this is Dr Mahathir Mohamad. Touching on his family background in his memoirs he says: "My father was a Penang Malay. Almost all Malays of the island of Penang have some Indian blood." He explains: "Culturally and linguistically, the Penang Malays are Malays. My father could not speak any of the languages of India and knew none of his forebears or relatives there. The connection was completely broken" (Mahathir Mohamad 2011, p. 14).

In the next chapter entitled "I am a Malay" he says, "I admit that some Indian, or more accurately South Asian blood flows in my veins, but from which part of the Indian subcontinent my ancestors came I do not know." Alluding to one possible reason he avoided talking about his ethnic background during office, he laments the double ethnic stereotyping he endured as Prime Minister; any "unpopular decision" was attributed to him being Malay, but "good decisions, those that brought progress and prosperity to the nation, it was always because I had Indian blood." Asserting that good leaders must challenge ethnic stereotypes, he writes, "I wanted to prove otherwise: that Malays were more than capable of thinking, progressing and leading" (Mahathir Mohamed 2011, p. 24). He then explains that being Malay is a formal legal construct unrelated to descent, and states his own position clearly and forcefully:

> My family and I have always fulfilled those formal criteria. But I am a Malay not just on paper. I am also a Malay in sentiment and in spirit. I identify completely with the Malays and their problems, their past and their present, their achievements and failures. I do not do so sentimentally and uncritically, but thoroughly and thoughtfully.
>
> (*A Doctor in the House: The Memoirs of Tun Dr Mahathir Mohamad*, 2011, pp. 25, 26).

A 2004 book on the history, role, and assimilation of the *Jawi Peranakan* written by two Malay academics identifies and speaks positively of a number of prominent Malays with *Jawi Peranakan* roots, including Dr Mahathir, who appears in a Hari Raya photo with one author (Halimah and Zainab 2004). The book is published by a local university formerly known as the Sultan Idris Teacher's Training College, once a bastion of Malay nationalism.

Najmudeen Kader, a respected middle-aged businessman who heads the fifty-year-old Penang-based Muslim League, a powerful coalition of Indian Muslim organizations, summarizes it thoughtfully: "The Malays are a heterogeneous people who are made up of many sub-ethnic groups, including Indian Muslims" (Interview, 31 May 2008).

Indian Muslim Permanent Residents: Not Acculturated nor Assimilated

These are non-citizen Permanent Residents (PRs) classified in their identity card records as Indians by race and Muslims by religion. They carry the patronymic *anak* — meaning "son/daughter of" — commonly used for Indians. The majority are older, male, Indian-born immigrants holding Malaysian permanent residency and Indian citizenship, with an Indian-born wife and children in India. They make a living in Malaysia as petty traders but maintain family, religious and — in the case of larger traders — business links with India. Tamil is their main language at home and among business colleagues, but they use bazaar Malay with customers and in dealings with the State. It is not known exactly how large this group is, but according to one grass-roots leader "there are thousands who are born in India and cannot get Malaysian citizenship" (Interview, Ibrahim Vengai, 16 June 2008).[16]

Not possessing Malaysian citizenship, voting rights or the ability for family reunions, many commute between both countries, maintain their Indian roots, and do not feel a complete sense of belonging to Malaysia (Shanker 2001, p. 50). This group remains trapped in transnational loyalties. They do not enjoy State recognition as Malays, and given their poverty and absence of political voice, are often the subject of ethnic stereotypes and jokes (Interview, Ibrahim Vengai, 16 June 2008).

They have not been helped by a once tough government stance on citizenship. Referring to complaints that many were unsuccessful in citizenship applications despite applying numerous times, in 1995 the then Deputy Home Minister Dato' Megat Junid Megat Ayub stated that sincerity will be judged by the number of times they reapply, and their ability to speak and write Malay. Though some had lived in Malaysia for several generations, he said this does not automatically qualify them as citizens, especially if they spend periods in both countries and have their family in India (*New Straits Times*, 20 February 1995).

Though some PRs have managed to obtain citizenship for their Malaysian-born children, most are unable to switch their children's official ethnic identity to Malay because they are classified as being of "Indian descent" (*Keturunan India*). Technically, the key device in achieving official recognition as Malay is to apply to the Registration Department to drop the patronymic *anak* or "son/daughter of". The patronymic is a give-away sign that they are of Indian origin and a sure way to be denied entry into the fold of the Malay and their constitutionally bestowed special position. However many applications in the past were rejected due to what appeared to be ad-hoc administrative decisions by individual civil servants in Registration Departments, where decisions varied widely from state to state. Applications have reportedly been rejected for a range of reasons — if parents are of "*keturunan India*", the applicant's Bahasa Malaysia is not seen to be fluent enough, or even for wearing Indian rather than Malay clothes (Nagata 2006, p. 527). Except for descent, the civil servants may be technically correct in rejecting certain applications since speaking Malay and following Malay customs are among the constitutional requirements of being Malay.

Indian Muslim Citizens: Acculturated but not Assimilated

This group comprises mainly children of PRs who remain classified in their identity cards as Indian. Despite being deeply acculturated to the Malay way of life through interaction in common locales, schools and workplaces, being Muslims, speaking Malay, and practising Malay customs, the State does not accept them as Malays, and they still have to carry the Indian patronymic *anak* in their identity cards. While some are content to remain Indian Muslims, many are anxious for State recognition as Malays in order to acquire a clearer cultural identity and better economic opportunities. As full-fledged citizens who are denied official recognition as Malays, this group is the most vocal about what they perceive as State discrimination.

The problem is so persistent that there are pleas for them to be classified as Malays before almost every national election.

In 1994, the Deputy Chairman of the Muslim League Council, Sheik Alauddin, complained that hospitals and State Registration Departments refused to allow Penang Indian Muslims to change their children's names from *anak* to *bin* and *binti* (Daud 1994). Just before the 2008 national elections, Malaysian Indian Muslim Youth Movement President Mohamed Kader Ali complained that despite conforming to the Constitutional definition of Malay, some Indian Muslims have tried, unsuccessfully for fifty years, to be reclassified as Malays. His son, Syed Osman Mohamed, 24, said:

> We feel uncomfortable to be known as Indians because people automatically think we are Hindus when we are actually Muslims. All our children do not even know how to speak Tamil. They only converse in Malay, and our wives wear *baju kurung* or *kebaya* nowadays, no more the *sari*.
> (*Expressindia*, 3 March 2008).

THE INDIAN MUSLIM "IDENTITY CRISIS"

The Dilemma of Dual Identities

The majority of Malaysians of Indian Muslim lineage have inter-married, fully assimilated into the Malay community, and are classified as Malay. However a minority remains Indian Muslim, sharing the religion of the Malay majority but the "race" of the Indian minority. Since they live in a society organized along essentialized ethnic and religious lines, this creates problems for some of them.

Firstly, they are accepted by the State as Muslims but not as Malays; they remain categorized as Indians in a State where Malays are prioritized in State affirmative action policies. This contributes to perceptions of State discrimination, and what community leaders refer to as an "identity crisis". Secondly, their anomalous position sometimes results in social stereotyping and social discrimination, partly because other Malaysians are not sure where to "place" them, but also because Indian Muslims are often forced to harness multiple identities in their quest for identity and opportunity.

Perceived State Discrimination: "Categorized as Indians"

The most affected are Indian Muslim citizens who cannot carry the patronymic *bin* or *binti* in their names because their parents are considered

Indians, not Malays. Despite being officially recognized as Muslims, they are still regarded by the State (and society) as Indians with Malay names. A.V.M. Haja, the lawyer who is Masjid India Mosque president, says this situation has sparked an "identity crisis", which he contends is "the single biggest issue facing the community today". He adds:

> The Malays worry that we will take away their rights, but many Indian Muslims want the "*bin*" and "*binti*" for cultural identity and educational access for their children. Some parents complain their children are ethnically ostracized in schools because of their names. Yet they cannot change their children's names. If some Indians from India have "*bin*" and "*binti*" on their names and Malaysian Chinese converts are allowed to do so, why not us? It's not too much to ask.
>
> (Interview, 17 June 2008).

Another community leader, Dr Mohamed Iqbal, says a perennial complaint is the reported inability of some to qualify for places, scholarships and loans reserved for Malays in tertiary institutions.[17] According to him, some cannot gain entry into government-run university matriculation courses — which are seen as a passport into local universities — despite being classified as Malays in their birth certificates and identity cards. "This is because they fail the ethnicity test when application forms demand information on their *keturunan ibu-bapa* (parent's ancestry)" (Interview, 17 June 2008). The researcher and writer Dr Neil Khor (2009) has also observed that "many Indian Muslims have been asked to produce their parent's birth certificates before they can qualify for places reserved for the *bumiputeras*. When it is learnt that they have Indian parents, they fail to obtain the desired scholarships." The respected Indian Muslim radio journalist and commentator Mydin Sultan claims that "Indian Muslims do not enjoy preferential quotas allotted to Malays when they apply to universities — they are categorized as Indians even though all their legal documents classify them as Malays" (Interview, 17 June 2008).

Despite these allegations, there are many cases where Indian Muslims have successfully obtained government loans, scholarships, and sponsored places in local and foreign universities. In Sarawak, for example, a sample survey of thirty Indian Muslims found that all those below the age of thirty classified themselves as Malays in applications. One respondent said:

Only *bumiputeras* can enter UiTM (University Technology Mara), and more easily (enter) other public universities compared to a non-*bumiputera*. I applied and got accepted to do a course in Science. I applied as a *bumiputera* — a Malay. So I'm *bumiputera* — a Malay because of my religion, even though both my parents are Indian Muslims and not Malays. There is no column for Indian Muslims in the application form.

(Survey respondent, quoted in Khemlani David and Dealwis 2009, p. 43).

The most likely explanations for these discrepancies is that while declared Federal Government policies are usually clear, actual decision-making at State, institutional and organizational levels can be ad-hoc, non-transparent and fluid, leading to unequal outcomes and perceptions of discrimination. Whether or not such discrimination exists is a moot point — the fact remains that powerful community leaders perceive, rightly or wrongly, that it does.

Social Discrimination: Negative Stereotyping

In addition to perceived State discrimination, the Indian Muslim community is often at the receiving end of negative stereotypes commonly expressed in private conversations and the Internet. For example, a letter written to the popular online news media *Malaysiakini* complained that Indian Muslims were often called "*Mamak*", associated with *roti canai* and *teh tarik* sellers, and treated derogatorily. The writer asked why "people who are loyal to this country are treated like foreigners despite having been here all their lives?" (GM 2001). Other comments came from an Indian Muslim who complained of bullying at religious classes, (Bashah 2009) and a writer who claimed that "Tamil-speaking Indian Muslims have been suffering in silence for the last 50 years" (Marginalised TMIM 2008).

The term "*Mamak*" is thought to have originated from "*Mama*", a respectful Tamil term for an older man. However when used in the case of Indian Muslims it can also have a neutral or negative connotation, depending on the context. "You're not Malay, you're *Mamak*," is a common taunt faced by Indian Muslims, especially in rural schools.[18] Translated into local parlance as "*U bukan Melayu, U Mamak*," it is often employed by a minority of rural folk who are less exposed to urban-based Indian Muslims, and who assume that just as all Malays are Muslims, all Indians are Hindus. An Indian Muslim is, in their minds, a social anomaly. In addition to *Mamak*, the term *Darah Keturunan Kling* (having Indian blood), is sometimes used to set them apart from Malays and Indians. The point is that these stereotypes simplify and vilify a complex community and deny and decry their vast contributions to Malaysian society.

OVERCOMING THE "IDENTITY CRISIS": ETHNIC, POLITICAL AND SOCIAL ROUTES

The Indian Muslim community has over time adopted a variety of individual and collective ethnic, political and social routes to overcome their perceived social and economic marginalization.

Ethnic Routes: Living With Multiple Identities

Most Indian Muslims prefer State-recognition as Malays because compared to other ethnic minorities, the political and economic stakes are highest for them — either they gain State recognition as Malays, belong to the politically dominant majority and enjoy a special position under the Constitution, or remain classified as Indians, a political minority. One scholar has noted that this aspiration is strong among both the working and business classes (Stark 2006, p. 387), but fieldwork for this book indicates that the desire for a State-recognized Malay identity is especially prevalent among the growing middle class, many of whom compete with the middle class from other ethnic groups — particularly Malays — for civil service jobs, government contracts, and university places and scholarships.

For "Indian Muslim" Permanent Residents and citizens, coping with the identity crisis can involve dual negotiations, one at the State level and the other at a social level. At State level, it involves registering themselves or their children as Malays and changing their ethnic status in their identity cards to Malay. However, at a social level they may present themselves as Malays or Indians without contradiction, as the situation demands. For instance one cohort of older "Indian Muslims" citizens are Tamil-educated and Tamil-speaking and have endogamous marriages. But since they cannot gain entry into the category of Malay, they present themselves as Tamil-Muslim culturally but "Malay" politically, in relation to the State. "I am a Tamil, Indian, Muslim," one trader says, "but when I deal with government departments I have to tell them I'm Malay. It's a question of survival." (Interview, Anonymous Respondent, Penang, June 2008).

In this context some comments by ex-premier Dr Mahathir Mohamad on the community are interesting. During the Kadayanallur Muslim Association's (KMA) sixty-fourth anniversary dinner in Penang in 2009, he was quoted by the national news agency Bernama as saying:

> The country is very liberal and I think they (Indian Muslims) will be accepted by all if they can pick either to become a Muslim or Indian. The Federal Constitution also define(s) a Muslim very clearly. If they want to become a Muslim then just follow the Constitution. The problem of Indian Muslims will be resolved if they can decide and choose to become either a Muslim or an Indian.
>
> (Bernama, 24 December 2009).

Since the group he was addressing was already Muslim, perhaps he was politely telling them that they should choose to be either Malay ("Muslim") or Indian, and that there are no two ways about it. Such a viewpoint fits clearly into his credentials as a Malay nationalist. Mahathir also said at the same gathering that Indian Muslims "must put aside their origin country and call themselves Malaysians for 1Malaysia to be successful" (Bernama 2009). His advice about being Malaysian also fits into his credentials as a leader who enunciated "Vision 2020" — the concept of a fully developed nation — and the idea of a "Bangsa Malaysia", or Malaysian nationality.

But Mahathir's comments raise two questions. Firstly, can Indian Muslims, or for that matter any other ethnic group, easily identify themselves as Malaysians if racial ideology, ethnic politics and State policy prioritize ethnicity? Secondly, why is it not possible to be Muslim and remain Indian, that is, Indian Muslim? Even a third permutation, the hybrid Jawi Peranakan, is possible. In other words, multiple identities are possible, without in any way detracting from being Malaysian.

Political Routes: Coalescing Fluid Identities

This involves political mobilization to gain opportunities for the Indian Muslim community. Like many other ethnic minorities, the community has tilted towards the political establishment for support. The Muslim League was an early political party affiliated to the United Malays National Organization (UMNO), and Indian Muslims first joined UMNO via the Muslim League in 1957. In its early days the Muslim League successfully fielded, among others, Mr S.M. Idris, a prominent businessman, who won the local council elections. In 1974 the Muslim League became a social body.

Subsequently a political party, the Indian Muslim based Kongres India Muslim Malaysia (KIMMA, or Malaysian Indian Muslim Congress), was formed in 1979. It teamed up with the UMNO breakaway party Semangat 46 and became part of an opposition coalition called Gagasan Rakyat, which lost badly in the 1988 general elections. Since then it sought to join the ruling coalition, and after six unsuccessful attempts, was finally accepted as an associate member of UMNO, with observer status in 2010 (*The Star*, Friday, 28 August 2010). Its president was also appointed a senator in July 2011, giving the community a direct line to the government and a greater say in public affairs.

Winning representation in government was difficult for the community partly because its fluid identities led to suspicion and confusion. Political analyst Hanapi Dollah comments:

> ......(the) identity of the Indian Muslims changes from Indian Muslims to Indian when they join MIC (Malaysian Indian Congress) and becomes Indian Muslim again when they form KIMMA and finally changes further to Malay when they join UMNO.
>
> (Hanapi Dollah, quoted in Seeni Naina Mohamed, 2001).

At the same time, there has been pressure from community leaders to move toward a Malay identity. In 1983, for example, Malaysian Indian Muslim Association (Permim) President Mohamed Ismail Sharif told members they had not benefited from their identity, and urged them to renounce their Indian identity and ally themselves with the majority Malay Muslims (Shanker 2001, p. 88).

Social Routes: Mobility and Marriage

Alternatively, or in conjunction with ethnic and political routes, individuals and families have improved their socio-economic status through educational, occupational and geographical mobility. Such mobility often involves moving out of their own ethnic spaces, leading to increased interaction, intermarriage and eventually assimilation into the majority-Malay community.

According to community leaders, increasing numbers of Indian Muslims are marrying Malays. Some segments of the Indian Muslim working class still tend to be endogamous but marriage to Malays is increasing among this group due to common schooling, shared neighbourhoods and workplaces, socialization outside the Indian Muslim community, and the passing on of patriarchs who would have otherwise frowned upon mixed marriages (Interview, Fatimah Hassan, 2 June 2008). Due to the country's rapid growth, thousands of educated children and grandchildren of once poor immigrants today work in the modern manufacturing and service sectors, while graduates work in the professions and the civil service, where they interact with and meet Malays.

Marriage to Malays is most common among middle-class Indian Muslim males whose parents are merchants, professionals or civil servants (Interviews, Mydin Sultan, 17 June, and Ibrahim Vengai, 16 June 2008). Couples usually meet in multi-ethnic educational and work environments locally and overseas. According to A.V.M. Haja this trend is due to the large number of Malay female graduates, a perception that Indian Muslim men are family-oriented, and the lack of emphasis on higher education for Indian Muslim girls in the past. "Indian Muslim parents are today more aware of the need to educate girls in order to make them financially independent and increase their choice of marriage partners," he adds (Interview, 17 June 2008). An enterprising retired Indian Muslim academic has also alleviated the problem through a successful free Internet matchmaking service (MalaysianMuslimMatrimonial.com).

Intermarriage to Malays is likely to lead to more and more Indian Muslims identifying themselves with the Malay community. Survey research among Indian Muslims in Sarawak indicates that when marriages are exogamous (that is, one parent is Malay), the children identify themselves with the dominant Malay community, but when it is endogamous (that is, both parents are Indian), the children tend to identify themselves as Indian (David and Dealwis 2009, pp. 38–39).

CONCLUSION: THE INDIAN MUSLIM QUEST FOR IDENTITY

The Indian Muslim impact on Malaysian life is the most influential compared to other ethnic minorities. This is due to their long history of contact with the region, their strong trade and political links, and their common religion with Malays. Even today their influence on religion, language, politics, literature, theatre, music, built heritage and cuisine remains strong and indelible. However these contributions have been largely overlooked as the role and influence of the community diminished over time, partly because many of them intermarried and assimilated into the heterogeneous Malay community.

While the majority are now clearly identified by the State as "Malay Muslim citizens", a minority — comprising "Indian Muslim" Permanent Residents and citizens — are still recognized as Indians rather than as Malays. Despite meeting the constitutional definition of Malay — being Muslim, speaking Malay and practising Malay customs — they are unable to change their official ethnic identity to Malay. While some are content to remain "Indian Muslims", the majority wish to be recognized as Malays to avoid social discrimination and to access State opportunities given to Malays.

Many younger Indian Muslims are able to improve their social status through educational, occupational and geographical mobility. In addition, those from the middle classes in particular have opportunities to interact, inter-marry and be assimilated into the Malay community. However a working class segment with PR status and their children remain trapped in dual identities; being neither "Malay" nor "Indian" they perceive both social and State discrimination.

Contrary to the stereotype of the prosperous Indian Muslim merchant, the majority of Indian Muslims remain wage earners. As with other communities in Malaysia, higher national economic growth rates have improved living standards for all, but it has also increased intra-ethnic wealth and income gaps. "Many people see a few rich Indian Muslim merchants and conclude that most of us are rich," notes Ibrahim Vengai, a community leader and businessman from the northern town of Teluk Intan. "They don't realize that only a few are businessmen — the rest are all wage earners" (Interview, 16 June 2008). Many second and third-generation Kadayanallur immigrants still work long hours as wage-earners or petty traders, often selling food, stationery and bread from lean-to sheds in narrow lanes and alcoves (Shanker 2001) in towns throughout the Peninsula.

While decades of State-led affirmative action have reduced absolute poverty and produced a larger middle class, grass-roots community leaders say that many Indian Muslim urban workers continue to struggle to make a comfortable living, competing for jobs and better wages with thousands of low-cost foreign workers from Indonesia, Burma, and the Indian sub-continent. In addition, in George Town and other urban areas in the Peninsula, the repeal of the Rent Control Act in 2000 hit many poor

Indian Muslims who for generations saved on rent and transport by living and working in pre-war shophouses.

Thus for the ordinary Indian Muslim worker today the dilemma of economic marginalization is conflated with that of dual ethnic identities and a perception of State and social discrimination. It is not surprising therefore that — like most ethnic minorities discussed in this book — some Indian Muslims see the acquisition of a State-recognized Malay-*bumiputera* identity, rather than a non-ethnic based economic and social policy, as the most effective means to improve their socio-economic position and social integration.

This perceived discrimination among segments of the Indian Muslim community is ironic given their deep-rooted contributions to Malaysian society. Indian Muslims, like all other ethnic minorities, should be encouraged not just to maintain but also celebrate their heritage and identity in the context of their historical and current role in nation-building. This can happen if they are accepted as part and parcel of a heterogeneous Malay community within a diverse multi-ethnic society. They can be Muslim, Indian, Jawi Peranakan, and yet remain Malaysian — without any contradiction — if Malaysia evolves from its ethnic-based political system to one where civic citizenship and economic needs take precedence over ethnicity.

APPENDIX 1.1
MOHIDEEN, A KADAYANALLUR TRADER*

Haja Mohideen has been making and selling *songkok*, the local Islamic headgear, for half a century. His shop sits in an alcove in the Nagore Shrine in Chulia Street. The shop, established by his father, a Kadayanallur immigrant, has been located here for almost a century. Mohideen, 58, wears a thin white singlet and thick spectacles, perhaps a result of years of intricate sewing. He is very busy using a small wooden hammer to staple the velvet of some headgear. The tiny shop is well equipped, with two worn out but functioning Singer sewing machines, one elongated to serve as a customer counter. A portable radio blaring Tamil music is his constant companion, while a suspended neon bulb, a Tamil calendar and two thread spittoons — one gold and one blue — complete his work ensemble.

A few minutes later, his grandniece arrives with her mother. He proudly introduces the girl, Sheerin, as "a doctor, just graduated from Dublin, just started working at the General Hospital." Both the *sari*-clad mother and daughter, who wears a Malay-style *baju kurung* and headscarf, look happy. Mohideen suddenly excuses himself and disappears down the backlane. After some small talk I venture to ask the doctor what ethnic group she identifies herself with: "Indian Muslim," she replies quickly. Ali, a friend of Mohideen who is at the shop, volunteers: "Both her mother and father are Indian Muslims and she has been brought up the Indian Muslim way, so she sees herself as one!"

Mohideen reappears with fifty food packets, and explains that they are to be distributed to the poor inside the nearby shrine as a thanksgiving offering for Sheerin's new job. He offers me a packet, saying, "just try, and tell me how." The rice came with mild chicken curry and meat, brinjal, and chunks of soft potato, and was delicious!

He is finally relaxed enough to talk. He recalls working by day and studying by night for the first four years of secondary school. However he could not continue his education as his father was unable to pay the school fees and needed his help in the shop. Their main clients were Indian Muslim immigrants who often took a few *songkoks* home as gifts. The *songkok* (headgear) worn by Muslim men for religious and official ceremonies, is believed to have originated from Achehnese migrants.

Mohideen is fifty-eight but looks much older. "When my kids were small I used to work 14–15 hours a day, often from morning till midnight. We lived in a rented room nearby. Now it's okay. My son is an engineer with Intel, my daughter is a teacher. Most of our clients were local Indian Muslims who lived in the city. There were more when Penang was a free port and before rent control was abolished in 2000. There was a thriving community in the city centre then, which was alive till late every night."

*This profile is based on several interviews in Penang in April 2008.

APPENDIX 1.2
FAZAL MOHD BROS:
PROVIDING FOR THE PILGRIM'S PASSAGE*

While Tamil Muslims from the south form the majority of Indian Muslims in Penang, many other Indians, including those from the north, have also contributed to its history, including its Islamic legacy. Across the road from the Nagore Shrine on Chulia Street are a row of ordinary looking textile shops. But one shop, Fazal Mohd Bros, is special. It serves a select clientele — Muslim pilgrims embarking on the haj. The items in this shop were once available only in the Port of Aden in Yemen, and the shop today symbolizes the historical role of Penang as a key location for Muslims in the region heading to Mecca to perform the haj. (From the nineteenth century to the 1970s Penang Port was a transit point for haj pilgrims from Southeast Asia, particularly the Peninsula, northern Sumatra and South Thailand (Abdur-Razzaq and Khoo 2003).)

The original founder of the shop migrated to Malaya in 1926 from Punjab in what was then India. He settled in Sungai Bayor, a one-street town in the Selama District of Perak where some relatives lived, and traded in textiles, clocks, bicycles, and prayer mats. In 1939 he went back to get married and returned with his wife, two uncles, and their families. Four years later, the three families moved to Taiping, the administrative capital of the Federated Malay States. In 1952 one uncle moved to Chulia Street to this shop, which was rented from a Chettiar (money-lender) for $175 a month. After 1957, when Taiping ceased to be the administrative and military centre, business became slack so all the families moved in stages to Penang.

In the 1960s the shop began specializing in pilgrimage items. Apart from Singapore, Penang was the only other place in the region where ships embarked on the journey to the Holy Land, and pilgrims needed to have certain items for the journey. Though pilgrims from the region now fly directly to the Holy Land, the State-run Pilgrims Board has enabled more Muslims to make the pilgrimage. This has aided the family business. Flights for the haj depart from Penang (in addition to Kuala Lumpur and Johor Bahru), and till this day pilgrims from nearby Kedah, Perak and Perlis purchase their items from the shop before leaving.

The shop sells at least twenty-five items related to the pilgrimage, in addition to standard textile items. The items range from two-piece white towel-robes for men and head-dresses and clothes for women to lip balm, pocket-sized Qurans, perfumes and prayer books.

* *Source*: Author's Fieldwork, 2008–09.

APPENDIX 1.3
SHOPS TO SUPERSTORES:
BARKATH, HABIB AND MYDIN

Kumpulan Barkath's history began in 1945 when an entrepreneur, the late Haji Abu Backer bin Mohd Hussain, founded a sundry shop called Barkath Stores at Union Street, Penang. The small family shop turned into a manufacturing venture with the local production of British "Hacks" sweets, other confectioneries, and frozen foods. Today, Barkath stores operates as part of Kumpulan Barkath, a group of twenty-two companies based in Malaysia, Singapore, Indonesia, India and the United Kingdom involved in manufacturing, import-export, distribution, property development, investment and communications (Kumpulan Barkath n.d.).

Habib Jewels began when Habib Mohamed Abdul Latif started his business in Penang in 1958. Today it has become a household name and operates a chain of jewellery outlets across the country. Habib's designs are a fusion of Malay, Chinese and Indian elements, and appeal to a wide cross-section of Malaysians (iGeorge Town Penang n.d).

Mydin Mohamed Holdings, a major retailer and wholesaler, had its humble beginnings in 1957 when its founder Mydin Mohamed set up shop in Kota Bahru, Kelantan, catering to the Indian Muslim community. Following his success there, he opened another branch in the heart of Kuala Lumpur in the Indian Muslim Masjid Jamek area. Today Mydin serves all ethnic communities and has 4,000 employees across twenty-eight branches nationwide (*Allied Telesis* 2007).

APPENDIX 1.4
LIST OF INTERVIEWS/FIELD VISITS

1. "Akbar" (religious official, Kapitan Keling Mosque), interview by the author, 5 April 2008.
2. Anwar Fazal (former UN official), interviews by the author, April and June 2008.
3. Asraf Fazal (proprietor of Fazal Bros), interview by the author, 7 April 2008.
4. A.V.M. Haja (lawyer, entrepreneur, and president of Masjid India Mosque), interview by the author at Bilal Restaurant, Kuala Lumpur 17 June 2008.
5. Dato' Dr Mohamed Iqbal (group executive director for FARLIM Group), interview by the author in Bandar Sri Subang, Kuala Lumpur (17 June 2008).
6. Fatimah Hassan (senior programme coordinator for Socio-economic and Environment Research Institute), interview by the author 2 June 2008.
7. Fidha Ulla (journalist for Nambikai Magazine, Kuala Lumpur), interview by the author, 17 June 2008.
8. Haja Mohideen (petty trader) interview by the author on Chulia Street, 7–8 April 2008.
9. Himanshu Bhatt (bureau chief of *The Sun*), interview by the author, 9 April 2008 and 1 June 2008.
10. Ibrahim Vengai (social worker and businessman from Teluk Intan), interview by the author in Kuala Lumpur, 16 June 2008.
11. Meera Nagore (book trader and local historian), interviews by the author, April and June 2008.
12. Mydin Sultan (radio journalist and commentator for RTM), interview by the author at *Nambikai* magazine office, Kuala Lumpur, 17 June 2008.
13. Najmudeen Kader (President of the Muslim League), interview by the author, 31 May 2008.
14. S.M. Mohamed Idris (businessman, President of Consumer's Association of Penang and former President of Penang Lighter Owners Association), interview by the author, 30 May 2008.
15. Random interviews with university and school students by the author, in Penang (June 2008) and Kuala Lumpur (February 2010).
16. Yousof Ghulam-Sarwar, Professor, University of Malaya, interview by the author, 21 April 2008.

Notes

1. Now known as Jalan Masjid Kapitan Keling.
2. A pseudonym.
3. This estimate was provided by community leader Ibrahim Vengai (Interview, 16 June 2008) and confirmed by the Indian Muslim corporate and community leader Dr Mohamed Iqbal (Interview, 25 June 2008).
4. There are other relics and ruins revealing the Hindu Pallava empire's fourth century contacts on the Penang mainland and its seventh century links in Kedah and Perak. There is also evidence of eighth and ninth century Buddhist Srivijayan influence in Kedah and Perak (Ghulam-Sarwar 2001).
5. Unless otherwise stated, details of the history of Indian immigration in Penang are based on a series of interviews with the late Penang-based local historian and book trader Meera Nagore in April and June 2008. Additional information is from the historian Khoo Salma Nasution (2001*a*, *b*).
6. Meera claims this is the origin of the pejorative *"Mamak Tongkang"* sometimes used on Indian Muslims. However a more credible version is that it refers to labourers who worked on lighters in Penang Harbour (S.M. Mohamed Idris, former president of Penang Lighter Owners Association, interviewed by the author, 30 May 2008).
7. From whence originates the popular P. Ramlee song *"Achi-Achi Buka Pintu"*, says Meera Nagore (Interview, April 2008).
8. The term "Kaka" is commonly used to refer to Malabar Muslims and is used in Kerala till this day (Narayanan 2002).
9. *Nambikai* magazine, published in Malaysia, is sold throughout Southeast Asia, including Laos.
10. Today Penang has at least fifteen long-established Muslim-based social organizations, including the Iqbal Islamic Association, the Central Muslim Society, and sports clubs. Among the more prominent ones are:
    • United Muslim Association, 1929
    • Anjuman Himayathul Islam, 1930
    • Persatuan Hidayathul Islam, 1941
    • Persatuan Nurul Islam, 1946
    • Kadayanathur Muslim Association, 1946
    • Penang Muslim League, 1954.
11. Fatimah Hassan says such cross-cultural influences are common among other ethnic groups in Penang. "It's not uncommon to find Penang Chinese who speak 'pure' Malay, and Indians and Malays who speak 'perfect' Hokkien," she adds. (Interview, Fatimah Hassan, 2 June 2008).
12. Masjid India was financed by Indian Muslim merchants who lived and traded in nearby Batu Road, now known as Jalan Tunku Abdul Rahman (Masjid India, n.d.).

13. "Sepoy" is a term of Portuguese-Urdu-Persian origin, referring a private serving in the army of a foreign conqueror, especially an Indian soldier under British command in India (The American Heritage Dictionary of the English Language, Fourth Edition, Houghton Miffin Company, 2009).

14. Variations, namely *Jawi Pekan*, referring to town dwellers, and *Jawi Bukan*, implying a lack of Malayness, have been used in different social context (Nagata 2006, pp. 519–20).

15. In January 2010 for example, I met a Kuala Lumpur-based Malay overseas-trained professional woman of Chinese-Malay parentage. She was married to a Malay of Indian ancestry, and both of them were originally from Penang. In the course of a casual conversation (she was not a research respondent), she teased her ten year-old son in the presence of her husband and me, saying, "He is half-*Mamak* because his father is a Merican." Her demeanour indicated she was proud of the fact. Her husband did not seem to mind. I could not help thinking that she was, perhaps unconsciously, socializing her son into being aware of his Indian ancestry.

16. Ibrahim Vengai (community leader/businessman from Teluk Intan, Perak), interviewed by the author in Kuala Lumpur, 16 June 2008.

17. Some Indian Muslim students from poor families who gain university and college places but are unable to secure government financial assistance turn to community initiatives, including one established by Dr Mohamed Iqbal and his friends in 1972, which provides loans to deserving students.

18. Random interviews with school students by the author in Rawang District, Selangor (February 2010), and Penang (June 2008).

2

THE CHITTY OF MALACCA
An Epitome of Cross-Cultural Influences

INTRODUCTION: KAMPUNG CHITTY, MALACCA

Ten minutes from historic Malacca's town centre is its best-kept cultural secret. It is Kampung Chitty, a quiet village of one hundred Malay-speaking Hindus, descendants of Malacca's fourteenth-century Tamil merchant community. Popularly known as *"Chitty"* but also referred to as Peranakan Indians (see Appendix 2.1), they reside in a five-acre village off a main road in Gajah Berang. On my first visit one evening I notice an old woman in *sarong kebaya* standing on the village road, deep in prayer. Her palms are clasped on her forehead and are pointed toward an old (1887) Shiva Temple at the village entrance, from which emanates the sounds of bells and Hindu devotional songs. At the end of the village road is a larger and older (1822) Mariamman Temple with intricate, colourful statues and figurines. An old Chinese man casually walks in to pray.

The houses are a mix of Malay, Chinese and Indian architectural styles. One small house built on stilts has a Sumatran Minangkabau-style roof, ornate concrete balustrades, and red lanterns in the veranda. Inside is an altar with photographs of Hindu deities. But there is also a table with very large black-and-white old photographs, similar to Taoist ancestor-worship altars. Some occupants of the house look "Indian", others "Malay" or "Chinese". The older women wear *sarong kebaya,* and everyone including the children speaks in Malay.

The Chitty are an epitome of the cross-cultural influences embraced by Malacca through six centuries. Through interaction, intermarriage and acculturation with ancient Malacca's cosmopolitan port population of Malays, Peranakan Chinese, Javanese and Bataks they have evolved a hybrid culture, with their language, cuisine, dress, dance and music incorporating diverse influences. Yet their identity has remained anchored in their deeply orthodox Saviate (Siva-worship) Hindu faith, their core residential space and Malay, their mother tongue (Dhoraisingam 2006, pp. xi–xii; Narayanasamy 2004, pp. 5–6).[1]

This is the story of how a tiny hybrid community, a "little tradition", has survived five "great traditions" (Redfield 1956), namely, a Malay Empire, Portuguese, Dutch and British colonial rule, and a Malay-dominated Malaysian post-colonial State. Despite colonial dislocation and dispersion, communal land ownership has saved their village. Though more youths have benefited from higher education and employment opportunities within Malacca State, a segment of the community within the village perceives itself as an economically and politically marginalized minority with indigenous roots, and seeks State-recognition and protection as *bumiputeras.*

SHARED HISTORIES: FACTORS FACILITATING ACCULTURATION

Hybrid Origins of the People

The community's roots go back to India's deep and long trade links with the Peninsula. Around 1402, Indian (Muslim and Hindu) traders played an important role in helping the Sumatran Hindu Prince Parameswara transform Malacca from a quiet fishing village into a thriving port. Islam was introduced by Muslim traders, mainly from India (Andaya 1982, p. 53), and when Parameswara converted to Islam the Indians remained influential traders and court advisors.

At its height the cosmopolitan port had a population of 40,000 to 50,000 people speaking eighty-four languages. They included 4,000 wealthy Indians living in the commercially strategic enclave of Kampung Kling near the river mouth in what is now Tranquerah.[2] Over the years, Indian traders who had to wait out the monsoons or who were domiciled due to the nature of their business married Malays, Javanese, Bataks and Peranakan Chinese women. Their children learnt Malay from their mothers, and the local bazaar Malay gradually became their mother tongue (Dhoraisingam 2006, pp. 1–6). However many traders did not convert to Islam despite marrying Malays because Islam had not fully taken root immediately after Parameswara's conversion. During this transitional period there were still pockets of Malay Buddhist and Malay Hindu communities in Malacca. This could be explained by the fact that Peninsular Malaysia had historically been part of the Buddhist (Srivijaya) and Hindu (Majapahit) Empires (Dhoraisingam 2008, p. 22).

Colonial Decline, Dislocation and Dispersion

After cosmopolitan Malacca produced a hybrid Chitty trading community, Portuguese, Dutch and British colonial rule induced its occupational decline, geographical dislocation and dispersion. This led to its further acculturation, but also created caste and class cleavages within the community.

(a) Side-Lined by the Portuguese

Malacca's prosperity attracted the Portuguese, who wanted to break its regional trade monopoly. A Malacca Chitty trader named Naina Chitty collaborated in the 1511 Portuguese conquest of Malacca, but despite his assistance Indian traders were sidelined, though Kampung Kling was retained and the trade with India remained important for some time. Many traders returned to India, but those who stayed on were mainly Chitty or their employees (Narayanasamy 2004, p. 3).

Towards the end of Portuguese rule many Chitty brought in domestic workers such as laundrymen, cooks and cleaners from India (Narayanasamy 2004, p. 7), contributing to the creation of castes within the community.[3] According to residents, today there is little caste consciousness, especially with more and more "love marriages". But caste remains a factor in arranged marriages. "Though some Peranakan Indians who are not from the Chitty caste may not be direct descendants of the early traders, many domestic workers later became traders or worked for traders and can therefore be considered part of the community," explains a village leader

(Nadarajan Raja, Interview, 28 September 2009).[4] His explanation underlines the heterogeneous nature of the community and the fluidity of ethnic definitions among ethnic groups, especially culturally hybrid minorities.

(b) *Dislocated by the Dutch*

While more than a century of Portuguese rule marked the decline of their trading influence, almost two centuries of Dutch Occupation led to their occupational and geographical dislocation from Kampung Kling. After conquering Malacca in 1641, the Dutch preference for Batavia and the rise of the British ports of Penang and Singapore added to Malacca's trading decline (Mearns 1995, p. 29). The Dutch, who viewed the Chitty as pro-Portuguese, imposed trade restrictions which forced more to return to India. Those who had married local women and had established families in Malacca remained, but switched from trading to agriculture (Narayanasamy 2004, p. 3). Chitty who had married locally could not return to India because caste-conscious Indian villagers would not accept their extra-caste and inter-ethnic marriages. Both colonialism and caste therefore combined to marginalize them from a trading community at the port city's centre to agriculturists and artisans at its periphery (Mearns 1995, pp. 29–31).

Remaining traders at Kampung Kling were moved eastward to Jalan Tukang Emas (Goldsmith Street) within the city. This remained the community's commercial centre for some time, as evidenced by the 1781 Dutch grant land on this street for the Sri Poyyatha Vinayagar Moorthi Temple (Narinasamy 1983, p. 240). This temple, the largest and oldest Chitty place of worship, is still owned by the community but maintained by the Natukotai Chettiars, an unrelated money-lending caste, some of whom still operate nearby (Narayanasamy 2004, p. 8). Today it is the oldest Hindu temple in use in Malaysia and Singapore (Dhoraisingam 2006, p. 12) and all Chitty communal property is registered under its name. The temple lies adjacent to the 1690 Kampung Kling Mosque and the nearby 1645 Peranakan Chinese Cheng Hoon Teng Temple.

While those who retained businesses continued to live in the newly relocated Kampung Kling, others resorted to farming and brick-making on land in the rural areas of Gajah Berang, Bacang and Limbongan northwest of the city (Dhoraisingam 2006, p. 12; Narinasamy 1983, p. 240). Dutch records indicate that this occupational and geographical dispersion began as early as 1678. Land grants for agricultural shrines in Bachang in 1754 and Gajah Berang in 1770 provide further evidence of early farming (Mearns

1995, p. 29). The Chitty are thus the first Indians known to be involved in agriculture in Malaysia and Singapore (Dhoraisingam 2006, p. 28), long before the British brought in Indian rubber plantation workers in the early twentieth century.

Mearns states that as occupational and residential locations coincided, "workspace became equivalent to ethnic space" and the geographical and occupational dispersion of the Chitty impacted their social and spiritual lives. The agricultural pioneers harnessed their native spiritual practices by building field shrines, each identified with a particular Hindu deity. These deities reflect both the community's Indian roots and the reciprocal social responsibilities between community, temple and land (Mearns 1983, pp. 30 and 70). The shrines are still in existence and in use today, particularly during the month of *Adimasam,* which traditionally marks the sowing season.

(c) *Dispersed by the British*

The geographical relocation of the Chitty was the result of Dutch, and to a lesser extent, late Portuguese trading practices. However the organization of their space today is the result of British and post-colonial market forces (Mearns 1995, pp. 72–73), which led to the emigration of the better educated, the sale of land, and eventually to the confinement of a largely working class segment to communal land where housing plots were offered at nominal rents. As the British colonial market economy penetrated the Straits Settlements, some educated Chitty began leaving agriculture and petty trading for secure — albeit low-level occupations — in British-run government departments in Malacca town, Singapore and Kuala Lumpur. This trend strengthened with better education and improved English fluency. Over the next few decades the Chitty in Malacca moved into geographical areas largely corresponding to class, caste, educational and occupational background. These areas defined them so strongly that they referred to themselves by location, as either "coastal", "hinterland" or "village" people (*orang pantai, darat* and *kampung,* respectively).

The *orang pantai* (coastal people) comprised families originally with a trading background, particularly those with Chitty caste surnames such as Chitty, Rajah and Naiker, who lived in coastal Tranquerah. In the course of the late nineteenth to mid-twentieth century, many of these old trading families emigrated to Singapore, and later Kuala Lumpur. In 2009, there was only one family left in Tranquerah. A senior community leader recalls:

After they were edged out of trading, these Chitty families worked for the British, through whom they acquired wealth and influence. They had enough money and influence to ensure that their children completed school and obtained clerical, supervisory and later semi-professional and professional jobs in British-run departments and firms. English fluency was their biggest asset.

(K. Arunasalam Pillay, Secretary, Temple Committee, interviewed by author, 14 July 2008).

The *orang darat* (hinterland people) of rural Bachang were farmers, while the *orang kampung* (village people) referred to those in the Chetti Village who comprised tradesmen and office workers:

Unlike the Chitty trading class, the two other groups were too poor to keep their children in school and were not so fluent in English. Therefore many of their children could not get good jobs and their families could not break out of the cycle of poverty.

(K. Arunasalam Pillay, 14 July 2008).

Portuguese, Dutch and British colonialism therefore contributed to the decline, dislocation and dispersion of what was once a thriving trading community and to the creation of caste and class cleavages within it. An educated group with better jobs moved to Singapore and Kuala Lumpur, while a less educated working-class component remained confined within their ethnic and spiritual space in Kampung Chitty.

Accountant M.K.T. Pillay, a Malacca community leader, was largely responsible for recommending many Chitty for government jobs in Singapore. There, many settled in enclaves in Chitty Road (off Serangoon Road), Dalhouise Lane, Kampung Kapor, Kinta Road, Rowell Road and Bencoolen and Selegie Road. Some women married Tamil Hindus, others Malayalees and Chinese, while many converted to Christianity through marriage. Inter-marriage was linked to the fact that many spoke English and Malay, but not Tamil (Dhoraisingam 2008, p. 29). Today there are an estimated 5,000 people of Melaka Chitty origin living in Singapore (Channel NewsAsia 2008).

Post-War Interaction and Intermarriage

Though of hybrid origin, the Chitty remained largely endogamous, and up to World War II many married cousins. Several factors explain why intermarriage became more common after the war. The terror unleashed by the Japanese Occupation in 1941 was the major turning point. "When we heard that Japanese soldiers were raping women, we got our daughters married off within days," recalls Madam Meenachi, a seventy-nine-year-old matriarch. "We didn't care who they married, as long as they had a good husband to protect them." Thus the war resulted in many young Chitty girls being hastily married off to Indians, Chinese and Eurasians (Interview, 10 July 2008).[5]

Secondly, in the post-war years intermarriages became more common as Chitty migrated to Singapore and Kuala Lumpur, where they worked, mingled and met Chinese, Indians, Eurasians and Malays. A third factor was language. Many Chitty spoke fluent Malay and English but not Tamil, and often had Malay and English-speaking Peranakan Chinese neighbours. This encouraged marriages with Chinese rather than Indians, who were mostly Tamil-speaking. A fourth factor was that many Chitty were fair-skinned, a colour preference bred by colonialism which made them sought after by other ethnic groups.

The trend towards exogamous marriages has persisted and today many Chitty youth marry non-Chitty Indians, and to a lesser extent, Chinese. More Chitty girls than boys make it to university, where they often meet and marry Indian non-Chitty Hindus. These women usually adapt to their husbands daily Hindu religious rituals and gradually drop their own Chitty religious and cultural practices. Trans-national marriages are not uncommon, with Chitty women who marry foreigners settling overseas.

While intermarriage was common among the pre-war generation and has picked up again as youths move out to study and work, a middle-aged cohort which grew up in the village in the 1960s and 1970s faced difficulties in obtaining education and finding spouses. "Our parents were not education-centric; they allowed their children to leave school early to work," recalls executive Amu Pillay, while noting that a lack of Tamil fluency prevented close interaction with Tamil-speaking Indians. Her personal experience makes her less sanguine about the future: "Our community is shrinking. More and more people, especially males, are marrying out of the community. A lot of daughters remain unmarried. Unless we marry our cousins, I'm not sure if we can last another three generations!" she laments (Interviews, 24 April 2010, Malacca, and 2 May 2010, Kuala Lumpur).

The Role of Peranakan Chinese as Cultural Intermediaries

Many of the Chitty's hybrid cultural influences did not come directly from the Malays but via Malacca's Peranakan Chinese, who served as cultural intermediaries in the process of acculturation. The Chitty interacted closely with the Peranakan Chinese and shared common elements in cuisine, dress and the performing arts. This intermediary role was facilitated by several factors. One was shared neighbourhoods. For example the Chitty trading class, like the richer Peranakan Chinese and well-to-do Portuguese Eurasians, lived in coastal Tranquerah. Another was a common language; the Chitty Creole developed from the Peranakan Chinese bazaar Malay. A third factor was common workplaces. These included government departments in the case of the more educated Chitty, and the homes of rich Peranakan Chinese families where some poorer Chitty (and Portuguese Eurasians) were often employed as housekeepers. A Chitty woman recalls:

> My 80-year-old mum was once a cook in a Baba (Peranakan Chinese) household. She not only learnt Peranakan Chinese dishes, which she cooked for us, but cooked Chitty cuisine for her employers. Not surprisingly, she's a gourmet cook today!
>
> (Ms Amu Pillay, Interview, 2 May 2010).

CULTURE AND IDENTITY: MANIFESTATIONS OF ACCULTURATION

Religion: Between Acculturation and Assimilation

Though other aspects of their culture — religious rituals, language, dress, cuisine, music and art forms — have imbibed strong indigenous influences, the core of Chitty culture comprises its orthodox Saviate Hindu beliefs. Among the pre-war generation, non-Chitty women who married Chitty men converted to Hinduism and assimilated into the community. For example, Chinese (Buddhist-Taoist) women who married Chitty men converted to Hinduism, took Hindu names and brought up their children as Chitty Hindus. The Chitty Village was probably the only place in Malaysia where Chinese women converted to Hinduism for marriage, assimilated rather than merely acculturated, and took on a new identity.

Today, though religion remains an important identity marker, being Chitty is considered being part of a culture rather than a religion, and newcomers are acculturated rather assimilated into the community. Since the Chitty are a patriarchal community, most Chitty men who marry Chinese (Buddhist-Taoist) or Indian (Hindu) women acculturate them into Chitty religious practices. Chitty women who marry out usually follow their husband's Hindu, Christian or Buddhist traditions.

"Look at my family", says K. Shanmugan Rajan, 40, an engineer who works in Kuala Lumpur but returns to the village for all religious events. (Interview, Chitty Village, 2 May 2010) "My mother is Chinese but she converted to Hinduism when she married my late Chitty father. One of my brothers married a Tamil Hindu, and another married an Indonesian Buddhist of Indian descent. I am married to a Chinese who remains a Taoist but 'became a Chitty' and practises Hindu rituals. But all of us are Chitty, and Hindu!" His wife retains her Chinese name on her identity card, unlike his mother who has both her Chinese and Hindu names recorded on it. (See Interview 1 in Appendix 2.3 for details.)

Although there has been a long history of close interaction and intermarriage with Malays and acculturation to their language and customs, the Chitty — like the Portuguese Eurasians of Malacca and the Peranakan Chinese of Terengganu — claim that very few of them marry Malays today (Fieldwork Interviews, 2008–2010). The reasons were similar to those given by the other communities, namely, that in the Malaysian context both the law and social norms dictate conversion and assimilation of the spouse and their children into the Malay Muslim community. The situation in Malacca is in contrast to that in Singapore where Chitty Muslim converts continue to identify with their Chitty heritage (Cempaka_s 2008, p. 8). The cosmopolitan environment of Singapore's secular city-state engenders the acceptance of a more heterogeneous Muslim identity. "Some Singapore Chitty have become Muslims but they keep their Chitty surnames. That's why in Singapore you get people with names like 'Anwar Pillay' who still proudly identify themselves as Chitty," says Nadarajan Raja (Interview, 28 September 2009).

Despite — or perhaps because of — their close cultural links with Malays, some Chitty fear their children may convert to Islam, and therefore discourage them from intermingling (and inter-marrying) with Malays. To achieve this, a high degree of social distance from Malays is engendered within some families through negative stereotyping (Fieldwork Interviews, 2008–2010). While stereotyping is a common strategy utilized to create exclusion and preserve identity in many multi-ethnic societies, in this particular case the aim is to preserve the identity of a hybrid minority which, rightly or wrongly, perceives itself as vulnerable to a demographically and politically dominant Malay Muslim majority.

The Chitty observe all spiritual events in the Hindu calendar including *Ponggal* (Harvest Festival), *Maha Shivaratri* (Lord Shiva devotions), *Navaratri* (dedications to the Goddess Sakti), *Varusa Pirapu* (Tamil Hindu New Year), and *Deepavali* (Festival of Lights). But there are two events they consider unique to their community and culture. One is their annual devotions to the Goddess Mariamman.

Known in the Chitty creole as *"Meggamay"*, this 200-year-old event held annually in April-May attracts thousands of devotees. They include Chitty who return to the village from various parts of Malaysia and Singapore, and local Indians and Chinese, including those around Kampung Chitty, whose ancestors traditionally participated in this event. The celebration is referred to in Malay as *Sembahyang Dato Chachar*, following a widespread belief that the ash used in temple prayers cures chicken pox and shingles.

The climax of the ten-day celebration is a spectacular procession which I witnessed on 25 April 2010. At dawn thousands of devotees in robes leave the village Mariamman Temple in batches and walk barefoot to the Sri Poyyatha Vinayagar Moorthi Temple, popularly known as "Kuil Melaka", on Jalan Tukang Mas in Malacca town. This 1781 temple, the oldest in Malaysia, is located adjacent the 1748 Kampung Kling Mosque, one of the oldest mosques in the country. Inside the temple hundreds of devotees conduct purification rituals. Outside, opposite the temple and mosque, a group of temple musicians play intense devotional music, using traditional instruments. A group of young people — Chitty, Chinese and Indians — are totally immersed in offerings of repentance involving the carrying of *kavadis*. Some men carry images of deities and have spikes in their bodies, while other men and women carry pots of milk. Several men and women enter into a trance. A procession of children, women and men slowly assemble, followed by a 200-year-old wooden chariot carrying a statue of Goddess Mariamman.

The procession then begins its return journey to the village. The chariot halts in front of the nearby 1645 Cheng Hoon Teng Temple, the oldest in Malacca, as a "mark of respect" to the deities there. All along the way, especially in the Tranquerah area where the Peranakan Chinese have lived for generations, Chinese onlookers clasp their hands in prayer. The chariot stops at several Chinese shophouses where traders make offerings and shatter coconuts. This is meant to symbolize the breaking of the ego and surrender to God. The procession finally reaches the Mariamman Temple in the village, where, to foster service and fellowship, free food is served to thousands of devotees. Prayers continue throughout the day, and in the late evening the Mariamman diety is taken from house to house in the Chitty village for families to make devotions and receive blessings. The deity, again accompanied by thousands, then returns to the temple in town, but this time — since vows have been fulfilled and repentance gained — the mood is less intense and there is some gaiety (Source: Participant observation, Author, Malacca, 24 April 2010).

The second event unique to the Chitty is their family ancestor worship ceremony called "*Parchu*", which is observed twice a year. The first and most important, *Parchu Ponggal*, is observed the day before Ponggal (Harvest Festival) in January, with prayers to the spirits of ancestors, and offerings including Chitty home-made food, cigarettes, betel leaves, tobacco and tea (details in Appendix 2.2). The second, *Parchu Buah-Buahan*, is celebrated between June and July during the fruit season, when offerings of fruit are made. The Chitty version of both these events incorporate some indigenous non-religious Malay and Chinese practices (Dhoraisingam 2006, p. 34), with regional and universal Hindu rituals common to Malaysia-Singapore and certain parts of South India.

All spiritual events are occasions where families return, reunite in the village and reaffirm their Chitty identity. As Kuala Lumpur-based engineer K. Shanmugan Rajan puts it: "I've never missed any festival here despite being out of Malacca for twenty years. Even when I was dating my wife (she is Chinese) I brought her here to help her understand my culture and religion. I will continue to come. I want my daughter to know her roots." (Interview, 2 May 2010).

Language: A Malay-based Creole

The mother-tongue of the Chitty is a Malay-based Creole that reflects their rich cross-cultural and cosmopolitan origins. In 2009 all the twenty-two households in the village used Malay as their main language of communication within the home (Interview, Nadarajan, 4 May 2010). The Chitty Creole developed from the "bazaar Malay" spoken by Malacca's Peranakan Chinese, and was originally used by Chinese, Arabs, Indians and Europeans in the seventeenth century. However the Chitty version includes Tamil words (Noriah Mohamed 2009, p. 59 & p. 65). Malay is such a critical part of their lives that the Chitty still pray in Malay, retaining some common Sanskrit and Tamil religious terms used by the majority Indian Hindu community (Narinasamy 1983, p. 256). Since the heart of Chitty culture is religion, the use of Malay in prayer demonstrates the depth of their acculturation. Dhoraisingam (2006, pp. 93–95) documents some fascinating examples of their prayers in Malay:

The Deity's Arrival
The Chitty call out: *Swami sudah datang!* (The deity has come). During festivals the deity it is carried around the temple courtyard.

Making an Offering
A devotee gives an offering at the temple. He *cuci kaki* (washes his feet), then walks around the temple to relax and *pusing koil* (prepare for reverence), before entering to *sembayang* (pray).

Devotee to priest: *Ayyah, saya mau arshaneh* (Sir, I want to make an offering)
Priest: *Siapa nama?* (What's your name?)
Devotee: *Kisna* (Krisna)
Devotee: *Ayyah, buat arshaneh* (Here is my offering)

Prayer for Healing
A Chitty was praying silently to the Deity Sri Mariamman, also known as Mother or *Ammah* in Tamil. When asked to verbalize his prayers, he explained it as follows:

Ammah, tolong-lah aku…badan sakit, kasi badan baik-baik-lah.
(Mother, please help me…I am sick, please help me to get better)

Prayer to Ancestors
During prayers to the ancestors (known as "Parchu" to the Chitty, "Padayal" to the Tamil Hindus) the head of the family uses both Malay and Tamil words:

Thatha, pahti, mama, mami
Ini hari ada parchu sulu
Mari datang makan; apa ada salah, minta maaf!
(Grandfather, grandmother, uncle and aunt,
Today is offering day,
Please come to partake in the food; please forgive us if there are any shortcomings!)

(Source: Dhoraisingam 2006, pp. 93–95).

In addition to the widespread use of Malay, English was used in five families where older parents had an English education; Chinese — mainly Hokkien — in three households; and Tamil in six or seven households, particularly where one household head was Tamil (Nadarajan Raja, Interview, 4 May 2010). The complexity of language use in the community is illustrated in this observation by engineer Shanmugam: "I speak to my mum in Chitty Malay, to my wife in Mandarin, and we all speak to our daughter in English — and a bit of Mandarin and Malay," he says (Interview, 2 May 2010).

Cuisine and Dress: A Malaysian Melange[6]

Chitty cuisine is a fascinating blend which has over centuries absorbed Indian, Malay and Peranakan Chinese influences. One Chitty describes their food as "more Malay and Indian-style, unlike Peranakan Chinese food which is more Chinese" (Interview, K. Shanmugan Rajan, 2 May 2010). Traditional Indian spices are freely used with Malay-based ingredients such as *belacan* (fermented shrimp paste), *serai* (citronella grass), and *lengkuas* (wild ginger). Their cakes are similar to those made by the Peranakan Chinese (Narinasamy 1983, p. 259; Narayanasamy 2004, p. 5; Dhoraisingam 2006, pp. 87–92). Beef, which is not consumed by Hindus, and pork, which is prohibited for Muslims, is not part of Chitty cuisine. This is an indicator of their cultural intimacy with Malay Muslims.

Among unique Chitty dishes are their version of *nasi lemak*, a traditional Malay dish of rice cooked with coconut milk and served with *sambal tumis*, *ikan bilis* (fried anchovies) and cucumber. The Chitty version involves cooling steamed rice and later boiling it with coconut milk and *daun pandan* (pandanus leaf). It is often offered for prayers (Hindu Tamils offer rice with vegetables). Other Chitty specialities include *nasi kembuli*, a rice dish made with ghee, cumin, coriander and pineapple,[7] served to brides three days after the wedding and as an offering during prayers, and *ikan pindang*, i.e. *ikan parang* (wolf herring) cooked in a clay pot. Salted egg — a Chinese/ Malay influence — is often served during ancestral rites.

Their traditional attire reflects centuries of Javanese, Bugis, Achehnese and Batak influences and has striking similarities to traditional Malacca Peranakan Chinese and Portuguese Eurasian wear. The men wore a *batik sarong* and tunic and a headgear of knotted *batik* cloth. Even today Chitty women, especially older folk, are easily distinguishable from Indians because they prefer the *baju* (Malay-style blouse) and *sarong*. For formal functions, the *sari* is more popular today, especially among the young. Youths prefer Western or Indian dress, though the *sarong* is often used at home.

For formal occasions Chitty women traditionally wore the *sarong kebaya* and *baju kurung* in the style of the Peranakan Chinese, fastened by *keronsang* brooches usually of silver, but sometimes with gold and tiny diamonds, depending on the user's status. Women wore some traditional Indian, but mostly Peranakan Chinese jewellery such as *keronsangs*, hairpins, and gold pendants made from British gold coins. Much of it comprised hybridized Malay-style jewellery with gold items set in Chinese, English and Dutch designs. The women traditionally wrapped their hair tight, with long protruding pins, in buns known as *"Sanggul Nyonya"*. Their footwear, like that of the Peranakan Chinese, comprises beaded slippers known as *kasot manek-manek*. These are handmade from beads and take weeks or months to weave. For both jewellery and footwear the status of the wearer is indicated in the intricacy of the patterns; the higher the wealth and status of the wearer, the more intricate the patterns (Narinasamy 1983, p. 259; Narayanasamy 2004, p. 5; Dhoraisingam 2006, pp. 80–81).

The Performing Arts: Shared Music and Dance forms

Like their cuisine, attire, jewellery and footwear, the Chitty shared music and dance forms with the Malays, Peranakan Chinese and Portuguese Eurasians. Their weddings were often followed by *dondang sayang* performances. These are interactive love songs sung in quatrains or *pantuns*, a genre first introduced into Malacca from Riau. The singers were accompanied by the *rebab* (violin) and accordion — which are Portuguese additions — and two Malay drums, the *rebana* and *tenawak*. Two well-known Chitty *dondang sayang* singers (1870–1920) were *Mamak* Kurnia and *Mamak* Redia (Narinasamy 1983, p. 259; Narayanasamy 2004, p. 6; Dhoraisingam 2006, p. 50).

The Peranakan Chinese and Chitty also enjoyed *ronggeng* and *joget* dances. The *ronggeng* is a social dance in which mixed sex couples dance and exchange verses to the accompaniment of a violin, frame drums and a gong. *Ronggeng* has been transformed from a folk genre of the Malay and Peranakan Chinese communities into a national form promoted by the Malaysian State, performed by and attracting audiences of different ethnic groups and classes (Tan Sooi Beng 2005).

The *joget*, a popular folk dance in Malaysia, is performed at cultural festivals, weddings and other social functions. A rhythmic dance performed by couples, it is an excellent example of how elements from various cultures can merge into a single form in the Malaysian setting. A syncretic dance with Portuguese roots, its music uses the Western violin, the Arab *rebana*, the Southeast Asian gong and a northeast Malaysian style of singing (Musicmall Productions Pte Ltd 2004).

In both Malacca and Singapore the *dondang sayang, ronggeng* and *joget* encouraged inter-ethnic interaction between the Chitty and Peranakan Chinese, and were a regular feature of their get-togethers up to the 1960s. For the Chitty, *dondang sayang* and *ronggeng* were once part of entertainment during the Hindu harvest festival of Ponggal.

ETHNIC SPACE: PEOPLE AND PLACE

Population: A Shrinking Community

The colonial dislocation and dispersion of the community has continued unabated through to the post-colonial period. The Chitty Malacca Cultural Society defines Chitty as those who come from families where both parents are Chitty and who still practise their religious customs and rituals, language, cuisine and way of life. In just over three decades — from 1976 to 2009 — Malaysia's Chitty population declined by almost half due to intermarriage, emigration and smaller family sizes (see Table 2.1 and Table 2.2). During the same period the number in Malacca State shrank by a third and those in the Chitty village by more than half.

In late 2009 there were an estimated 340 Chitty left in Malaysia, about one third of whom still lived in the village. There are another 250 persons of "Chitty origin", mainly outside Malacca, from families where one spouse, usually the mother, is Chitty. In such cases the mother and children follow the husband's beliefs (Nadarajan Raja, Interview, 28 September 2009).

The trend towards emigration for jobs, education and marriage in the British colonial and immediate post-colonial era has been mitigated by better educational and job opportunities in Malacca State in recent years. Unlike their parents' generation, about 60–70 per cent of those below twenty-five years of age now continue their studies beyond post-secondary education, often in Malacca-based educational institutions. More school-leavers now also manage to find work within Malacca, with

TABLE 2.1
Chitty Population, Malaysia, September 2009
(Families where both parents are Chitty)

Location	Houses	Persons
Chitty Village	22	110
Rest of Malacca	16	80
Rest of Malaysia	30	150
TOTAL	68	340

Source: Nadarajan Raja, Malacca Chitty Cultural Society (Interview by the author, 28 September 2009). Mr Nadarajan is the full-time Secretary of the society and has lived in the village all his life. This data is based on his mailing list of Peranakan Indian families in the country.

TABLE 2.2
Chitty Population, Malaysia, 1976
(Families where both parents are Chitty)

Location	Families	Persons
Chitty Village	32	255
Rest of Malacca	24	130
Rest of Malaysia	40	240
TOTAL	96	625

Source: Compiled from survey data by Narinasamy (1983), p. 246.

the rest moving to Singapore and Kuala Lumpur. This is mainly because Malacca, once dubbed the "sleepy hollow", has managed to attract foreign — including Singapore — investments and create many local jobs. Most school-leavers from the village become mid-level employees in the private sector in Malacca, with half of them working in its export-oriented plants, the other half in services, while a few run small businesses. Job entry is facilitated by the Chitty community's multi-lingual skills. "Firms prefer to hire us because many of us can speak Malay and English in addition to Tamil and Hokkien," said one youth leader (Interview, Temple Committee, Malacca, 13 July 2008).

Creating Ethnic Space: The Temple Trust

The dispersion of the community persisted after independence, and by the 1960s out-migration coincided with the rising value and loss of most of the community's residential and agricultural land in Tranquerah, Gajah Berang, Bachang, and Limbongan. Chitty who had given up agriculture or had emigrated sold their land to Chinese businessmen at inflated prices. Land transactions were also fuelled by a government warning that idle land would revert to the State (Narayanasamy 2004, pp. 3–4; Mearns 1995, p. 72).[8]

As land sales and fragmentation continued, community leaders, fearing eventual loss of their ancestral property, placed sixteen plots totalling about eight hectares into a trust deed under the Sri Poyyatha Vinayagar Moorthi Temple in 1962. It included village land and houses donated to the temple by villagers in the nineteenth and early twentieth century, in addition to graveyards, temples and shrines. The land was donated to avoid inheritance disputes or because owners were emigrating (Arunasalam Pillay, Interview, 14 July 2008).

The trust is managed by an elected committee of fifteen, including three trustees, in what is akin to the traditional Hindu Panchayat system of village councils. Meetings among these Hindu committee members are conducted in Malay and English (Dhoraisingam 2006, p. 26). The head of the committee is by default the village headman. The committee manages village affairs, including all rituals such as marriage, death and daily temple prayers. Its decisions are often binding and community members who defy them can be penalized. Though seldom exercised, this power remains a potent force, deterring a critical attitude towards the village leadership (Narinasamy 1983). Just as the trust deed "underpins" the physical existence of the village, the layout of the village has cultural and symbolic meaning, with houses within it "delineated by three important Hindu temples which define the Chitty socially as well as geographically". (Mearns 1995, p. 75). (See Figure 2.1 for location of temples and shrines, and Figure 2.2 for village layout.)

Today, except for community land held through the trust, the Chitty do not individually own any land in Gajah Berang or Bachang. The temple trust owns and manages the entire two-hectare village and fifty house-plots where villagers have built houses. In addition, it manages ten temples and shrines — the Sri Poyyatha Vinayagar Moorthi Temple in town, three within the village, four in the village periphery and two in Bachang — plus a four-hectare community graveyard in Batu Berendam (Fieldwork, 2008–10).

FIGURE 2.1
Location of Chitty Village and Its Temples and Shrines, Malacca

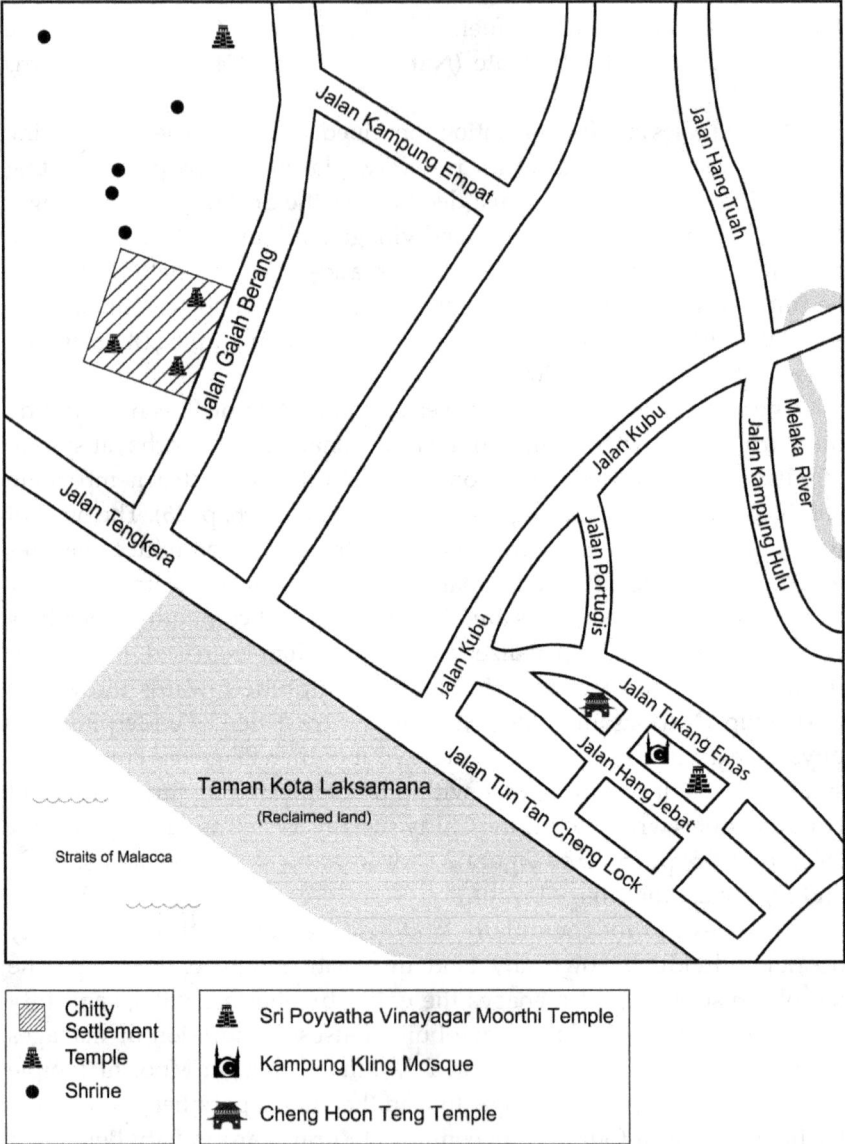

Jalan Kampung Empat

Jalan Hang Tuah

Jalan Gajah Berang

Jalan Kubu

Melaka River

Jalan Kampung Hulu

Jalan Tengkera

Jalan Portugis

Jalan Kubu

Jalan Tukang Emas

Jalan Hang Jebat

Taman Kota Laksamana
(Reclaimed land)

Jalan Tun Tan Cheng Lock

Straits of Malacca

	Chitty Settlement		▲	Sri Poyyatha Vinayagar Moorthi Temple
▲	Temple		Ⓒ	Kampung Kling Mosque
●	Shrine			Cheng Hoon Teng Temple

FIGURE 2.2
Layout of Chitty Village

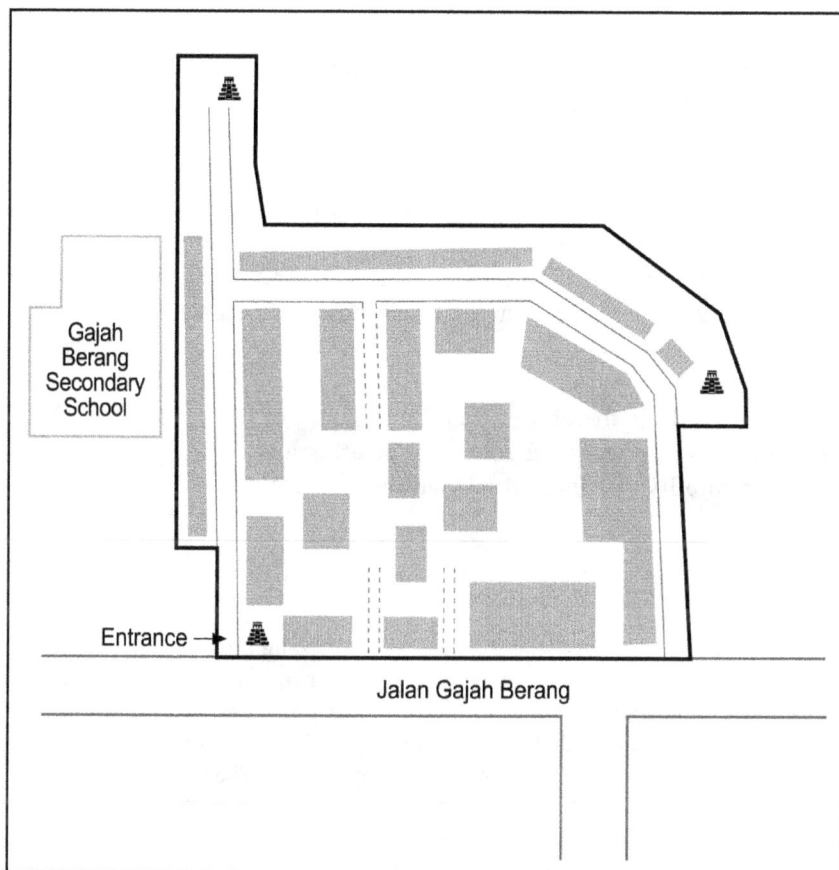

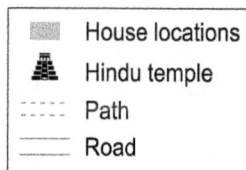

Gajah
Berang
Secondary
School

Entrance →

Jalan Gajah Berang

House locations
Hindu temple
Path
Road

This is a list of temples and shrines owned by the Chitty:

1. Sri Poyyatha Vinayagar Moorthi Temple, Jalan Tukang Emas (1781)
2. Sri Kailasanathar (Sivan) Temple, Gajah Berang (Kuil Baru) (1887)
3. Sri Maha Mariamman Temple, Gajah Berang (Datuk Cacar) (1822)
4. Sri Anggalamman Temple, Gajah Berang (Kuil Kolam) (1888)
5. Sri Ayyanar Temple, Bacang (Kuil Gajah)
6. Dharma Rajah Temple, Gajah Berang (Kuil Dharma) (1770)
7. Sri Amman Temple, Gajah Berang (Kuil Amman) (1770)
8. Sri Kathayee Amman Temple, Gajah Berang (Kuil Kattai Amman)
9. Sri Kaliamman Temple, Bacang (Kuil Kaliamman)
10. Lenggadariamman Temple, Gajah Berang (Kuil Nenek).

(Source: Narayanasamy 2004, p. 8).

Kampung Chitty is therefore a core living and spiritual space and there is a keen consciousness of its role in delineating and defining the identity of the community and individuals within it, as well encapsulated by this observation:

> Like the Portuguese Eurasians, our culture is easier to preserve because we have our own place, our own *kampung*, where we can bring our children. But unlike the Portuguese, our living space and religious space coincide. Our temples are located in the same village where we stay. Every time we have a big festival — like *Meggamay* — many families reunite and the entire community is involved in organizing it. This brings us together.
>
> (Kuala Lumpur-based engineer K. Shanmugan Rajan,
Interview, 2 May 2010).

Perpetuating Ethnic Space: Housing and Identity

While Chitty emigrants see the village as a cultural and spiritual base, for the villagers it is also a residential area which provides cheap housing on communal land. Housing is a major problem, particularly for the less skilled, poorer and younger Chitty who cannot afford alternative housing outside the village. In late 2009 the Chitty village contained fifty houses, of which twenty-two were owned and occupied by Chitty and twenty-eight by Chinese (Nadarajan Raja, Interview, 4 May 2010). The entry of Chinese has its roots in British land policy.[9]

The villagers find the Chinese houses too costly to purchase. "Most of us cannot afford to buy Chinese houses in our village when these are available because they cost as much as 30,000 Malaysian Ringgit each", one Chitty villager complained. He is in his thirties, holds a manual job, and has a family to support.[10]

However low rentals imposed by the temple trust have helped the villagers. In 2010 each household paid a mere 25 Malaysian Ringgit per month to the trust for the right to rent the plot of land on which a house stood. Villagers would have to pay many times more in a similar location. These low rents allow poorer Chitty to save for their children's education, maintain their own and their extended families, and yet keep aside something for their old age. The central location of the village in relation to the town also facilitates access to workplaces and schools.

While older villagers are content with the low rentals, younger villagers fear they may be denied a chance to rent or buy homes in the village. Since decisions of the temple trustees are often binding and community members who defy them can be penalized, this fear engenders strong loyalty to older, traditional community leaders (Fieldwork, 2008–10). At a local level, these leaders have not been able to unite the community or harness its communal land bank to alleviate the housing shortage. In terms of public discourse, they have not linked the housing issue to low skills and low wages, or insufficient State-financed public housing. Instead, given ethnic-based politics in Malaysia, housing — a non-ethnic issue — is expressed in ethnic and cultural terms, including a fear of loss of identity.

A scholar notes that the Chitty fear loss of their "core ethnic space" and identity to Chinese entrepreneurs and the Malay-dominated State government (Mearns 1995, p. 73). Fieldwork for this book (2008–10) confirms this, especially since most villagers now comprise working-class Chitty and retirees who cannot afford alternative housing outside the village. Thus Chitty attachment to their space — linked both to their need for cheap, accessible housing, and fear of loss of identity — has found expression in appeals to the State for indigenous *bumiputera* status. (Interviews, Sithambaram Pillay (Jeeva) 13 July 2008; Nadarajan, 4 May 2010; News Report, *The Star*, 15 March 2011). Such ethnic "rerouting" is seen as a way to not only preserve their land and housing, but also regain their cultural pride and improve education and job opportunities for their youth. The need to protect their land has taken on a new urgency given threats to the village over the last few years.

Threats to Ethnic Space: A Heritage Ignored?[11]

The central location of the village within a fast-growing city and the consequent rise in land prices make it a ripe picking for property developers. In recent years several proposed projects have threatened the village and its heritage character. Despite the community's 500-year link to the Malacca Sultanate, its 250-year-old village and ancient temples, the village's State-endowed heritage status, and Malacca's prestigious UNESCO heritage standing, the State government's response to these threats have worsened the perception of neglect and vulnerability felt by this minority community.

In 1991 a housing developer, in cahoots with one of the three temple trustees, attempted to buy the entire village for several million Malaysian ringgit. The other trustees managed to obtain a court order to prevent the sale. The agreement to sell was later revoked. Then in 1995 the developer of a nearby shopping complex managed to obtain permission from the Malacca State government to construct a wide road right through the village. Residents were neither informed nor consulted. They only knew of the plan when surveyors arrived to take measurements and put yellow markings on the narrow road which runs through the centre of the village. The residents fought back. They formed a sub-committee, lodged formal appeals to the State, and had meetings with the local council, local planners, the Public Works Department, the ruling coalition's Malaysian Indian Congress, and the Chief Minister. "The response was upsetting," recalls Nadarajan (Interview, 4 May 2010). "The Malacca local council told us our village was not unique, the road will boost the economy, and the heritage arch marking the entry to our village can easily be replaced!" In 2000 when the Malacca Chief Minister visited the village to attend a function, the residents presented him a memorandum appealing against the highway construction. He verbally assured them that the project would be cancelled.

Subsequently in 2002 the State government gazetted the village as a heritage site. A notice near the Chitty Museum next to the village today reads: "Kg. Chitty is a Residential Area Gazetted under the Preservation and Conservation of Cultural Heritage Enactment 1988." Other areas of

Malacca similarly gazetted were Malacca's Portuguese Settlement, the urban Malay village of Kampung Morten, and Heeren Street, a Peranakan Chinese area in town. The conservation order, though likely meant for heritage-tourism rather than for the residents welfare per se, was nevertheless a victory for the villagers since it seemed unlikely that the highway would be built. However, their happiness was short-lived and seven years later the character of their village was in jeopardy again.

In August 2009, a private builder initiated plans to construct a high-rise hotel cum condominium on private land next door to the village and immediately adjacent to its 187-year-old Mariamman Temple, and the State government confirmed that it had approved the project (Carvalho and Chen, *The Sunday Star*, 22 November 2009). At the time of writing (April 2011) it was not clear if the access road to the project would run through the middle of the village or by its side entrance. Either way the project will drastically increase the population and vehicle density in the area and permanently damage the social ecology and historical character of the heritage village and its adjacent temples. This will not only affect residents negatively but also the State and the nation's tourist revenue.

SEEKING *BUMIPUTERA* STATUS

The fear of land loss and lack of access to cheap housing is already expressing itself in ethnic and cultural terms. One well-known community leader feels that granting *bumiputera* status to the community will secure their land and improve the village:

> *Bumiputera* status can give our land similar protection as Malay Reserve Land, which is only saleable within the community. It can also bring improvements to our village. Unlike the Portuguese Settlement, it took so many years for us to get a simple community hall (recently built). The government has also upgraded Kampung Morten (a nearby riverside Malay heritage village); we have been neglected.
>
> (Nadarajan Raja, 48, Secretary, Malacca Chitty Cultural Society,
> Interview, 4 May 2010).

While local village leaders worry mainly about the status of the land on which their temples and homes are located, educated Chitty who have moved out of Malacca see indigenous status as a means to overcome perceived marginalization. "Politically, we've got no influence — we are like the Chinese and Indians. Economically, it's the same — we are like the Indians," claims Shanmugan Rajan (Interview, 2 May 2010). Others perceive neglect and a lack of political channels. "It's taken so long for people to know that we even exist!" complains Amu Pillay. "The Portuguese were seen to have 'hard-core' poor and were given *Bumi* (indigenous) status. People thought we were rich; they missed out the many poor among us. Only later did we too realize our position. But we can't turn to the MIC, MCA or UMNO. So whom do we turn to?" (Amu Pillay, Manager, Interview, 2 May 2010).

Without a clear ethnic-based political channel to turn to, some leaders have begun to state both privately and publicly that only *bumiputera* status can improve their social mobility, especially through better higher education opportunities:

> Most of us have to take the tougher route of studying for the local Malaysian pre-university course STPM (*Sijil Tinggi Persekolahan Malaysia*) since we usually cannot get into matriculation courses (run by public institutions), which provide an almost automatic route into local universities. Those are mostly reserved for *bumiputeras*. *Bumiputera* status will help us gain entry into matriculation courses and into universities.
>
> (Sithambaram Pillay (Jeeva), village youth leader,
> Interview, 13 July 2009).

There are also indications that the appeal for indigenous status is moving to the national level. In early 2011, Chitty leader Nadarajan Raja announced that community leaders planned to meet the Prime Minister and State Chief Minister to appeal for *bumiputera* status. He added:

> Our forefathers assimilated with the local population by marrying Orang Laut, Malays, Chinese, Javanese and Bataks, creating a unique new culture.... We are appealing for *bumi* status as a way to preserve our identity as a community which existed here since ancient times.
>
> (Nadarajan Raja, quoted in "Chitty Seek Bumi Status",
> *The Star*, 15 March 2011).

CONCLUSION

The Chitty are an epitome of cross-cultural influences embraced by Malacca through six centuries. Through interaction, intermarriage and acculturation with Malays, Peranakan Chinese, Javanese and Bataks they have evolved a hybrid culture, with their language, cuisine and art forms incorporating highly diverse influences. Their main identity however remains rooted in their Hindu belief, their ethnic and spiritual space, and Malay, their mother-tongue.

Descendants of traders who helped Parameswara and subsequent Sultans make Malacca one of the wealthiest and most cosmopolitan ports in the world, they were sidelined by the Portuguese, dislocated by the Dutch, and dispersed during British rule. The colonial market economy contributed to class cleavages, with an educated and occupationally mobile group emigrating to Singapore and Kuala Lumpur and a working class component confined to their ethnic and spiritual space in Kampung Chitty.

The village continues to serve as a spiritual and cultural base for the widely dispersed and shrinking community, whose identity remains largely defined by its communally-owned space and temples. Despite their long history, their intimate links with the indigenous population and their deep acculturation, some Chitty, particularly those in the village, feel trapped in a society where many issues — national, community and even individual — are often perceived and expressed in ethnic terms, through an ethnic-based political system in which they lack a clear ethnic identity, numerical strength and influence.

Given Malaysia's ethnic-based politics, its *bumiputera*-Malay dominated State, and a perceived *bumiputera*-Malay bias in government policy, it seems logical to them that indigenous status provides the fastest route to land security, social recognition and economic opportunity. The success of the Portuguese Eurasians in accessing some *bumiputera* related benefits, and the Thai Malaysians in gaining full *bumiputera* status encourages them to pursue this path:

> How come the Portuguese and Dutch who first arrived here as conquerors have been given *bumiputera* status, while we Chitty who arrived much earlier as traders are not regarded as *bumiputeras*? We are equally qualified for *bumiputera* status. In addition to having Malay ancestry, we speak Malay, practise Malay customs and have been settled in the Peninsular Malaysia for at least 500 years!
>
> (Sithambaram Pillay (Jeeva), village youth leader,
> Interview, 13 July 2009).

The reality is that despite seeming advantages, there are practical short-term problems and long-term challenges in taking the *"bumiputera* route". For one, Chitty is a hybrid identity which is difficult to define. This was one reason for the rejection of the community's first application for *bumiputera* status submitted two decades ago through the Malaysian Indian Congress (MIC), a partner in the ruling coalition. Secondly, unlike the Portuguese who are classified and registered in their identity card data profile as "Eurasians", the Chitty come under the category "Indians". This makes it difficult to identify a Chitty (K. Arunasalam Pillay, 14 July 2008). Thirdly, to make matters worse, there is no village registry despite the fact that the temple committee oversees all major religious rituals, including weddings, births and deaths.

Taking the *bumiputera* route will not in any case solve the community's problems in the long run. In addition to opening the doors to claims from other historical minorities and contributing to a perception of threat from segments of the Malay population, it may worsen intra-ethnic inequities within the Chitty community, as it has for the Malays. This is because, other things being equal, it is the relatively wealthy among them who are more likely to be able to save and invest in higher yield equity funds, property discounts and preferred shares. The children of the more well-to-do are also more likely to benefit from education quotas compared to children from poorer families, who are usually less likely to qualify for university places.

Economically the immediate short-term need of the community is to gain access to existing houses within the village and to public housing units near it. In the longer term what is required is improved quality of school education, and upgraded skills, employment and wages. These are needs that go beyond ethnicity and apply to all groups, especially the poorer segments of the Malaysian population.

POSTSCRIPT

In 2015 high-rise apartments were built next to the Chitty Village. Construction proceeded despite community objections, a promise by the previous Chief Minister to shelve the project, and a pledge by the new Chief Minister to probe how the project was approved adjacent to a State-recognized heritage site. A private builder is constructing two 22-storey condominiums, a 12-storey hotel annex and a multi-storey car park. Community leaders expressed deep concern over the impact of the high-density project on the social, spiritual and physical ecology of their tiny heritage village (Murali 2014; Malaysiakini 2014).

APPENDIX 2.1
CHITTY OR PERANAKAN INDIAN?

Most community members refer to themselves as "Chitty" and prefer the term, but "Peranakan Indian" is in fact a more accurate description of the community. Both terms are used interchangeably in this chapter. "Chitty" and "Chetty" are Anglicized forms of Malay *Cheti* and *Chiti*, said to be derived from the Malayalam term *Chetti*. Also referred to in Tamil as *Shetti*, the term originally denoted a member of any of the trading *jati* (castes) in South India (Narinasamy 1983, p. 239). Community leaders, especially a segment which seeks indigenous (*bumiputera*) status for the community prefer the term Chitty, whose ethnic boundaries are, they argue, relatively easier to define. "The term 'Peranakan' is too loose — we fear other Indians may one day also claim Peranakan status and we will not be entitled to the special position enjoyed by *bumiputeras*," explains Nadarajan Raja, the Secretary of the Malacca Chitty Cultural Society (Interview, 28 September 2009). However there are several reasons why the term Peranakan Indians is more accurate. Firstly, Chitty originally denoted and is still associated with Malacca's once dominant trading caste, few of whom now live in the village. The trading chiefs and community headmen were Chitty, who subsumed other castes which came to Malacca in subordinate capacities (Narinasamy 1983, p. 249). As a result the use of the term Chitty to describe the entire community is resented by some villagers who say it is a caste term that is not representative of them (Arunasalam Pillay, Interview, 14 July 2008). Secondly, Chitty is often confused with Natukotai Chettiars, a South Indian money-lending clan/caste group. Thirdly, *Peranakan*, a Malay word which refers to those who are locally born and acculturated, is a more historically descriptive and meaningful term. The term is used in *The Peranakan Indians of Singapore and Melaka: Indian Babas and Nyonyas-Chitty Melaka*, the first ever published book on the community (Dhoraisingam 2006).

APPENDIX 2.2
PARCHU PONGGAL: CHITTY ANCESTOR WORSHIP

A week before *Parchu Ponggal* the Chitty pay respects to deceased relatives by visiting ancestral graves. Unlike other Hindus who cremate their deceased, the Chitty, following Malay and Chinese practices, traditionally buried their dead. (In recent years however, both cremation and burial have been practised). Following Chinese custom, graves are cleaned and joss sticks and incense burnt. However, unlike the Chinese, no food is offered. Instead the Chitty observe the Malay practice of offering scented flowers and leaves. These comprise sliced *pandan* leaves mixed with *bunga butang* and *bunga saintain* (flowers) and *ayer mawar* (scented water) (Nadarajan Raja, Interview, 14 September 2009).

On the day itself *Parchu Ponggal* is celebrated as a home and family-based event. In addition to prayers, offerings of elaborate home-made Chitty-style food, cigarettes, betel leaves, tobacco and tea or coffee are made to the spirits of the ancestors. I witnessed the *Parchu Ponggal* ceremony at the home of S.K. Pillay in the village on Tuesday, 13 January 2009. Pillay's spotless home was decorated with festive lights and filled with the fragrance of fresh fruits and incense. It is a large airy house, with cement floors and wooden walls. Like many Chitty homes, it has several old cupboards filled with family antiques and black and white photographs of ancestors. A large altar has Hindu deities but also one of Kuan Yin, the Chinese Goddess of Mercy. "We pray to her too," he says.

At 6.30p.m. sharp he calls out to his three children: "Come-come-come!" The entire family gets to work. Seven freshly cut and washed banana leaves are meticulously arranged in a circle. An oil lamp, known to the Chitty in Malay as *pelita duduk* and to Hindu Tamils as *kutuveluku* is lighted. The eighth banana leaf, which is placed nearest to the oil lamp, is different. This is meant for the ancestors, especially Pillay's father and grandfather. There is also one large tray comprising a wide selection of cut fruit, and another with an array of Chitty deserts. "Rice first," Pillay commands. Mounds of steaming *nasi lemak* are scooped very carefully on each leaf. The womenfolk then carefully begin serving a spoonful of each of thirteen dishes around the rice. These include freshly cooked mutton, fish and chicken curry, cabbage, long beans and ladies' fingers (okra). All are placed neatly around the mounds of rice. "Don't stand on one leg!" Pillay's wife warns their twelve-year-old son. There are many strict rules of behaviour to be observed because the souls of the ancestors are due to make an appearance. "Manners, manners! ....arrange nicely," Pillay adds sternly, as he walks around with a frown. "Pa, can-ah appa?" asks his young daughter as she checks if her layout of the vegetables is acceptable. He nods in agreement.

The whole village is quiet. Other families in the village are busy with similar ceremonies. Suddenly a strong cool breeze blows outside. I wonder if the ancestors have arrived. But my fears are put to rest when I am told that such breezes are common in Malacca in early January.

The food is finally laid out. Then four cups and saucers are placed on the left of the oil lamp, another four on the right, and one in the centre. Coffee is poured into them. They are filled to the brim, without overflowing. Milk is then poured in the centre cup until it overflows. Lastly, some durians are pried open as an offering too. His sister, who by this time had gone outside the house to evoke the souls of the ancestors to enter the house, now comes in with a tray of burning incense which gives off a sweet fragrance. *"Pasang pelita!* (Light the lamp!)," someone screams. Pillay carefully relights the oil lamp. Then he lights two long red candles on brass-stands. These are similar to those used by the Hokkien Chinese in prayer ceremonies. Pillay now prays to Lord Shiva to ask permission for his ancestors to visit the house and accept the offerings. "Children, come here and sit down, let Grandpa see you!" he calls out. They come out and sit, silent and still. Everyone is quiet.

Soon the ceremony is over. Pillay finally has time to talk. "We have carried out this ceremony for generations," he says proudly. "We believe our ancestors can guide us: that's why we asked Lord Shiva permission for our ancestors to visit us and accept our offerings." I inquire about the huge variety of food being offered. "When we lost our jobs as traders and became farmers we used to grow a large variety of food. That's one reason why we have such an elaborate cuisine," he explains.

(*Source*: Participant observation by author at home of S.K. Pillay, Chitty Village, Malacca, 13 January 2009).

APPENDIX 2.3
INTERVIEWS OF CHITTIES

In 2010 four members of the community were asked two open-ended questions: (1) What is your personal experience of "being Chitty" in terms of uniqueness, advantages and opportunities, disadvantages and dilemmas? (2) How do you negotiate your identity? (This was explained using the analogy of a "social GPS".). These were their responses, in their own words:

1. K. Shanmugan Rajan, Engineer, 40

Shanmugan is very proud of his Chitty heritage. He works in Kuala Lumpur but returns to the village for all the main festivals:

(i) *Personal Experience of Being Chitty*

Uniqueness: So many things — our religion, language, food, village, temples. We don't speak any Indian language but remain Hindus. That's special. When I was growing up in Malacca I took all this for granted, but when I went to Kuala Lumpur I realized I was different.

Look at my family. My mother is Chinese but she converted to Hinduism when she married my late Chitty father. One of my brothers married a Tamil Hindu, and another married an Indonesian Buddhist of Indian descent. I am married to a Chinese who remains a Taoist but "became a Chitty" and practises Hindu rituals. But all of us are Chitty, and Hindu!

I spent half my life in this village in Malacca. This is my origin. This is my temple. I own it. We own it. We own the festivals. When I attend the Thaipusam festival in Kuala Lumpur I am a spectator, but here, I'm the host. I return to Malacca every year. My cousin who moved out of Malacca when he was very young returns too, but as a spectator.

I've never missed any festival here despite being out of Malacca for twenty years. Even when I was dating my wife I brought her here to help her understand my culture and religion. I will continue to come. I want my daughter to know her roots. My wife is a Taoist. She did not let go of her previous religion though she takes part in Hindu rituals now. She officially took an Indian name by going to an Indian priest, who selected an appropriate name for her by looking at her birth date, like what I did for my daughter. But my wife only has her Chinese name on her identity card, unlike my mum who has both her Chinese and Hindu names. My wife and I both pray at the same Hindu altar at home.

I also look different. People expect an Indian to turn up when we speak on the telephone but they get surprised when they meet me in person. Others ask how come I can't speak Tamil. Our language has Malay, Tamil and Hokkien inside it! And our food, it's more Malay and Indian-style, unlike Peranakan Chinese food which is more Chinese.

Advantages/Opportunities: Our culture is cross-cultural and unique. Take language for example. I speak to my mum in Chitty Malay, to my wife in Mandarin, and we all speak to our daughter in English and a bit of Mandarin and Malay! Like the Portuguese Eurasians, the Chitty culture is easier to preserve because we have our own place, our own *kampung,* where we can bring our children. But unlike the Portuguese, our living space and religious space coincide. Our temples are located in the same village where we stay. Every time we have a big festival — like *Meggamay* — many families reunite and the entire community is involved in organizing it. This brings us together.

Disadvantages/Dilemmas: Politically, we've got little influence. We are like the Chinese and Indians. Economically, it's the same, we are like the Indians. In terms of perception, people sometimes get confused when they meet us. Our names are very Indian but we don't look Indian. Also, Tamils cannot understand how we can practise Hinduism without speaking Tamil. They sometimes find it hard to integrate with us because we have this language barrier.

(ii) *How Do You Negotiate Your Identity?*

Our identity cards indicate we are Indians. But I prefer to sit in the centre because it's very easy for me to mix with Chinese or Indians! And we continue to explain to Tamil Hindus that you don't have to know Tamil to practise Hinduism. We tell them that in India, for example, there are many Hindus who are non-Tamil speakers.
(Interview, K. Shanmugan Rajan, Chitty Village, Malacca, 2 May 2010).

2. Ms Amu Pillay, Public Relations Executive

Amu Pillay's family left the village for Malacca town when she was a schoolgirl ("the best thing we did"). After leaving school, she worked but studied part-time until she obtained a Master's degree. She now works at a leading Malaysian multi-national. I met her at the *Meggamay* Festival in April 2010, the first time she had returned for the event in twenty years. Without much prompting she spoke with verve and vitality about her heritage:

(i) *Personal Experience of Being Chitty*

Uniqueness: Our religion, language and food are very different from other Tamil Hindus in Malaysia. Ancestor worship or Parchu is very special to us. Ponggal too, the harvest festival, since we were farmers once. Malay is our mother-tongue. Yes, that's the only language our mothers taught us! At home we have both Hindu and Chinese altars, but we pray in Malay. Our food is totally different — it's a blend between Malay, Peranakan Chinese and Indian cuisine. Those who live in the village eat this traditional home-made cuisine daily, while those who have migrated still consume it regularly.

Advantages/Opportunities: I can't think of any! It's taken so long for people to know that we even exist! Many Malays I talk to on the phone are so impressed with my Malay they refuse to believe I am Indian. I explain I am an Indian version of Baba-Nyonya (Peranakan Chinese). They find that fascinating! Generally most of us get along quite easily with Malays, Chinese and Indians.

Disadvantages/Dilemmas: Many! There's not much advantage economically. The Portuguese were seen to have "hardcore" poor (among them) and were given *bumiputera* (indigenous) status. People thought we were rich; they missed out the many poor among us. Only later did we too realize our position. But we can't turn to the MIC, MCA or UMNO. So whom do we turn to? Secondly, many of our parents were not education-centric; they allowed their children to leave school early to work. I was lucky. My mum emphasized education. Thirdly, most of us don't speak Tamil, so we sometimes can't easily integrate with Tamil-speaking Indians. But perceptions change once they know and appreciate us, particularly our family values. Lastly, our community is shrinking. More and more people, especially males, are marrying out of the community. A lot of daughters remain unmarried. Unless we marry our cousins, I'm not sure if we can last another three generations!

(ii) *How Do You Negotiate Your Identity?*

It's important to first get out of the village; at least that's my personal experience. That's how my family got exposure and experience in the world outside. Secondly, education; during my time at most a few girls became nurses. It's good to see that today more and more young people, especially women, are going to university.

(Interviews, 24 April 2010, Malacca, and 2 May 2010, Kuala Lumpur).

3. Sithambaram Pillay (Jeeva), 25, Safety Officer

Jeeva is a young, bright and upcoming village leader who takes a deep interest in both his career and his village culture. He could not get a place at university, so he studied while working, completing his local and overseas industrial safety examinations through distance learning. He says he faces curiosity rather than discrimination as a Chitty.

(i) *Personal Experience of Being Chitty*

Uniqueness: We are different from the ordinary Indians. Our culture is an adaptation of both the Indian and Malay culture. You can see this in our cultural practices and our religion. In terms of identity this can be confusing to people. When people meet me they think I am Malay, then they see my name and think I am Indian. Later they wonder how come an Indian can be so fair. Once they know I'm a Chitty, they become very interested. Some think I'm a Chettiar (Natukotai Chettiars, a clan of moneylenders). Indians are curious about my religion, Malays about my history. This is a chance to explain to them about my community.

Advantages/Opportunities: People are now curious about us, and the government now recognizes our existence.

Disadvantages/Dilemmas: We still do not have the status of the *bumiputera*. Our community exists because of intermarriage between the Indians from Kalinga in India and local women here. Yet, the Portuguese who came here as conquerors managed to get it (*Bumiputera* status). Another disadvantage we have is that we don't speak Tamil.

(ii) *How Do You Negotiate Your Identity?*

We have to work in the private sector and we don't gain any benefits that the *bumiputera* are entitled to. I guess we will have to learn and pick up the Tamil language for future generations.

(Interview, Malacca, 2 May 2010).

4. Nadarajan Raja, 48, Secretary, Malacca Chitty Cultural Society

Nadarajan is Secretary of the Malacca Chitty Cultural Society. He was previously curator of the State-run Chitty Museum located next to the village, and now works full-time as a tour guide specializing in the Chitty heritage. He is married to an Indonesian Indian who converted from Buddhism, and they have a daughter. They live in his family home in the village.

(i) *Personal Experience of Being Chitty*

Uniqueness: There are so many things; I don't know where to start!

Advantages/Opportunities: Our hybrid culture and our unique language.

Disadvantages/Dilemmas: Bumiputera status can give our land similar protection as Malay Reserve Land, which is only saleable within the community. It will also improve our village. Unlike the Portuguese Settlement, it took so many years for us to get a simple community hall (recently built). The government has also upgraded Kampung Morten (a nearby riverside Malay heritage village). We have been neglected.

(ii) *How Do You Negotiate Your Identity?*

The only thing we can do is to work with local officials and our elected representatives. We also need to upgrade education in the community. More people also know of our existence now.

(Interview, Malacca, 4 May 2010).

Notes

1. "Narinasamy" is spelt "Narayanasamy" in his subsequent 2004 publication. It refers to the same author. I have kept to the original spellings used in the respective publications.
2. Officially spelt as "Tengkera".
3. There were originally eleven historically based caste groups, but a liberal attitude has allowed new groups to enter the community. Firstly, most are middle-order castes and therefore the social distance between each is limited. Secondly, given its small size, the community could not have functioned without cross-caste marriages. Thirdly, many early marriages were with indigenous women to whom the concept of caste was meaningless. Lastly, the temple constitution allows any individual — male or female — who marries a Melaka Chitty to be treated as an equal member of the community (Narinasamy 1983, pp. 249–50). A 1976 survey identified nine castes. These were the Chitty, Pillays, Neikers, Rajahs, Padayachis, Mudaliars, Patters, and the Konars and Kallans, the last two being new entrants through marriage during the British period. Two other castes, the Pandaran and Retti, were no longer represented due to inter-caste marriages and emigration (Narinasamy 1983, pp. 249–50; Narayanasamy 2004, p. 7). Another study in 2004 found that there were still nine historically recognizable groups, with the Pillays being the single largest group (Dhoraisingam 2006, p. 25) through marriage and choice, since it was considered a respectable caste (Narinasammy 1983, p. 249).
4. Nadarajan Raja, Secretary, Malacca Chitty Cultural Society (Interview, 28 September 2009).
5. Madam Meenachi, Chitty resident of Taman Laksamana, Malacca, interviewed by author, 10 July 2008.
6. For more on Chitty cuisine, see Dhoraisingam (2006), p. 87 and Veni Rengayah-Knight, *Foods of My Ancestors: The Best of Peranakan Indian-Chitty Melaka Cuisine* Singapore: Glenn Knight, 2007.
7. Peranakan Resource Library, <peranakan.hostoi.com/IndianPeranakans. html>.
8. Another reason for land loss was the conversion of the status of some land plots to Malay Customary Land (MCL). "Some pioneer Chitty settlers had rented their land to Malays, but over time as Chitty died, emigrated or could not produce documentary evidence of ownership, the Malay tenants managed to obtain customary titles to this land," says Nadarajan Raja, the Secretary of the Malacca Chitty Cultural Society (Nadarajan, Interview, 28 September 2009).
9. In the 1950s the government threatened to impose additional taxes on idle Chitty land. The Chitty, who had given up agriculture, were not able to cultivate

or afford to build houses on it. As a result those with capital, who happened to be Chinese, rented the house plots from the temple and built houses on them. Consequently, the better houses in the village were mostly Chinese-owned, and some were used as business premises. This caused bitterness among newly married Chitty couples and young families who could not get a house in the village and were forced to pay higher rentals outside (Narinasamy 1983, pp. 253–54). Despite pressure on housing, the Chitty bear no grudges against the Chinese, many of whom are long-time neighbours who participate in Chitty religious ceremonies and rituals. The Chitty are also free from stereotypes and myths about Chinese since many Chitty themselves have some Chinese ancestry or relatives. In addition, some Chitty see the Chinese in the village as people who protected their land when it was in danger of being taken over by the British. "In a way, the Chinese protected our land," recalls supervisor S.K. Pillay (Interview, 13 January 2009). "By occupying the land when we could not afford to do so, they prevented the British from taking it over. The rent they paid over the years was also a small source of income for the temple."

10. Anonymous villager, Kampung Chitty, Interview, 17 July 2008.
11. Information here is based on an interview with Nadarajan, 4 May 2010.

3

BUMIQUEST[1]
Malacca's Portuguese Eurasians and the Search for Identity

INTRODUCTION: A VILLAGE BY THE SEA

At first sight there is little "Portuguese" about the Portuguese Settlement, a seaside village outside Malacca town. Most people have brownish complexion, some women wear sarongs, and their homes are more akin to those in an urban Malay *kampung* than an exotic "Portuguese" village. But a closer look reveals a crucifix and an image of the Virgin Mother Mary at house entrances. Children play barefoot on narrow streets, speaking a strange mixture of English and Malay, interspersed with screams of "Alleluia!" (Fieldwork 15 September 2008). The people here speak a Portuguese Creole called Kristang, practise a common Catholic religion, and live a culture which, through long interaction within Malacca's diverse cultural milieu has became a Malay-Portuguese-Eurasian hybrid, with Chinese, Indian, Dutch and English influences. This hybridization is also evident in their ethnic origins, family names, language, religion, cuisine, dress, and performing arts and varied descriptions of them as Malaysian Portuguese, Portuguese Eurasians, Luso-Malays, *Serani* (*Nesrani* or

Christians in Malay) or simply *Kristang* or Christian in their own language (Sarkissian 2002).

Set by the sea on 11.5 hectares two kilometres south of the city, the settlement was built in 1934 by the Catholic Church, elite Eurasians and the British to improve housing and living conditions for poor fishermen of Portuguese descent who lived as squatters in overcrowded seaside villages. Today it remains a vibrant community. "We have 120 houses and 1,200 residents, but only forty depend on fishing for a livelihood," says Peter Gomez, the headman or *regedor* (Interview, 15 September 2008). The majority of young wage earners today work in services and manufacturing; the rest comprise housewives, students and pensioners. Housing is still a problem among some poorer families, especially those involved in fishing, and in the poorer streets of the settlement it is common for one house to be occupied by several families. In addition about 300 Portuguese Eurasians occupy private and public low-cost flats around the settlement, and 1,000 others reside in nearby Ujong Pasir and suburbs such as Bukit Baru (Interview, Michael Barnerji, 26 July 2011).

The community is widely dispersed, with a diaspora of over 10,000 members living in other Malaysian towns, Singapore, and Perth.[2] Despite their dispersion, many return yearly to the settlement and to churches and chapels linked to it for family reunions and religious festivals. This is the only Christian community in Peninsular Malaysia with a place which simultaneously serves as its occupational, residential and cultural space. In addition it has become a tourist site, a role now closely linked to its existence and survival.

Before the settlement was established, inter-ethnic interaction with Malays, Chinese and Indians was more spontaneous and organic due to occupational inter-dependence, shared neighbourhoods and intermarriage. This created a hybrid community distinguished by a common Creole and Catholic faith, its key identity markers. In later years, especially after 1934 when the working class segment of the community was confined to the settlement, interaction with other ethnic groups was limited. Instead the settlement became the site of a deliberate and intense process of cultural production and reproduction, expressing itself in Portuguese cultural performances and unique "Portuguese Eurasian" religious events involving the participation of thousands of Portuguese Eurasians, Malaysians and tourists.

For example during the one-week St Peter's (San Pedro) Festival celebrations in June 2011, in addition to a church service, hundreds turned up daily to enjoy "Portuguese" cultural shows and cuisine. The Malaysian visitors were truly multi-ethnic, multi-religious, and from all classes. Portuguese Eurasians comprised a minority. The rest were Chinese, Indians, Chitty and Malay Muslims, including *tudung*-clad women. There were visitors from nearby housing settlements, couples visiting after work, families on outings, students, company employees and overseas visitors. They ranged from humble fishermen to powerful royalty — the prince of a neighbouring state, a regular visitor, arrived with a large entourage to enjoy Portuguese Eurasian cuisine at the seaside stalls run by residents. The mix of people reminded one of the cosmopolitan Malacca of old. There was also a curious blend of overseas visitors. A couple from Portugal turned up at the home of a family to show them a photograph of their visit to the same house forty years ago. Portuguese Eurasians from Singapore, Perth and Adelaide were also enjoying local food in the stalls. Horace Sta Maria, 90, a Malacca teacher now retired in Perth, visits several months every year. "I don't step out of the house in Perth, but here I am out late every night, having a good time!" he exclaims. In contrast John De Alvis, 61, from Adelaide, recently retired from the IT business and was returning to the settlement with his Australian wife for the first time after forty-seven years (Fieldwork, Malacca, 21–23 June 2011).

The carnival-like atmosphere during such celebrations belies the conscious process of cultural production which has ensured the community's solidarity and survival. Visiting the settlement one evening one finds residents relaxing in their verandas, enjoying the sea breeze. It is difficult to understand how this seemingly easy-going community survived Dutch religious persecution, the Japanese Occupation, the British era, global culture, ethnic-dominated politics and the juggernaut of State-sponsored seaside reclamation to reinvent themselves from fishermen into private sector employees, from squatters to permanent residents of State owned land, and from marginalized Malaysians to citizens with State-recognized indigenous roots. The story of their journey is intriguing, an illustration of how a minority with little political or economic capital harnessed its multiple identities to survive as a village, community and culture, and utilized its "Malay" roots to eventually gain access to some benefits reserved for the Malay majority. To better understand their story

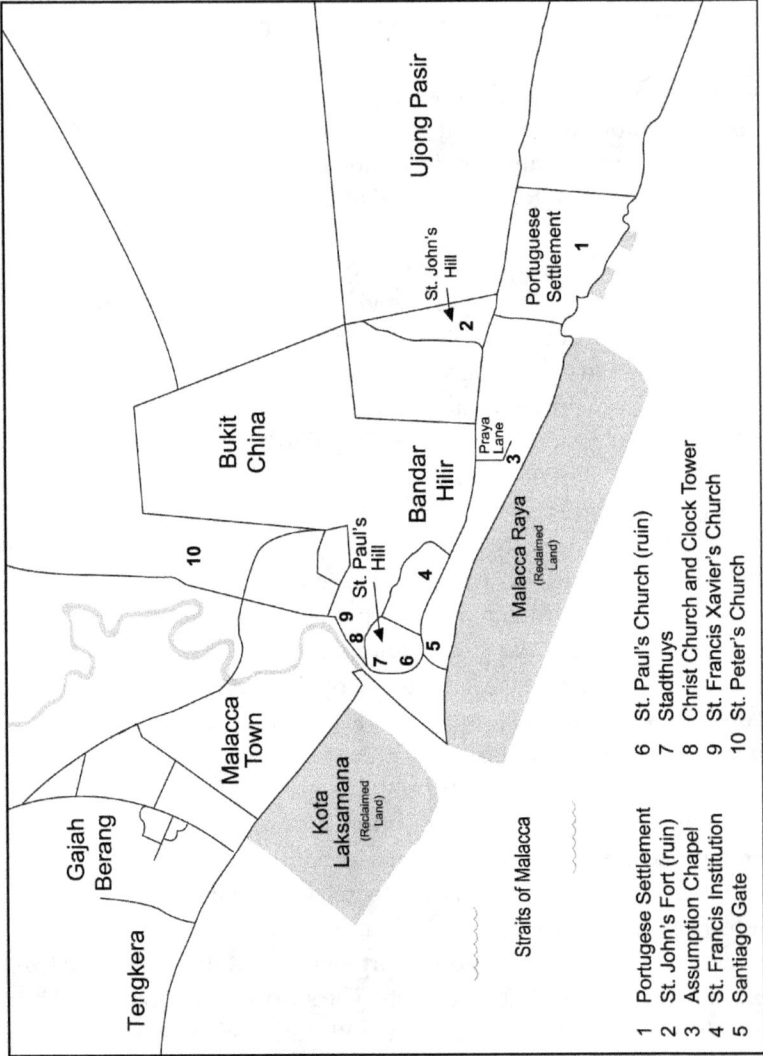

FIGURE 3.1
Location of Portuguese Settlement and Related Landmarks

Tengkera

Gajah Berang

Malacca Town

Kota Laksamana
(Reclaimed Land)

Bukit China

St. Paul's Hill

Bandar Hilir

Praya Lane

Malacca Raya
(Reclaimed Land)

St. John's Hill

Ujong Pasir

Portuguese Settlement

Straits of Malacca

1 Portugese Settlement
2 St. John's Fort (ruin)
3 Assumption Chapel
4 St. Francis Institution
5 Santiago Gate

6 St. Paul's Church (ruin)
7 Stadthuys
8 Christ Church and Clock Tower
9 St. Francis Xavier's Church
10 St. Peter's Church

FIGURE 3.2
Layout of the Portuguese Settlement, Malacca

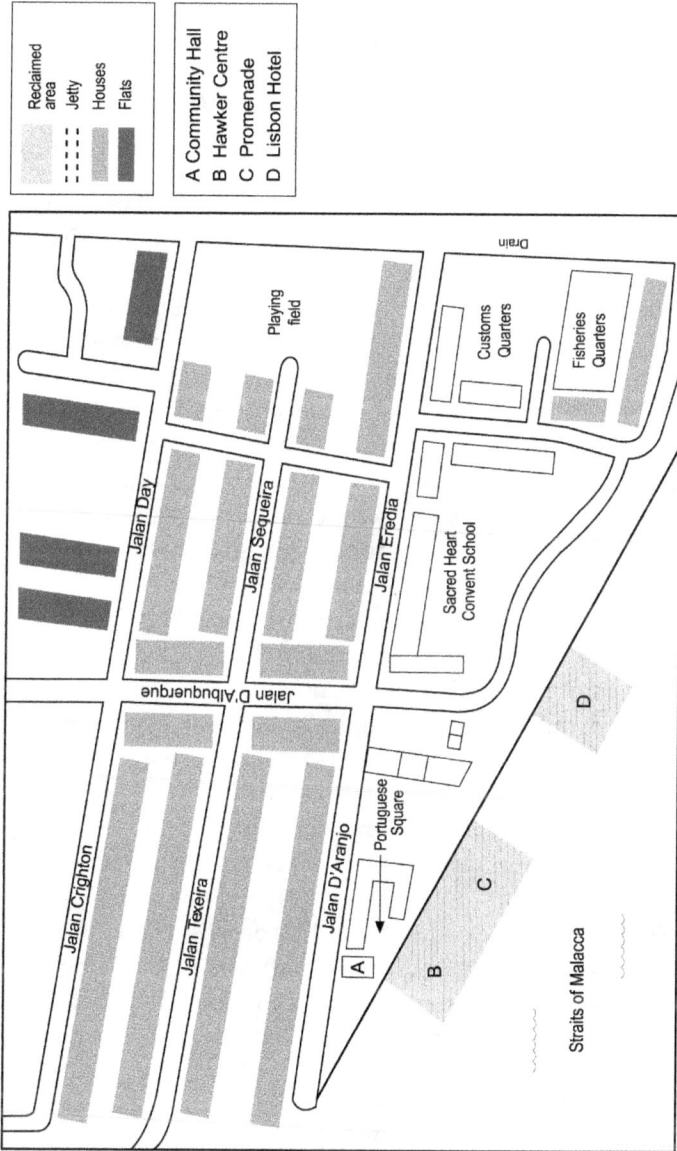

Reclaimed area
Jetty
Houses
Flats

A Community Hall
B Hawker Centre
C Promenade
D Lisbon Hotel

we need to examine their shared histories, fluid cultures, identities and ethnic space against the broad context of the colonial and post-colonial State.

SHARED HISTORIES: FACTORS FACILITATING ACCULTURATION

Marrying and Mixing: Intermarriage and Acculturation

The history of the community begins with the Portuguese conqueror Alfonso de Albuquerque. Five hundred years ago, in 1511, he captured Malacca, then Southeast Asia's busiest and most cosmopolitan port, built a walled city, and tried to populate it with locally born Portuguese who could serve as a reserve army and a social bridge to the local population. The plan failed but a Eurasian community did evolve over the years as housing, land, cattle and orchards — previously owned by Malay noblemen — were offered as dowries to Portuguese to encourage them to intermarry. This gave rise to the popular view that the Portuguese Eurasians are descendants of marriages between Albuquerque's men and local women, particularly Malays. But scholars are divided on this issue, with some suggesting that Portuguese Eurasian bloodlines are far more diverse.

The anthropologist Margaret Sarkissian (2000, pp. 24–26) suggests that original settlers came from four groups. The first comprised soldiers, sailors and ex-convicts from Portugal. The second comprised non-Portuguese conscripted sailors, soldiers and slaves from other Portuguese trading stations. The third was made up of non-Portuguese who were given Catholic names upon conversion and were granted Portuguese citizenship. The fourth comprised mixed-race children who were absorbed into the Portuguese community to escape negative Dutch and British attitudes towards them.

The historian Thomaz (2000, p. 123) proposes that the early Portuguese Eurasians are descendants of mixed marriages between the Portuguese and Malacca-based Indian traders who converted to Catholicism. He claims that most of the 7,400 Christians at the beginning of the fifteenth century were mainly of Indian origin, who "must be the ancestors of a large part of the present Portuguese-speaking Catholic community of Malacca". The linguist Alan Baxter (1995, p. 49), who did his PhD on Kristang, implies that intermarriages with Europeans were common since it was the indigenous wives and their Eurasian children who played a key role in the emergence of the language. Creolization occurred when these children heard Malay-speakers use Portuguese (and Hokkien) as a second language. Since the children were also learning Malay, they helped increase its influence on Kristang. The departure of the Portuguese further increased the influence of Malay — and later Dutch and English — on this Creole.

Working and Living Together: Inter-dependence and Interaction

In addition to intermarriage, interdependence in trade and manpower among a highly diverse population encouraged interaction and acculturation during the 130 years of Portuguese rule (1511–1640). For one, it made it necessary for locals and Europeans to speak each other's languages, creating a fertile environment for the emergence of Kristang. The trade routes — which included Malacca and its regional ports — were controlled by Malays and Javanese, and Malay was their lingua franca. The trade system — involving the organization and distribution of goods — was controlled by Gujeratis and Arabs, Tamils and Javanese, and Malays, Chinese and Filipinos. To facilitate trade Portuguese merchants and missionaries spoke Malay, while local rulers used European and Eurasian translators (Baxter 1995, pp. 44–47).

The lack of manpower also contributed to interaction and acculturation. While Portuguese influence was widespread their numbers were small, with no more than 200 to 600 Portuguese in the city at any time. They therefore depended on a diverse local population within the port to sustain their trade. These included Portuguese Eurasians (offspring of Portuguese marriages to local women); slaves (Javanese, Balinese, Makassarese and Bugis); soldiers and sailors; merchants (Indian, Chinese, Malay and Javanese); and local Christians (indigenous, Chinese and Indian). All the members of this cosmopolitan population spoke colloquial Malay, but were influenced directly or indirectly by Portuguese (Baxter 1995, pp. 43–45), which was the official language in schools and churches. The early Portuguese lived in three areas. Soldiers — who comprised half their population — stayed in the fort, traders in Tranquerah near the port, and farmers and fishermen in coastal Banda Hilir south of the city. These occupations and locations provided numerous opportunities for intermingling, interaction and acculturation with Malacca's diverse multi-ethnic population.

The Dutch Period: Dispersion and Dislocation, Acculturation and Assimilation

During the Dutch conquest in 1640 there were more than 20,000 Christians, including a few hundred Portuguese soldiers, but after the siege only 3,000 survived. Portuguese Eurasians with means fled to south Thailand, Penang and Indonesia by sea while the others escaped by river and took refuge in rural areas such as Melaka Pindah (literally translated as "Relocated Malacca") to the north, Kesang to the south (near Muar in Johore), and Malim and Krubong to the northeast of Malacca town. Here they blended into village life and interacted with Malays to avoid detection. (Fernandis, 1995a, pp. 96–97; Horace Sta Maria, Interviews, 22 and 23 June 2011). Not all escaped. Ninety-year-old Horace Sta Maria, a Malacca Portuguese-Eurasian local historian and former teacher, says one group of refugees in Melaka Pindah hid in a cave, and upon its discovery the Dutch "sealed the cave and entombed them". The site was discovered at the turn of the twentieth century when rubber planters stumbled upon dozens of skeletons inside the cave, nicknamed *Gua Tengkorah* (Skeleton Cave) by local Malays. "The *penghulu* (village headman) confirmed this story when I visited the village as a young man," he recalls (Interviews, Malacca, 22 June and 23 June 2011).

The dispersion of the Portuguese Eurasians into the Malay rural heartland contributed to further acculturation and eventually the assimilation of some Portuguese Eurasians, who became Muslims. Tales of these assimilated Portuguese abound. "A few of Malacca's rural Malays were still able to speak Kristang, even in recent years," says Michael Carvalo, a prominent local Portuguese-Eurasian journalist (Interview, Malacca, 14 January 2009). Ann Nunis, a settlement resident, recalls sharing an outstation taxi with an old Malay man in neighbouring Johore when she was a young student. "He was very fair and had a Muslim cap. When I told him I was Portuguese Eurasian, he suddenly switched to Kristang! I got the shock of my life! He said his village near Muar in Johore was originally made up of Portuguese who converted to Islam. He claimed some older villagers still spoke the language." (Interview, 23 June 2011).

During the Dutch Occupation a minority fled overseas and a few blended into Malay communities, but most Portuguese Eurasians who remained had to endure religious persecution and educational and economic neglect. The severity of persecution varied with various governors. For example, in 1665 the Dutch commander Balthazar Bart prohibited Catholicism, with violators facing property confiscation and bodily punishments; many resisted and kept their Catholic faith alive, operating underground (Muzzi 2002, p. 38). The Dutch also deprived them of schools, books and Portuguese language teachers during almost two centuries of rule (1641–1824). In addition they suffered economically when their lands were seized, sold and distributed to Dutch descendants and officials. In the face of such persecution the Catholic religion became a unifying force, a source of hope and identity "through which they developed a propensity to survive"[3] (Muzzi 2002, p. 44). Persecution gradually abated, initially because Dutch officials had married widows of Portuguese nobles, and later due to political realignments in Europe after 1710 (Muzzi 2002, p. 38). As persecution diminished, refugees returned to the city, but since many had lost their properties, were deskilled or lacked education, they were forced to resort to fishing and farming. The damage inflicted by the Dutch remained for a long time, and it took several generations for the community to fully recover.

The British Era: Classes and Chasms

The late eighteenth and early nineteenth century marked the entry of British colonialism and the market economy into the Peninsular Malaysia, beginning with the British takeover of Penang in 1786, Singapore in 1819 and Malacca in 1824. This was followed by their increasing influence over the Malay States after 1874. In 1827, three years after the British takeover, the Portuguese Eurasian population was 2,289 (Fernandis, 1995a, p. 100). Initially the British restored some of their land titles, and subsequently there were Portuguese Eurasian landowners in Tranquerah and Banda Hilir, up to Bukit China (Muzzi 2002, pp. 44–45). Over the next 133 years (1824–1957) the British education system and the market economy created chasms within the community, as reflected in an educated, mobile elite group serving British interests, and an uneducated, immobile working class — mostly fishermen — confined to the coast.

The British facilitated the establishment of Catholic missionary schools. The Holy Infant Jesus Convent was established in 1865 and a La Salle Brother's School, renamed St Francis Institution, in 1880. The Cannosian Convent, set up in 1905, opened a branch in the settlement in 1950. With schooling restored, educated Portuguese Eurasians sought employment in

British departments and firms both in Malacca and the colonial centres of Penang, Singapore and Kuala Lumpur. There were three main outflows — in the late 1800s; after 1910 when males joined government departments and formed the core of teaching staff in Catholic schools; and during the Japanese Occupation. Women also began working as telephone operators, typists and stenographers in the public and private sectors (Muzzi 2002, pp. 46–47).

Despite improved educational and employment prospects, poverty was kept persistent by a high school dropout rate. "Many fishermen just couldn't afford to keep their kids in school; they needed their help at home or with fishing," recalls Horace, who as a St Francis Institution teacher taught many Portuguese Eurasians. Lack of education and poverty thus became endemic among its working class segment. While Dutch rule had led to dislocation, dispersion and economic decline, British colonialism fragmented the community further. Residential locations overlapped with education, occupations and class in the following areas:

- Tranquerah, the coastal enclave north-west of the city, where educated Portuguese Eurasians — who worked as government clerks — lived inland, and some fishermen by the shore. The Chitty and Peranakan Chinese elite also lived here.
- Jalan Portugis (Portuguese Street) in Kubu, also in the northwest, was settled by Filipino musicians brought in by the British to perform on occasions such as Empire Day and the King's Birthday. These musicians took Portuguese Eurasian wives, and a community developed. "This explains family-names like Zazadius or Zuzartee among Portuguese Eurasians. These are Spanish-Filipino names," explains Horace.
- Kampong Tengah and Kampong Praya, on either side of Praya Lane, south of the city, where the majority of the Portuguese fishing community lived.

  (Interviews, Horace Sta Maria, 22 June and 23 June 2011, and Percy D'Cruz, 26 July 2011, Malacca).

These class schisms endured, buttressed by the inter-marriage of some Portuguese Eurasians to Dutch and British officials, which led to a social distance between "Dutch/British Eurasians" and "Portuguese Eurasians", most of whom were fishermen. The late social activist Bernard Sta Maria, who grew up in Praya Lane and was not a member of the elite, spoke scathingly of the social fragmentation induced by British colonialism:

> The contradiction within the Eurasian Community began when the English took control in 1824. Pigmentation began to be the differentiating qualities within a fragmented community aping the white Masters....synthetic diction and a predominating inclination to emigrate to England grew in rapid proportions....
>
> (*Source*: Bernard Sta Maria 1979, pp. 8–9).

SHARED CULTURES AND IDENTITIES: MANIFESTATIONS OF ACCULTURATION

Eclectic Family Heritage and Names

> The Kristang population is a unique, hybrid specific phenomenon — an agglomerate of varying influences over almost five centuries, in which a Portuguese base prevails, but in which Malay, Chinese, and Indian elements have been absorbed.
>
> (Brian Juan O'Neill 1995, p. 69).

The hybrid influences on the community are reflected not only in their appearance but in their family names. Anthropologist O'Neil's analysis of family photographs of settlement residents is revealing. Despite intermarriage and over sixteen generational links since 1511, a Portuguese audience in Lisbon when shown these family photographs almost unanimously commented that "those are practically Portuguese faces." Settlement residents, when shown photos of O'Neil's wife's Portuguese grandparents, reacted similarly, saying they looked "very Kristang" (O'Neill 1995, pp. 71–72).

The hybrid nature of the community is most clearly reflected in their family names. Most Portuguese Eurasians today carry a fascinating potpourri of Portuguese, Dutch and British family names, but call themselves "Malaysian Portuguese". Intermarriages with the Dutch occurred during the Dutch Occupation, and subsequently the British took spouses who were of Portuguese-Dutch heritage, leading to an infusion of British surnames (de Silva 2003, p. 2). To this one must add surnames reflecting Chinese, Indian, and even Kadazan family links (See Table 3.1 for sample of Malacca Portuguese Eurasian family names).

However, as O'Neill reminds us, those who have Portuguese names may not necessarily be of direct Portuguese descent because surnames are

TABLE 3.1
Some Malacca Portugese Eurasian Family Names

Portuguese	Dutch	British	Others
1) Collar	1) Danker	1) Lowe	1) Banerji (Bengali)
2) De Costa	2) De Witt	2) Farnel	2) Gimino (Filipino)
3) De Mello	3) Frederick	3) Marsh	3) Aeria
4) De Roche	4) Goonting	4) Savage	4) Singho (Burger)
5) De Rozario	5) Hendricks	5) Scully	5) Tan (Chinese)

Sources: de Silva, Patrick, "Culture". Paper presented at the Malacca Story Seminar organised by the Malacca Museum Board, Malacca, Malaysia, 14 January 2003, p. 2, and Fieldwork Interviews, Author, 2009–11.

only transmitted through the paternal line. The names could also have been given upon conversion to Catholicism (O'Neill 1995, pp. 67–69). Religion, rather "race" or language, is the key factor in assimilation through inter-marriages; most spouses readily convert to Catholicism.

The combined influence of both ethnic diversity and religious commonality mean that "Portuguese Eurasian" is seen more as a broad cultural rather than a narrow ethnic identity. This explains why someone like Edgar Ovaree, 80, says: "I am pure Portuguese. I am not mixed" and in the same breath informs me that his great-grandmother was Burmese (Interview, 22 June 2011). He also has a Dutch surname. Virtually every Portuguese Eurasian family possesses diverse ethnic origins, and spouses from non-Portuguese Eurasian backgrounds are common.

Philomena Singho Tan, 57, of Burger (Dutch Eurasian) and Burmese parentage, is married to a Chinese and reckons her children are "culturally Portuguese Eurasians" though they observe traditional customs during Chinese festivals. She reflects on her hybrid background, her children's dual Portuguese Eurasian and Chinese identities and how religion and rituals are flexibly shared, regardless of conversion and culture:

> My great-grandfather, a Sri Lankan Burger, emigrated to Alor Gajah, Malacca, where he met and married a Burmese. My father is therefore of Burger Burmese background. He married a Portuguese Eurasian — a Nunis, worked with the police force in Singapore, and moved into the settlement in 1957. I was brought up and educated here in the settlement. After school I worked as a clerk, a teacher, and then in the training section of an electronics firm. Today I work in a centre catering to settlement children with learning difficulties. We have about forty students. My husband is Chinese, from a Malacca Peranakan Chinese family. Our two

children are registered as Chinese, following the father's ethnicity, but I think they are culturally Portuguese Eurasians. They are Catholics and enjoy Portuguese food. My husband has not converted but he attends mass with us and prays. My children observe the Chinese *cheng beng* or All Soul's day, and during Chinese festivals they wish him in the traditional *Baba* style, kneeling down and clasping their hands.

(Interview, Portuguese Settlement, 23 June 2011).

Another resident, Stevie Tobin bin Sikim, 15, a settlement schoolboy, feels "more" Malaysian than the average Portuguese Eurasian because his father is an indigenous Kadazan from the East Malaysian state of Sabah, and he also carries the patronymic *"bin"*, only used by Muslims in Peninsular Malaysia (Interview, 24 June 2011).

There are many other examples of people with a hybrid heritage and interethnic marriages. During one field visit for example, I met three women of mixed heritage. One was of Punjabi Portuguese lineage and spoke Malay, English, Portuguese and Punjabi. The other was of Portuguese-Indian-Malay descent, and a third was an "acculturated" Filipina married to a Portuguese Eurasian at the settlement. (Fieldwork, Malacca, 28 June 2009). It is also increasingly common to marry outside the community. Teacher Sara Sta Maria says she and her five siblings are all married to non-Portuguese. "All of us have a diploma or degree and my father insisted that we marry graduates, but there were very few Portuguese Eurasian graduates. So we married out." Sara herself married a Kadazan, two siblings married Indians, one a "non-*Peranakan* Teochew Chinese", another a "*Peranakan* Chinese" and one a "Filipino Japanese", she says proudly (Interview, 24 June 2011).

In addition to Malaysian, Portuguese, Dutch and British influences over the centuries, after independence some Portuguese Eurasians intermingled and inter-married with foreign soldiers at a military camp in Malacca. Historian Horace Sta Maria explains:

Just before and after the war we retained our identity for a reason; if you married outside the group you were ostracized. What changed the situation was the establishment of a Commonwealth Army Camp at Terendak, sixteen miles (25.7 km) north of Malacca, in 1957–59. Many of our girls worked in their shops, supermarkets and nightclubs, met white soldiers, married and eventually moved to Australia, New Zealand and the U.K.. For a time this upset the female-male ratio in the Portuguese Eurasian community, and more males married out. Today, though the sex ratio is balanced, people are open-minded and there are many more intra-marriages.

(Horace Sta Maria, Interview, Malacca, 23 June 2011).

Catholicism: A Permeable Identity Marker

Catholicism is an important identity marker, but one which is permeable, allowing outsiders to enter the community through conversion and marriage. Membership is therefore based on self-ascription, with religion rather than "race" being a defining factor (Sarkissian 2000, p. 26). While Portuguese Eurasians adopted elements of Malay in their language, dress, food and performing arts, they retained their religious beliefs, and like the Chitty and Peranakan Chinese, were acculturated but not assimilated. Christianity was germane to their social identity; they were referred to as *Jente Kristang* (Christian people) by the Portuguese, and as *Serani* or *Nasrani* (people of Nazareth) by the Malays. Their strong Christian identity is manifested in their history as the earliest Christian community in Peninsular Malaysia, their links with Malacca's many Catholic churches, chapels and mission schools, and their celebration of numerous local religious events (Fernandis 2003, p. 1) (See Appendix 3.1 for historical context of Christianity in Malacca). In addition there was a regional Christian connection due to the fact that for many years Malacca came under the Macau diocese, which provided Portuguese priests to the community.

Their religious events are significant in several ways (Appendix 3.2 details these events). Firstly, they illustrate the hybrid and heterogeneous nature of the Portuguese Eurasian community and the wide diversity of people linked to the community and the settlement through birth, belief, marriage and family. In addition to Portuguese Eurasians, these events attract Catholic (and non-Christian) Indian, Chinese and mixed couples with children of mixed descent. There are also hundreds and in some cases thousands of pilgrims and tourists from Malaysia and abroad, including members of the diaspora from Singapore and Australia, who attend these events regularly. Secondly, many of these events have been conducted for generations, often in the same locations, with local rituals unique to the Portuguese Eurasians. They therefore provide the community a deep sense of place and a strong sense of pride in their spiritual and cultural heritage.

A third point to note is that some religious events in the settlement — Christmas, St Peter (San Pedro) and St Johns Feast Days' in particular

— have become commercialized and politicized in the sense that they have become tourist attractions, and top politicians often officiate. In addition to being church-based events fulfilling the spiritual needs of residents and visitors, they have become huge tourist events involving the support of the Malacca State government, national tourist promotion agencies and the tourist industries. In other words, the culture of the community has been co-opted for political and economic gain. Such commercialization is seen as crass by some older folk who miss the prayerful atmosphere of a once organic community, and irksome by younger members who are discouraged from returning to the settlement by the sheer overcrowding. Yet, as we will show later, without such co-option and commercialization, the settlement may never have survived.

A good example of such an event is Christmas. There is both a private and public Christmas at the Portuguese Settlement. The private Christmas is a home-coming event where hundreds of former residents return from all over Malaysia, Singapore, Australia and New Zealand join families for Christmas mass. This is followed by a family dinner, often comprising traditional dishes such as *acar chili* (chilli pickles), *curry debal, feng* (finely sliced pork offal), and *sebak* (a Portuguese pork salad). Traditional cakes include *bolu koku* (coconut sponge cake), *bluda* — which uses toddy as a rising agent, pineapple tarts and sugee cake (Selvarani 2009).

The public Christmas is the biggest event in the settlement, having overtaken San Pedro in scale and size. As with other major festivals, the prospect of the tourist dollar has led to State government sponsorship, which from the mid-1990s has expanded Christmas in the settlement from a family and community-based religious event into a national-level celebration. In addition to festive lights in homes, the settlement itself has a 7.5-metre Christmas tree with almost 20,000 bulbs, transforming the settlement into a fairyland attracting thousands of revellers, including local and international tourists (Interview, Michael Barnerji, 17 September 2008). The biggest highlights however are the visits of top officials, and public performances. In 2008 for example, the visitors included the Prime Minister, the Malacca Governor and the Chief Minister. There were performances by Portuguese dance troupe and top local singers such as Francisca Peters, Nurin Aziz and David Arumugam of Alleycats. An unusual crowd puller was the presence of forty beauty pageant contestants from all over the world, who were specially flown in for the occasion (Mahavera 2008).

Kristang: A Cosmopolitan Creole

> I am proud of being Portuguese Eurasian because 500 years ago my ancestors came here and we spoke the language. Although it has become bastardized, we are still the smallest community in the world speaking it.
>
> (Horace Sta Maria, Interview, Malacca, 22 June 2011)

The Kristang Creole is one of the clearest reflections of the deep interethnic interaction of the Portuguese with other groups in culturally diverse Malacca. Though Kristang is 95 per cent Portuguese-derived and recognizable to Portuguese speakers, Malay has influenced its grammar and has in turn borrowed words from it. Today there are between 300–400 Portuguese-derived words in Malay, such as *bantal* (pillow), *butang* (button), *buyang* (water jar), and *tiras* (fringe, pillow-border) (Baxter 1995, p. 55). A little known fact is that Malay also has about 1,000 Arabic, 400 Sanskrit and 77 Persian words (Beg 1982 and Beg 1983, as cited in Baxter 1995, p. 54). They include Arabic loan words in Portuguese which have entered Malay, given that Portugal was once occupied by the Arabs. These comprise words such as *algoja* (executioner) and *zetun* (olive). There are even loan words from the Brazilian Indian language Tupi, such as *buah gajus* (cashew) and *buah nanas* (pineapple), the result of the fact that Brazil was once a Portuguese colony (Baxter 1995, p. 58). (See Table 3.2 for examples of Bahasa Malaysia words derived from Portuguese.)

According to cultural activist and former Settlement Secretary, the late Patrick de Silva (1979, pp. 12–14), other Malay words of Portuguese origin include *kampung* (village), *kereta* (car), *sekolah* (school), *kebaya* (long blouse), *mesti* (must), *limau* (lime), and *bolo* (sponge cake). "Kristang has enriched the national language," he argued, and proposed that the Malaysian government reciprocate this contribution by documenting traditions, vocabularies, idioms and stories, and producing a Kristang-English dictionary. Today Kristang is still widely used in the settlement especially among fishermen, middle-aged and older residents, though younger people use English and Bahasa Malaysia. "People are amazed at how we have maintained our language despite the absence of Kristang books and teachers," says Michael Singho, president of the Malacca Portuguese Eurasian Association. "I guess it's part of a self-preservation mechanism, related to our need for a sense of identity," he adds (Interview, 26 April 2010).

TABLE 3.2
Bahasa Malaysia Words Derived From Portuguese

Local Portuguese	Malay	English
Arang	Arang	Charcoal
Agar-agar	Agar-agar	Seaweed Jelly
Bangkuk	Bangku	Bench or stool
Basi	Basi	Stale
Butang	Butang	Button
Cubek	Cubit	Pinch
Cucuk	Cucuk	To Poke
Janelak	Jandela	Window
Kacang	Kacang	Peanuts
Kebayak	Kebaya	Traditional Dress
Kerang	Kerang	Cockles
Longkuas	Lengkuas	Galangal
Pulut	Pulut	Glutinous Rice
Sakuk	Saku	Pocket
Skolak	Sekolah	School
Tabong	Tabung	Money-box
Tukah	Tukar	Change
Tualek	Tuala	Towel
Tepuk	Tepuk	To clap

Source: Sta Maria, Joseph. "Culture" (p. 13), Festa San Pedro Programme, 23–29 June, Portuguese Settlement, Malacca, published by Pesta San Pedro Organizing Committee, 2011.

Cuisine and Dress: A Malaysian Mix

Portuguese Eurasian hybridism is best experienced in their cuisine, which has over the centuries absorbed a delightful mélange of Malay, Peranakan Chinese, Indian, Dutch and British influences. Dishes popular among Portuguese Eurasians include *pongeteh* (a Peranakan Chinese dish) and cakes such as *kuih giggang* and *apom berkuah* (also common to Peranakan Chinese and Chitty). Popular Malay deserts such as *dodol* and *wajek* have become traditional Christmas cakes. The Indian impact is seen in *vindalu* and *debel curry*, nicknamed "curry devil" due to the spiciness of the Portuguese version, while Dutch influence is apparent in the Portuguese Eurasian cake called "*bruda*" or "*blunda*". Their British version of chicken stew comprises a thick spicy soy sauce gravy. *Portugal*, a cake made with grated tapioca, sliced bananas and grated coconut, seems to have been invented by the Portuguese Eurasians (de Silva 2003). Malay seafood-based flavourings popular with the Portuguese Eurasians include *sambal tumis*, *sambal belacan* and *cincalo*.[4]

Many local and foreign — especially Singaporean — tourists visit the settlement at night to enjoy Portuguese cuisine, particularly Portuguese baked fish and curry devil, two adaptations of Malay and Indian styles typical of Portuguese Eurasian food. *Pikadel* or fried shrimp patties is also popular during the shrimp season. It is made by mixing a handful of flour and a pinch of salt with water in a light batter. Clean shrimps, chopped spring onions and red chillies are added, and tablespoons of the batter are deep fried to a golden crisp. "It is best eaten with home-made chilli sauce, and downed with a glass of ice-cold beer" (Marbeck 2004, p. 104). Both the young within the settlement and families outside the settlement still enjoy traditional home-cooked Portuguese-type cuisine.

In terms of attire, some claim that early Portuguese influence in the region was so extensive and enduring that even today it is still manifested in the wedding coats of the Minangkabaus, the ceremonial attire of the Kadazans and Bajaus of Sabah and the Ibans and Dayaks of Sarawak (Bernard Sta Maria 1986). Attire remains an important identity marker for older settlement women. Like the Peranakan Chinese and Chitty, they still wear the *sarong kebaya* (short blouses over long Malay-style sarongs) at home, for social functions and religious events. Traditionally the older Portuguese Eurasians wore the *kebaya kompridu* (*kebaya* is Malay for blouse and *kompridu* is Kristang for long) while younger and single women wore the *dabaia kurtu* (short *kebaya*) (de Silva 2003, p. 8). Another traditional piece of clothing is the *banian*. This is a collarless short-sleeved shirt popular among fishermen and poorer Portuguese Eurasians; the clothing and the term is believed to be of Tamil origin (de Silva 2003, p. 8).

For the young however, ethnic identity is not marked by dress and everyday practice but by wearing special costumes and performing on stage. During cultural performances both men and women wear Portuguese folkloric costume, displaying a "Portuguese" face to their hybrid identity. However in mock weddings grooms wear Western-style clothing and the women don Malay costumes, reminding us of the community's hybrid past. While the other women wear the *kebaya kompridu* fastened by three *keronsangs* (gold pins) over *saias* (long skirts), the bride wears a white silk *kebaya* and *saia* with elaborate golden headdress and ornate necklace, reflecting Malay influences (Sarkissian 2000, pp. 137–38 and 146).

Student Stevie Toby bin Sikim, 15, has current interests typical of those his age — Western pop music, football, and Internet surfing — though he says many of his older friends are into Portuguese dance, due mainly to the influence of a local dance teacher. He lives in the family home in the settlement, where he enjoys mostly Portuguese food, his favourite being curry devil and *ambilak*, a meat-fish curry with brinjal and long beans (Interview, Portuguese Settlement, 24 June 2011).

The Performing Arts: "Playing Portuguese"[5]

> During the 130 years of Portuguese rule, the community inherited a priceless jewel... local Portuguese culture (through) the blending of the artistic culture of the indigenous people with the exotic culture of Portugal. The *Branyo* is of Portuguese origin, and has inexplicable similarities to the *Ronggeng*. The *Keronchong* originated from the Portuguese Eurasians living in Java, who were once in Malacca. The song *Jinklie Nona* is always linked to the Malaysian Portuguese of Melaka, and the *Mata Kantiga* is similar to the Malay pantuns.
>
> (de Silva, Patrick 1979, p. 15)

The community's performing arts are a clear example of how multiple identities have been mobilized to showcase their culture, secure their space and win State recognition of their heritage as unique and worthy of preservation. A confluence of factors, initially outside their control, resulted in once traditional, hybrid (Malay-Portuguese *and* Chitty-Peranakan-Chinese) art forms morphing into "pure" Portuguese performances. These were staged for local, national, foreign audiences and tourists, thus providing an exotic "Portuguese" face to a deeply hybrid people.

The community's traditional music, song and dance in fact provide clear evidence of long, close and deep interaction and acculturation with Malays. Before the 1960s certain aspects of settlement culture were more "Malay" than "Portuguese". Women wore sarongs and *kebayas*, while residents practised traditional but hybridized genres of *branyo* dances and *mata kantiga* song duels. The *branyo* is a dance in which couples advance and retreat but avoid touch, while *mata kantiga* (sung to *branyo* music), is a male-female song duel.[6] *Branyo* is closely related to Malay *joget* and *mata kantiga* to *dondang sayang*. Popular *branyo* songs such as *"Jinkly Nona"*[7] are called *jogets* when performed by Malay musicians. *Joget* itself was greatly influenced by Malacca's Portuguese Eurasians over four centuries. This interaction resulted in the adoption of the *joget* as a national social dance and the acceptance of *"Jinkly Nona"* as a national rather than a purely Portuguese song. *"Jinkly Nona"* has been described as a "critical symbolic cultural link over time and space", linking the "settlement-as-housing estate" to the "settlement-as-historical monument", and connecting the community to its Malaysian context and its Portuguese diaspora (Sarkissian 2000, pp. 98, 101, 181).

The transformation in the settlement's performing tradition from a hybrid Malaysian variety involving residents into distinct "Portuguese" cultural shows staged for the public is closely linked to history and politics. The independence movement had forced elite Eurasians to distance themselves from the British and present themselves as "Portuguese". For this purpose they imported twentieth century Portuguese performing arts, including dress, music, dance and song. As elite Eurasians emigrated after independence, these arts forms were passed on to working-class settlement residents who merged them with elements of traditional performances to create their own genre. In this way, a once hybrid Portuguese Eurasian performing arts tradition incorporating Malay influences became "Portuguese" (Sarkissian 2000, pp. 11, pp. 51–66).

A cultural performance today includes songs, dances, and on important occasions, a mock wedding. These are packaged, presented and perceived as authentic and "pure Portuguese" performances inherited and passed on over the last 500 years. But this is an invented, not an inherited performing tradition. Cultural production and reproduction began formally with the establishment of the Portuguese Cultural Society in 1967. These efforts were complemented by independent cultural groups. In 1990, for example, the Tropa De Assunta group in Praya Lane in Bandar Hilir, the organizers of the San Juang celebrations, stated in an advertisement that they specialized in organizing traditional Portuguese mock weddings, music, dance, and Portuguese food catering (Festa San Juang Booklet, 1990).

Together with Portuguese imports and adaptations, local creations and Western popular music, performances in the settlement have taken a life of their own (Sarkissian 2000, pp. 146–47). At the feast of St Peter at the settlement in 2009 for example, there was a well attended mass after which there was a traditional blessing of fishing boats. Later in the evening there were Portuguese dances and songs, followed by a performance by the "Connie Francis of Malaysia" — a Portuguese Eurasian singer from Penang. But the real crowd-puller was a Michael Jackson impersonation by a young man from the settlement (Author's Fieldwork, 28 June 2009).

A prime example of music syncretism is octogenarian Horace Sta Maria, 90. Though he grew up outside the settlement he was closely associated with the community as a school teacher, musician, and in the evening of his life, as an amateur historian. In Malacca he was best known as a musician and leader of a band called *Trez Amigos* (Three Friends). Formed in 1949, their popularity grew once their recordings of six country-and-western songs hit the airwaves from Singapore's Radio Malaya. The group then performed on radio shows in Malacca, Penang and Kuala Lumpur, with Horace in particular gaining a large following as the "best yodeller in the country". They made their first commercial recording in neighbouring Singapore under the His Master's Voice label with the songs "*O Bulan Cemerlang Di Malaya*" and *O Maria* on 78rpm records. *O Bulan Cemerlang Di Malaya* was also featured by the British Broadcasting Corporation (BBC) in its Overseas Coronation radio programme, which was broadcast to Australia, New Zealand, Canada, South Africa, Indonesia and Portugal. In 1954 the Malayan Film Unit produced a documentary entitled "Malayan Variety" featuring the group (D'Cruz, 2002).

SECURING ETHNIC SPACE AND POLITICAL PLACE: PORTUGUESE AND *BUMIPUTERA* ROUTES

A Place for the Poor: Creating the "Portuguese Settlement"

As mentioned earlier the Portuguese settlement was established in 1934 by the Catholic Church, elite Eurasians and the British as a public service project to improve housing and living conditions for the Portuguese Eurasians poor. These elite Eurasians were mostly of Dutch and British origin, educated, English-speaking and employed by the British, in contrast to the Portuguese, the majority of whom were working class, illiterate Kristang-speaking fishermen. Both lived in separate worlds. The elite Eurasians lived in Tranquerah, a wealthy area north of the town, while the Portuguese, mainly fishermen, resided in Bandar Hilir in the south (Sarkissian 2000, pp. 30, 31, 37). Similar class divisions related to education, language, occupation and location existed in the case of the Chitty, whose trading class resided in Tranquerah and working class comprising farmers lived in rural Gajah Berang (see chapter 2). Though the context and factors differed, the Portuguese Eurasians, like the Chitty, were dislocated by the Dutch and later socially fragmented by British colonialism.

The idea of an improved housing settlement for Portuguese Eurasian fishermen was initially proposed in 1926 by two Catholic priests and supported by the British resident commissioner. A mangrove swamp was drained, reclaimed and readied by 1934, with roads named after Portuguese historical figures such as Alfonso de Albuquerque, Godinho de Eredia, Diego Sequeira, Ruy de Araujo and Hieronymous Texeira. A headman or *regedor* was appointed and residents entered the settlement in 1935. Response was slow because many could not afford to build their own houses; the British therefore built and rented out houses at nominal sums. In 1940 the settlement comprised sixty-two houses rented at $2 per month, and by 1952 the population was 557 people. Most were fishermen, some were clerks. The houses had *attap* roofs and mud floors, but by the mid-1950s these were replaced by zinc and concrete with financial support from the Rural Industries Development Authority (RIDA), precursor to MARA (Majlis Amanah Rakyat), a body which today assists *bumiputeras*. Home electricity arrived in the late 1950s and piped water by the late 1960s. A hall was built through donations and self help in 1961 (Sarkissian 2000, pp. 37–40).

The Land Dispute: "Saving" the Settlement

The dilemma of the Portuguese Eurasians was that they lost the security of their land — specifically the freehold status of their land — barely fifteen years after being granted it. This led to a forty-year dispute with the State and a quest for land security which first engendered a cultural resurgence and later political action, culminating in the granting of partial indigenous benefits to the community in 1984, a visit by the Prime Minister in 1985, and finally a State announcement in 1990 that the Portuguese Settlement would be preserved as a heritage site.

The dispute had its roots in a British move to set aside 0.8 hectares for the Canossian Convent, which catered to children of residents. Since foreign-based institutions could not own freehold property in colonial Malaya, the convent was given a 99-year lease plot in the freehold settlement. This created an anomaly between the school plot and the original land, which was remedied by changing the status of the entire settlement from freehold to State land in 1949. The State-owned status led to acquisition of plots in the settlement three times over the next fifteen years — in 1953 for the Customs and Excise Department staff quarters;

in 1962 for a proposed La Salle Brothers trade school; and in 1964 for the Fisheries Department staff quarters. These moves shrank the size of land available for housing in the overcrowded settlement and made residents anxious about their future. Discontent flared up again in 1976 when residents were offered ninety-nine-year leases; in 1979 when there were reports that the government planned to replace the existing ground-level Customs staff quarters with a high-rise apartment; and once more in 1987 when residents were offered sixty-six-year leases and asked to pay temporary occupation licences.

In August 1979 community leaders established the "Save the Portuguese Community Committee", which launched a campaign to gain permanent land tenure for settlers and halt plans for the high-rise. A few weeks later they organized a seminar on the history and evolution of the community, followed by a "solidarity dinner" attended by 1,000 people (Save the Portuguese Community 1979), including Portuguese Eurasians from various parts of Malaysia. To raise awareness of the issues involved, the seminar papers were distributed in booklet form during the dinner. A major grievance among residents was that the existing Customs quarters reduced the size of their overcrowded settlement, where family sizes were still growing. Resident Rachel Sta Maria told the seminar: "We believe we are entitled to that land because the sole intention in acquiring the 28 acres (11.3 hectares) was for the creation of a Portuguese-Eurasian settlement and no other purpose whatsoever" (Rachel Sta Maria 1979). In a telegram to Prime Minister Hussein Onn, the committee stated:

> The erection of the Customs quarters on our land in 1953 was a grievous error, but the proposed erection of multi-storey flats would destroy us. For Customs, it is a matter of relocation; for us it is a question of survival of our culture, heritage and community.
>
> ("Plea to PM Over Flats Move in Settlement",
> *New Straits Times*, 5 August 1979).

Linking People to Place: Saving the Portuguese "Community"

The key issue was the proposed government use of part of the settlement's land; there was no immediate threat to the existence of the community. However the panel was not named "Save the Portuguese *Settlement* Committee" but instead "Save the Portuguese *Community* Committee" (emphasis mine). The leaders had astutely tied the future of the community to the settlement. The entire campaign was premised on the argument that the settlement was the only place in the country where a unique "Portuguese" culture survived; allowing non-Portuguese (government staff) into the settlement would dilute its character. The key person highlighting the link between ethnic space and cultural identity was Bernard Sta Maria, the late Portuguese Eurasian community leader and politician. This is how he put it:

> As a community of Portuguese descendants we would cease to exist, because a community can only claim to be one if it possesses a cultural heritage and an identity. For this to exist, we have to live in a homogeneous environment, and a Portuguese settlement is the only area where it exists.
> (Bernard Sta Maria, "Plea to PM Over Flats Move in Settlement", *New Straits Times*, 5 August 1979).

Bernard Sta Maria had sown the seeds of a cultural revival as early as 1967 when he founded the Portuguese Cultural Society, which presented "Portuguese" cultural performances throughout the country, portraying an exotic and unique "Portuguese" image of the village. In the ethnically fractured elections of 1969 he was elected an Opposition (Democratic Action Party) State Assemblyman, and consequently re-elected in 1974 and 1978. In 1981 he consolidated his community work by setting up the Malacca Portuguese Development Trust and the Malacca Portuguese Development Centre, which offered tutorials, vocational classes and university loans to students.

National political leaders were not insensitive to the plight of the community, especially after the land issue received publicity in the national media. In 1981 Dr Mahathir Mohamad became Premier, and in reply to a congratulatory note from Bernard Sta Maria, he promised to give attention to the community. Months later his deputy Musa Hitam made a surprise visit to the settlement, the first minister to do so (Goh 2002, p. 127). Despite these political gestures, the campaign continued unabated. The pressure was kept up through protests by Eurasian associations throughout the country, appeals to top government officials, and publicity in the media, eventually forcing the government to abandon the high-rise plan. The community had halted further intrusions into their ethnic space. But they had yet to secure land tenure.

Mobilizing Dual Identities: Portuguese *and* Malay-*Bumiputera*

The cultural resurgence, which began as a means to strengthen community solidarity in the struggle for land tenure, had over time become a force of its own, increasing in subtlety and intensity. Community leaders soon began portraying and exploiting *two* overlapping aspects of their identities — their unique, exotic "Portuguese" origins *and* their part-indigenous "Luso-Malay" (Portuguese-Malay) identity. This was despite the fact it was difficult for non-Malay, non-Muslims in Peninsular Malaysia to gain State recognition as Malays or *bumiputeras*.

One reason for this "Bumiquest" (a term first used by Fernandis 2000, p. 1) was that as a minority the community had no direct political representation in Parliament, nor could they join the dominant Malay, Chinese or Indian-based political parties. Moreover, there is no single State or Parliamentary constituency with a Eurasian majority. Though Bernard Sta Maria became the first Portuguese Eurasian elected to the State Assembly, the Portuguese Eurasians had no representative in the Parliament or Senate since 1946–47, when Eurasian Union President G. Shelly was the nominated Senator for minorities (Muzzi 2002, p. 53). As a minority lumped into that amorphous category "Others", their best alternative was to emphasize their common roots and links to the Malay majority.

By the early 1980s the cultural resurgence had radiated from the settlement to the Peninsular Malaysia's wider Eurasian community and was reflected in speeches, papers and books available to the community. Bernard Sta Maria, in a paper presented at the 1979 seminar at the height of the land controversy, acknowledged that the community is "a mixture of intermarriages..." and that "no race in this whole wide world is a pure, unmixed and intact race." Significantly, he highlighted the Arab and Malay roots of Portuguese Eurasians through two types of early intermarriages. He argued that the first Portuguese settlers who married local girls were in fact "Moz-Arabs", descendants of the 500-year Arab colonization of parts of Portugal. The second type of mixed marriages, he said, involved Malays and Javanese who converted to Catholicism, took Portuguese names and married Portuguese Eurasians. One such well-known convert was the Malay nobleman Panglima Awang, the first Malay who circumnavigated the world on Ferdinand Magellan's ship. He took the name Dom Hendrique (Bernard Sta Maria 1979, pp. 6–9).

Another paper highlighting the Malay roots of the community was written by the late Gerard Fernandis, a university graduate and cultural activist from the settlement. In a 1993 presentation to a State government panel assessing the community's eligibility for full *bumiputera* status he propounded three arguments. Firstly, he emphasized, the early Portuguese settlers "lived in a totally Malay environment". They lived in Malay-style houses, their women maintained Malay lifestyles, and they mixed freely with other native groups, including the Minangkabaus, who were described as "friends of the fortress" (Fernandis 1995a, p. 95). Secondly, he said, the government's move to grant *bumiputera* status to Malaysian Buddhists of Thai-Malay heritage "raises the possibility" of the same recognition for Portuguese Eurasians, who are of "mixed Luso-Malay parentage". Thirdly, he argued, it is difficult to physically distinguish a native Malay from a Portuguese Eurasian; they have "turned native" and can no longer be termed "Portuguese" (Fernandis 1995a, p. 92).

Besides these papers, two texts published around the same period drew attention to the community's indigenous roots and national contributions. One was a 1981 booklet *Bygone Eurasia: The Life Story of the Eurasians of Malaya*, the memoirs of James Augustine, President of the Kedah Eurasian Association. It highlighted the hybrid origins of northern Peninsular Malaysia Eurasians, their teachers' contributions in Christian missions schools, their use of Malay as a medium of instruction and UMNO founding-president Onn Jaafar's belief that Eurasians could claim to be "sons of the soil" (*bumiputeras*) (Augustine 1981, pp. 19, 26). The other was Bernard Sta Maria's 1982 book, *My People, My Country*, a lengthy treatise emphasizing the Malay "racial roots" of the Portuguese Eurasians, their mutual linguistic and cultural acculturation, and the critical importance of the Portuguese settlement as their sole ethnic space (Sta Maria 1982).

The swerve from the "Portuguese" toward the "Malay-*bumiputera*" route coincided with shifting notions of Malay identity following a power struggle in UMNO in the mid-1980s, when, according to one scholar, some UMNO leaders tried to increase their support base by co-opting minorities (Goh 2002, pp. 134–37). Groups which had cultural, social, and linguistic affinities with Malays were courted and endowed with benefits reserved for the indigenous community. In the early 1980s the Thais of Kedah — a non-Malay, non-Muslim and non-*bumiputera* group — were given full *bumiputera* status and thus access to Amanah Saham Nasional (ASN), a blue-chip State-run equity fund reserved for indigenous people. (Renamed Amanah Saham Bumiputera or "ASB" but still popularly referred to by settlement residents as "ASN".) This was seen as a sign of a loosening of the official Malay-*bumiputera* identity, and Kedah Eurasians,[8] who share some similarities with Thais in terms of language and customs, also began pressing to enter the "*bumiputera* route". The lobbying in Kedah coincided with a "heightened political atmosphere" (Goh 2002, p. 135) among Portuguese Eurasians in Malacca due to the land issue. In 1982 Bernard Sta Maria switched political allegiance to Gerakan, part of the ruling National Front. Two years later, on 3 August 1984, the ASN was opened up to Portuguese Eurasians. Though the Portuguese Eurasians did not enjoy full indigenous status, their eligibility for ASN shares was politically symbolic and economically important; the state now recognized their indigenous roots and allowed them to benefit from the State-run equity fund. The land campaign and the "Portuguese" cultural resurgence had veered into the *bumiputera* route, resulting in nominal *bumiputera* recognition. But land tenure was still not in sight. That had to await the official visit of Dr Mahathir Mohamad, Malaysia's most influential Prime Minister, to the settlement.

Showcasing Culture, Securing Space: The "Portuguese Square"

In 1985 Dr Mahathir fulfilled his promise to Bernard Sta Maria to "give the community attention," by visiting the settlement and opening the Portuguese Square, a tourist attraction which was his brainchild. No bigger than a football field, it comprised an arch-like entrance leading to a small paved courtyard with souvenir shops and cafes. Dr Mahathir's interest was not merely political; he appeared to have a cultural if not intellectual interest in the community.

Dr Mahathir, according to Bernard Sta Maria, believed that many of the region's traditional songs originated from the Portuguese "*fado*" (Bernard Sta Maria, 1986). A widely recognized urban-folk musical genre in Portugal to this day, *fado* is melancholic, akin to the American blues (worldmusic.nationalgeographic.com.), and is said to originate from a community of Moors who lived outside Lisbon after the Christian takeover (www.lisbon-guide.info/about/fado). *Fado* translated into English means fate, but the music style reflects nostalgia and longing. The mournful tunes originate from the sorrow felt by sailors and their families due to separation. (LisbonWeekendGuild.com)

Scholars confirm that *keroncong*, a syncretic music form employing the ukulele and other stringed instruments and popular in the archipelago and the Peninsular Malaysia up to the 1960s, has its roots in *fado*, introduced by the Portuguese into Malacca and later perpetuated by Portuguese refugees who fled to Indonesian islands after the Dutch attack (Ferzacca 2006, p. 336). Two other music ethnologists state that *keroncong* originated in Betawi (Jakarta) in the sixteenth and seventeenth century, where it was first sung by Portuguese called Mardijkers, and later by those of Dutch Portuguese descent (Matusky and Tan 2005, p. 342).

Fado music enchanted Dr Mahathir so much that he reportedly spent two whole days visiting Lisbon listening to the *fado* singers, bought some tapes and, on "one of his visits to the Portuguese settlement, he offered those tapes to anyone wishing to emulate the *fado* singers" (Bernard Sta Maria, 1986). When he opened the settlement's Portuguese Square, the Prime Minister, who flew in three *fado* singers from Portugal for the event (Interview, Barnerji, 26 July 2011), indicated that the culture of the community should be preserved:

> I hope the uniqueness of this settlement (can) be perpetuated because the settlement will show everybody that Malaysia is made up of different races, and even though they are different, they are all Malaysian citizens who have a place in Malaysia. *As a unique race we must perpetuate the Portuguese culture here.* (Emphasis mine)
>
> (Malaysian Prime Minister Dr Mahathir Mohamad,
> speaking at the opening of the Portuguese Square,
> Portuguese Settlement, 1985. (Translated from the original speech
> in Bahasa Malaysia, as cited in Joseph Sta Maria 1994, p. 83).

By saying that Portuguese culture "must" be perpetuated, one could deduce that he meant the Portuguese Settlement should be preserved. Dr Mahathir's advice would have been impossible for the State government, or the Malacca Chief Minister — whose appointment depended on the Prime Minister — to ignore. Consequently in 1987 the Chief Minister announced the settlement would be preserved, in 1988 a State conservation law was drawn up, and in 1990 the settlement was declared an official historical monument (under the Malacca Preservation and Conservation of Historical and Cultural Heritage Enactment 1988).

The Chief Minister said residents "need not fear anymore as the settlement will remain there forever now that it is protected by the enactment" (*New Straits Times*, 23 August 1990). The move met several goals at one go; it fulfilled the Prime Minister's wish, boosted tourism, and met the residents demand for land security. However the Chief Minister specifically mentioned that "Portuguese Reservation status" requested by the community was not possible (*The Star*, 10 October 1987). Presumably this was because granting land reservation to a community with a colonial heritage would arouse Malay nationalist sentiments, particularly since many urban Malays themselves sought freehold titles for State land they were occupying.

The Portuguese Square soon became the settlement's main tourist symbol. One scholar has described it as a clear attempt to convert the settlement into a "historical monument" and to use tourism to co-opt it for "political and economic gain" (Sarkissian 2000, p. 158). In the initial years the food stalls were more attractive than the square, but gradually the whole area became increasingly popular among local, Singaporean and foreign tourists seeking to experience Portuguese cuisine and culture, particularly during weekends and major festivals. Given its heritage status and tourist pull, it was highly unlikely that the residents, the living representatives of Portuguese culture, would lose their land. The older community leaders, especially those who were involved in the land campaign, are fully cognizant of this, and it is one reason why they are insistent on publicizing cultural events and keeping the settlement on the tourist map.

The residents had finally gained land security, though through a somewhat unusual route. But this was not the end of their land woes. Despite being officially declared a historical monument, there were attempts in the mid-1990s to reclaim the settlement seafront for property development. The move would have land-locked the seafront fishing settlement. The residents fought back. They set up a Reclamation Action Committee, arguing that the move would destroy the character of the village, the livelihood of settlers, their culture and its tourism value. This new strategy directly linked their interests to that of the tourist industry and the State. To add intellectual ballast to their campaign, in 1995 the committee organized an international conference with foreign scholars testifying to the historical significance of their culture in Malacca. Referring to the loss of their seafront, one speaker said:

> For us it is not just a matter of losing a beautiful view or selling concepts. It is a question of losing a cherished natural feature that has been a part of our lives for centuries. We are the last bastion of Portuguese and Eurasian identity and existence. Our wealth and treasures do not lie in gold, diamonds or silver; they lie in our language, religion, culture tradition, songs, dances....there is no price tag to these elements. If we lose them, then we would be no more.
>
> Michael Singho, member of the *regedor*'s panel and vice-chairman of the Reclamation Action Committee, in Fernandis 1995*b*, p. 28.

Their campaign coincided with the recession of the late 1990s, which forced the proposed private sector reclamation project to be called off. Though the government later reclaimed a part of the settlement seafront for the State-run Lisbon Hotel and a hawker-food centre run by residents, the seafront was preserved and the settlement — unlike the old Malacca town-centre — was saved from being land-locked.

"BUMIQUEST": Toward A State-Recognized Identity

As mentioned earlier, the State's long delay in granting land security to settlement residents sparked a cultural resurgence which strengthened their cultural identity and communal solidarity. However, before the land issue was resolved (in 1990), partial *bumiputera* benefits were granted to the community (in 1984), thus imposing a State-defined cultural identity on them. Thus both the community and State-defined identities coalesced to further reinforce Portuguese Eurasian ethnic consciousness.

Expectations of full *bumiputera* status were raised in 1991 when Prime Minister Dr Mahathir announced that Portuguese Eurasians could apply for membership of UMNO, the key Malay-Muslim ruling coalition partner, which had just admitted Sabah Christian-*bumiputeras* as members. However the party's supreme council decided that Portuguese Eurasians should be considered for full *bumiputera* status first; to this end a State-level panel was set up, but its findings were inconclusive (Fernandis 2000, pp. 264–65).

The pining for a State-recognized full-fledged *bumiputera* status ran deep, however, as reflected by statements by influential community leaders. Gerard Fernandis, a respected cultural activist and university graduate from the settlement, published a journal article in 2000 entitled, "The Portuguese Eurasians in Malaysia: Bumiquest, A Search for Self-Identity", which began with this poem:

> The last few acres of land,
> This last bastion of cultural stand.
> Echoes of cannon's roaring,
> Drowning the cries, casting nets
> In muddy water, shrimp people,
> Once Conquerors,
> Now Fishermen.
> Where do we go from here?
> Identity in confusion
> Bumi status we seek.
> Why only invest?
> Why under 'Others'?
> Portuguese Eurasians Indigenous,
> *Papia, Relijang e tradisang.*
> (Gerard Fernandis 2000, p. 262)

Others like Joseph Sta Maria, advisor to the village headman's panel, hopes that the current partial *bumiputera* benefits are merely a precursor to full *bumiputera* status.

> The debate (to determine) if the Portuguese community should be granted *bumiputera* status lives on today, and perhaps the decision made to grant members of the Portuguese community the privilege to invest in the ASN in 1984 (renamed Amanah Saham Bumiputera (ASB) in 1990) was a beginning towards the Melaka Portuguese attaining full *bumiputera* status.
>
> (Joseph Sta Maria 2011, p. 13).

The partial benefits now enjoyed by the community are a mixed blessing. At an individual level the chance to invest in blue-chip State equities is welcomed by most, but at the community level it has its pros and cons. Philomena Singho Tan is grateful for the opportunity and feels that eligibility to invest is a consolation since the community does not get any other "special help" from the authorities:

> Though my children are registered as Chinese, they are eligible to apply for ASN shares. If one parent is Portuguese they are eligible. They (the government authorities) are more flexible now. People apply via the headman or *regedor*, but most go directly to the ASN office these days. ASN eligibility is one of our few privileges. We do not get any special help with housing or university places. We have very few graduates from the settlement, perhaps two dozen in the last thirty years. Perhaps there are three times more Portuguese Eurasian graduates in Malacca state as a whole and five times that number for the country. Most youths in the settlement join the workforce after school. Most work in the private sector. Very few of us get government jobs.
>
> (Interview, Portuguese Settlement, 23 June 2011)

Even those unable to invest realize its potential usefulness. Fisherman Napolean Fernandez, 58, was sanguine: "Even if some of us cannot afford to invest, our relatives and friends can, and the community benefits." Others feel that the partial benefits give the impression that the entire community is progressing when in fact opportunities are limited by various factors. "ASN is good — if you have money," says musician Francis Decosta, 58. "We do not enjoy any other benefits. Nothing comes on a tray. We have to work for it," he adds. (Interviews, 23 June 2011, Portuguese Settlement).

Law student Carissa Stephens, 21, says "the Thais and the indigenous people of Sabah and Sarawak are *bumiputeras*, but we are not recognized as *bumiputeras*. This is one reason why we do not get any preferences when entering public universities." She says she was denied a place in a public university of her choice despite good pre-university results, and thus opted for law at a private university in Malacca. "However I managed to get a loan from a government agency because my father is a pensioner," she adds. (Interview, Portuguese Settlement, 24 June 2011).

At the community level the ASN investment opportunity has potential to both unite and fracture the community. While it provides an incentive for the middle class — many of whom live away — to reclaim their Portuguese roots and reconnect to the settlement and community, it also contributes to increasing income inequality by favouring the wealthy over the poor, who are unable to save and invest. It thus connects the community culturally, but divides it socio-economically.

The chasm is worsened by residential and sub-ethnic differences. The majority of investors, including those who identify themselves simply as "Eurasians", live outside the settlement. Though many of these "Eurasians" have contributed to the Portuguese Eurasian cultural heritage, the settlement residents' quest for land, and the public services, there remains a residue of resentment against them, linked both to old class schisms spawned during the British period and the new investment opportunities made available by the State.

Joseph Sta Maria noted in 1995 that many Portuguese Eurasians outside Malacca — including State Eurasian Association leaders of Portuguese extraction — had earlier preferred to be identified simply as "Eurasians". But, he added, "this Eurasian perception was immediately transformed after 3 August 1984 when the government announced that the Portuguese community (was) permitted to invest in the ASN." As soon as they realized the economic benefits of being "Portuguese", many Eurasians reclaimed their Portuguese roots, he said. He described their actions as "the highest form of leadership betrayal". Though most investors lived outside the settlement, the benefits they enjoyed were the result of decades of effective leadership of local leaders within the settlement, he argued (Joseph Sta Maria 1995, pp. 14–15).[9]

CONCLUSION

Malacca's diverse cultural influences are richly reflected in Portuguese Eurasian language, cuisine, dress and performing arts. Like the Chitty, religion is their strongest identity but not one that precludes inter-marriage, acculturation and assimilation into their community.

Constant threats to their land and fishing grounds galvanized the community over the years. In the 1970s residents rallied against proposed high-rise government quarters in the settlement. In the 1980s discontent arose over the temporary status of their land titles. In the 1990s they successfully protested against the State's proposed land reclamation, a project which incensed the community because of its threat to their coastline, fishing grounds, livelihoods, and way of life. However these responses expressed themselves as a "Portuguese" cultural resurgence and a "Bumiquest" rather than a direct legal challenge to preserve their land and fishing rights.

Being a tiny minority lacking economic capital and political power in an ethnic-based political party system, they exploited their cultural capital by harnessing their dual identities as both "pure" Portuguese and as "Luso-Malays". The "Portuguese" identity allowed them to carve out an exotic image of themselves as a small but vulnerable community requiring their own ethnic space to survive, while boosting their potential as a heritage and tourist site; the "Luso-Malay' identity allowed them to identify with the indigenous Malay majority and project themselves as a people eligible for *bumiputera* status and State assistance. Through a confluence of factors they managed to win both land security and partial *bumiputera* benefits.

The cultural resurgence first manifested in the 1960s as a means to broaden and strengthen community solidarity in the face of uncertainty over their land. As part of this strategy, traditional religious festivals, which for centuries had been observed within the community, were publicized beyond the settlement and soon became State, national and international-level events incorporating both church services and traditional Portuguese and contemporary Western performances.

The community appears to have made gains only when their interests coincided with the State's. This happened twice — once when they gained partial indigenous benefits (eligibility for State equity funds) in 1984, and again in 1990 when the settlement was gazetted as heritage land, a move consolidated in July 2008 when UNESCO recognized the settlement as part and parcel of Malacca's newly bestowed world heritage status.

Like most historical minorities discussed in this book such as the Indian Muslims, the Chitty and Indonesians, the Portuguese Eurasians sought the *bumiputera* route as a way out of their perceived socio-economic and political marginalization. But this move has its weaknesses. In the case of the Portuguese Eurasians, as with other groups, ASN eligibility confers far greater benefits to the wealthy than to low-wage earners, and does not solve the problem of their perceived marginalization in a holistic manner.

Today the settlement is the lifeblood of the community. It is not only their residential, ethnic, spiritual and occupational base, but has also become, through their own efforts and State interests, a cultural museum and tourist site. Its survival appears ensured by its continued value to the local and national tourism industry, to the Portuguese Eurasians and their diaspora, and to other Malaysians. The real value and national contribution of the Portuguese Eurasians of Malacca is best encapsulated by a scholar, who notes:

> The Kristang population of Malacca afford living testimony to the open and flexible orientation of Malaysia towards diversity in cultural form. Any and all forces posing danger to this living heritage, by definition, poses threats to the heart of Malaysia itself.
>
> (Dr Brian Juan O'Neil 1995, p. 95)

POSTSCRIPT

In 2014–15 the sea facing the tiny settlement was being reclaimed. This was part of a huge 245 hectare (600-acre) project involving further reclamation of the Malacca coastline. Community leaders complained that reclamation was affecting the sea-access and livelihood of fishermen, and eliminating the sea-view which was part and parcel of their heritage. They alleged residents were not consulted, that the project was not preceded by up-to-date environmental and social impact assessments, and that it would affect Malacca's status as a UNESCO World Heritage Site. "For us, it is not only a matter of our livelihood but also the survival of a 500-year old culture and heritage which we cherish and are proud of," said Save Portuguese Community Action Committee (SPACC) chairman Martin Theseira, who presented a memorandum to Parliament in early 2015 appealing for Federal government intervention (Cheah 2015; Singho 2014).

APPENDIX 3.1
THE PORTUGUESE EURASIAN CATHOLIC HERITAGE

To appreciate the impact of religion on Portuguese Eurasian identity, it is important to examine the historical context of Christianity. Malacca became a thoroughly Christian city during the 130 years of Portuguese occupation, with nineteen churches and chapels occupying virtually every hill and street (Lee 1963, as cited in Sibert 2003, p. 2). Catholic religious orders including Jesuits, Dominicans and Franciscans set up branches in Malacca, which became a half-way house for missionaries on their way to the Spice Islands, China and Japan (Fernandis 2003, pp. 1–6).

These included a Franciscan monastery on Bukit China, an Augustinian hermitage and a Jesuit chapel just outside town, the church on St John's Hill and another on St Paul's Hill next to the Stadhuys. Another church which catered to the early Portuguese Eurasians was St Stephen (later renamed St Lawrence) on Jalan Bunga Raya in town. This was the precursor to the 1710 St Peter's Church, which until today remains the main parish of the Portuguese Eurasians. St Peter's is the oldest functioning Catholic Church in Malaysia, and is considered the "mother-church and the last historic and sacred vestige of Portuguese presence" (Fernandis 2003, p. 6). It is still referred to as the "Portuguese Church", probably because it was run by the Portuguese Mission out of Macau, as opposed to St Francis Xavier's, which was run by the French Mission, and is still sometimes called the "French Church" (Fieldwork 2009–11).

Since Catholic influence first came with the Portuguese, the Eurasians enjoy the distinction of being the founding members of the Malaysian Catholic Church (Sibert 2003, p. 2). As the majority of Malaysian Christians are Catholics, their collective role, particularly through the establishment of mission schools in virtually every town throughout the country, is also a heritage that the Portuguese can associate with. Though much of this developed under British colonialism, the earliest influences were Portuguese.

During the Portuguese Occupation, there were churches catering to a population of 20,000, mainly Portuguese Eurasians. However, only 3,000 people survived the 1641 Dutch attack of Malacca while others succumbed to injuries, hunger and disease. The Dutch persecuted the Catholics; many homes and almost all churches were destroyed, except the one on St Paul's Hill, which was temporarily used for Dutch Reformed Church services. Half of the 3,000 who remained, particularly the clergy, were expelled to the region, or migrated to neighbouring Malay states. Others took refuge in Malacca's rural areas, particularly Melaka Pindah and Kesang, where they blended into the Malay community and took up farming. Some worked for and intermarried into Chinese families, as evidenced by church records. The Chapel of the Holy Cross in Malim and the Chapel of Our Lady of Hope in Melaka Pindah are examples of places of worship built by these refugees (Fernandis 2003, pp. 5–6).

Out of this climate of persecutions emerged a society called the *Irmoes da igreja* or Brothers of the Church, which organized secret masses. When Dutch persecutions abated, the society helped build a chapel on the bank of the Malacca River near the former Federal Theatre on Jalan Bunga Raya. When St Peter's Church was built in 1710, the society relocated there. The society is still active today, though its work is mainly confined to organizing the Lent celebrations at St Peter's and the San Pedro (St Peter's) Feast in the settlement (Fernandis 2003, pp. 4–5). It is believed to be the oldest-surviving church organization in Southeast Asia, with membership passing from father to son.

APPENDIX 3.2
KEY PORTUGUESE EURASIAN RELIGIOUS EVENTS

Feasts of St John the Baptist (25 June) and St Peter (29 June)

Both these events are usually celebrated together. These were once private, community-based church celebrations, but after the mid-1960s they were transformed into public events. Today, apart from Christmas, they are the biggest public events, involving the participation of thousands of Portuguese Eurasians and people from all faiths outside the settlement.

St John the Baptist is the patron-saint of the Bandar Hilir area, where a large number of Portuguese Eurasians once lived. According to local journalist Percy D'cruz, the celebration, termed Festa de San Juang, was initially celebrated only at the small Assumption Chapel in Praya Lane in Banda Hilir. "During the Portuguese period, a prayer service was held on St John's Hill. Hundreds came to pray and the gathering ended with a picnic late at night." (Interview, 23 April 2010). Martin Theseira, a long-time resident of Praya Lane notes that before most Catholics moved out of the area, traditional *branyo* was also a highlight of the festival (Interview, 25 April 2010).

The Feast of Saint Peter, or Festa San Pedro, is held a week later. This celebration has deep cultural, social and spiritual significance for the community because St Peter is the patron saint of fishermen, who once dominated the settlement. It is still celebrated as a religious event though an annual State financial grant has commercialized it. The highlight is a mass at the community hall, a procession of St Peter's Statue, the blessing of boats and a competition for the best decorated boat. In the evenings, there is a carnival-like atmosphere, with traditional and popular Western-style cultural performances. In 2009 there were regular Portuguese cultural performances, traditional games, songs and dances, but the most popular item was a local impersonation of Michael Jackson, illustrating the fusion of local pop culture into their performance tradition (Fieldwork, 28 June 2009).

The Feast of Saint Francis Xavier (3 December)

This religious event has been observed in Malacca for centuries. St Francis Xavier, a Jesuit missionary, was one of the earliest and best-known Christian missionaries in Asia. He visited Malacca five times between 1545 and 1553 and established a formal, systematic educational institution termed "*escola*" in Portuguese, a term that entered Bahasa Malaysia as "*sekolah*". The *escola* he established is said to be the first school in the country (Muzzi 2002, p. 30), but it should be remembered that for hundreds of years prior to Western colonization there was informal mosque and temple-based teaching of Islamic, Hindu and Buddhist tenets by visiting missionaries.

St Francis Xavier's Feast Day is observed on his death anniversary on 3 December on St Paul's Hill, where he was once buried. An annual mass conducted by bishops and priests from all over the world is attended by thousands of Catholics and non-Catholics from Malaysia and Singapore, and foreign tourists. "For Catholics in Malacca this is a very meaningful event," observes Percy D'cruz. "St Francis Xavier is the only saint with a connection to Malacca. The church on St Paul's Hill was his headquarters for his missionary work in Indonesia, Flores and the Far East. He made five visits to Malacca between 1545 and 1553, walking and preaching on these streets." After his death on Sancian Island off China in late 1552, his body was temporarily interred at St Paul's Church in 1553, but later exhumed and moved to Goa. "The ruins of the St Paul's Hill church are therefore considered a sacred place. Two of his sacred relics are also kept at the St Francis Xavier's Church nearby, and are taken out during the feast day," adds D'cruz (Interview, 23 April 2010).

The Santa Cruz Festival (14 September)

This festival is held at the quaint Santa Cruz Chapel in Malim, a semi-rural area eight kilometres from the settlement. People have been praying at this spot for more than a century. The chapel is located on a hillock between a shady old rubber plantation and a serene Chinese cemetery. When I attended the event in 2008, hundreds of people were queuing to climb the steps to the church, stopping to pray at an old wooden cross at the altar before rejoining the crowd below. This cross and the chapel hold special meaning for the thousands of Portuguese Eurasians who gather here every year. Legend has it that the cross was left there by Catholics who fled to Malim to escape religious persecution by the Dutch. A chapel was later built on the site, whose spiritual reputation was enhanced when a group of pilgrims reported an apparition of Mary in 1880 (Fieldwork, 14 September 2008).

The festival is one of many which tie spiritual belief, customs and traditions to history, drawing Portuguese Eurasians from Malacca and the region, reinforcing community and identity. The pilgrims were from very diverse ethnic backgrounds. In addition to Portuguese Eurasians, there were Indian and Chinese families, and couples and children of mixed Chinese-Indian-Portuguese-Eurasian parentage. Most interesting of all were two Malay-looking church wardens conversing in Peranakan Chinese Malay. "I don't speak Chinese or English," one of them said. "My parents were Peranakan Chinese — my mother was Indonesian and my father a Malaccan. In Malacca there are a few dozen Chinese families where Malay is the only spoken language." (Interview, Church Warden, 14 September 2008).

The Feast of the Assumption (15 August)

The Feast of the Assumption is celebrated at the tiny Chapel of the Assumption on Praya Lane, which is decorated for the event. Sugarcane is often used to decorate the churchyard; this is an influence of local Chinese neighbours. In addition to mass, a wooden statue of Mary, believed to be first found floating in the sea facing the chapel and widely believed to be miraculous, is carried in procession.

Intrudu (March–April)

"*Intrudu*" means "Introduction" to the season of Lent. It is celebrated a week before Palm Sunday as a water festival, water being a symbol of washing away sins to prepare for Lent (Fernandis 2003, p. 9) and is linked to pre-Lenten traditions such as the carnival in other parts of the Iberian Catholic world. The water-splashing is done in a festive spirit and the evening often ends as a celebration, with traditional cakes and *branyo* dancing. This event too was re-introduced in the mid-1990s and has become a big public celebration.

Holy Week

During Holy Week the community's Palm Sunday and Good Friday services at the 1710 St Peter's Church include some Portuguese and Hispanic rites and rituals first introduced by Augustinian missionaries during the Portuguese era. The survival of these traditions is attributed to the work of the Brothers of the Church, the *Irmaos de Igreja*. As part of these ancient rites the Passion of Christ is enacted twice, on both Palm Sunday and Good Friday. Life-size wooden statues of Jesus and Mary — which are washed in wine for preservation and used only during Holy Week — are carried in a candlelight procession. The procession stops as a girl (Veronica) wipes Jesus' face, and when three boys — the *tres Marias* (three Marys) — sing a Latin dirge. These procession scenes are repeated on Good Friday, with the statue of the deceased Christ mounted on a wooden bier. Easter is a time of prayer and family get-togethers. In addition to high mass, most Portuguese Eurasians have special curries like *lardeh* with rice and salads. A leftover pickle from the Lenten Season called *pesi tambrinyu* is often served.

(*Sources*: D'cruz 2008; Fernandis 2003, p. 8 and Fieldwork 2008–11).

Notes

1. "Bumiquest" refers to a quest for State recognition as *Bumiputeras* (indigenous people). The term was first used by Gerard Fernandis, the late Portuguese Eurasian cultural activist (Fernandis 2000, p. 1).

2. According to Horace Sta Maria, there are about 3,000 Portuguese Eurasians in Perth today. The Eurasian Club alone has 300 members belonging to 150 families, 60 per cent from Singapore, and the rest from Malacca and elsewhere. "We comprise all ages. We have lunch every fortnight, and volunteers cook Portuguese-Malacca dishes such as devil curry and *nasi lemak*" (Interview, Malacca, 22–23 June 2011).

3. A phrase originally used by the late Malacca Portuguese-Eurasian community leader Bernard Sta Maria (Muzzi 2002, p. 44).

4. *Belacan*, a daily staple, is a shrimp relish with chillies and lime, while *sambal belacan* is a wet paste mixture of fresh red chillies, sugar, and toasted *belacan*. The *belacan* is burned on a charcoal fire or roasted in the frying pan before being pounded with fresh chillies in a huge granite pestle and mortar (*tumbok-tumbok*) (Marbeck 2004, p. 102). *Cincalo*, another fermented shrimp relish, is an acquired taste. Cooked rice is mixed with salted cleaned shrimps and left to ferment for three days. In the Portuguese-Eurasian version, the mixture is then put into a bottle laced with brandy. "It is delicious when garnished with sliced onions, red chilies, kaffir lime leaves and fresh lime or lemon juice. *Cincalo* is often eaten with steaming rice and hot curry" (Marbeck 2004, p. 104). (Note: Marbeck, a Portuguese Eurasian of Dutch origin, is not from the settlement; nevertheless her book is a useful reference).

5. This phrase was first used by Sarkissian (2002). This section draws from her earlier seminal work on their performing arts (Sarkissian 2000).

6. Aside from *mata kantiga*, there were also Portuguese Eurasian nursery rhymes, cradle songs and lullabies, much of which are almost extinct. One cradle song which survived and was popularized by the Dutch-Indonesian singer Aneke Gronloh was *Nina Boboi Nina*. It was brought to Indonesia by Portuguese Eurasians fleeing the Dutch occupation of Malacca in 1641 (De Silva 2003, p. 1).

7. This song has its origins in a mixed-race Portuguese diasporic past. This is evidenced by "*Jinkly Nona*"'s broad unconnected geographical presence, its use of rare Portuguese words, its title, and evidence of links stretching from Kerala to Sri Lanka, and Malacca to Macau. In Malacca, "*Jingly Nona*" is referred to as a "beautiful young girl with jingle bells on her ankles". Scholars suggest she may be of Indian, Sri Lankan, or even Chinese origin, with "Shingly" referring to the Chinatown of a coastal city in Kerala. The tale is about an exotic local girl desired by a Portuguese suitor (Sarkissian 2000, p. 99).

8. Thais and Eurasians in Kedah share similarities — both emigrated from Thailand and practise a mixture of Thai-Malay and Eurasian-Malay customs. The Thais speak a Malay-Thai hybrid, and the Kedah Eurasians once spoke a Malay-Siamese-Portuguese Creole (Goh 2002, pp. 134–35).
9. Joseph Sta Maria repeated these points in a casual conversation with the author in mid-2008.

4

BETWEEN "CINA-KAMPUNG" AND "CHENG-HO" CHINESE: Terengganu's Peranakans

INTRODUCTION: GLIMPSES OF A FAST-DISAPPEARING HYBRID WORLD

Businessman Soh Teck Soon,[1] 39, grew up in a mixed Malay-Chinese village, abstains from pork, is circumcised and speaks the local Malay dialect perfectly. "I also don't look typically Chinese, so when people meet me for the first time they assume I'm Terengganu Malay," he says. (Interview, 18 March 2009). Koo Ong Jin, 60, a retired construction supervisor and leader of the Chinese in Kampung Tirok, a village located amidst Malay settlements outside the state capital Kuala Terengganu (KT), speaks the Terengganu Malay dialect fluently, enjoys Malay food with his fingers, and could easily pass off as Malay. His acculturation is a result of what sociologists refer to as "primary" links of friendship with Malays. "I have at least twenty very close Malay friends. We visit each other's homes and attend family weddings and funerals. They all attended my father's funeral. We are very close." (Interview, 18–20 March 2009).

Both Soh and Koo are part of a long-settled but virtually unknown acculturated Chinese community in the east coast state of Terengganu.

Unlike the better known west coast urban-based Peranakan Chinese of Malacca and Penang, little is known about this group.[2] What is clear however, is that centuries of deep interaction with Malays via shared occupations, living spaces and schools shows itself in their adoption of Malay language, attire, cuisine, performing arts and Malay-style housing. Most of them live in rural pockets and small towns and are easily mistaken for Malays.

Terengganu Chinese like Soh and Koo are referred to as "Peranakan-type" — despite Peranakan characteristics, they do not identify themselves as Peranakan but as Chinese, while making a cultural distinction between themselves and non-Peranakan Chinese (Tan 2002, pp. V, 1–3).[3] This distinction is sometimes expressed through the use of the Malay term *Cina Kampung* (Village Chinese) to describe Chinese — particularly Peranakan-types — living in or near a Malay village.[4] (Lua Yik Hor, Interviews, 2 and 5 April 2009).

The oldest acculturated Chinese settlement in Terengganu is the small village of Kampung Tirok, but the single largest concentration of Chinese, mostly non-Peranakans, is found in KT's Chinatown (Appendix 4.1). Although the Peranakan-type community is shrinking due to out-migration, Mandarin education, and urbanization, those who remain provide fascinating glimpses into a fast-disappearing hybrid cultural world where the lives of Chinese and Malays were once closely intertwined.

They also provoke interesting questions about ethnic relations in Malaysia in general and Chinese identity in particular. What factors encourage acculturation among Chinese? Will the Peranakan-type community remain a distinct group harnessing their multiple identities, be absorbed into the Malaysian Chinese mainstream, or assume transnational identities? Can their experiences of acculturation provide some creative ideas on improving interethnic relations in Malaysia? To answer these questions, we first need to examine the factors which facilitated interethnic interaction and acculturation among the Terengganu Chinese, the manifestations of such acculturation, and how they manage to harness their multiple identities to buttress both their deep Malaysian roots and their old Chinese origins. This chapter analyses the process of acculturation of the Terengganu Chinese as a whole and the Peranakan-type Terengganu Chinese in particular, using Kampung Tirok as an illustration.

FIGURE 4.1
Terengganu: Towns and Villages Where Peranakan-type Chinese Live

FIGURE 4.2
Kampung Tirok and Surrounding Villages on Terengganu River Banks

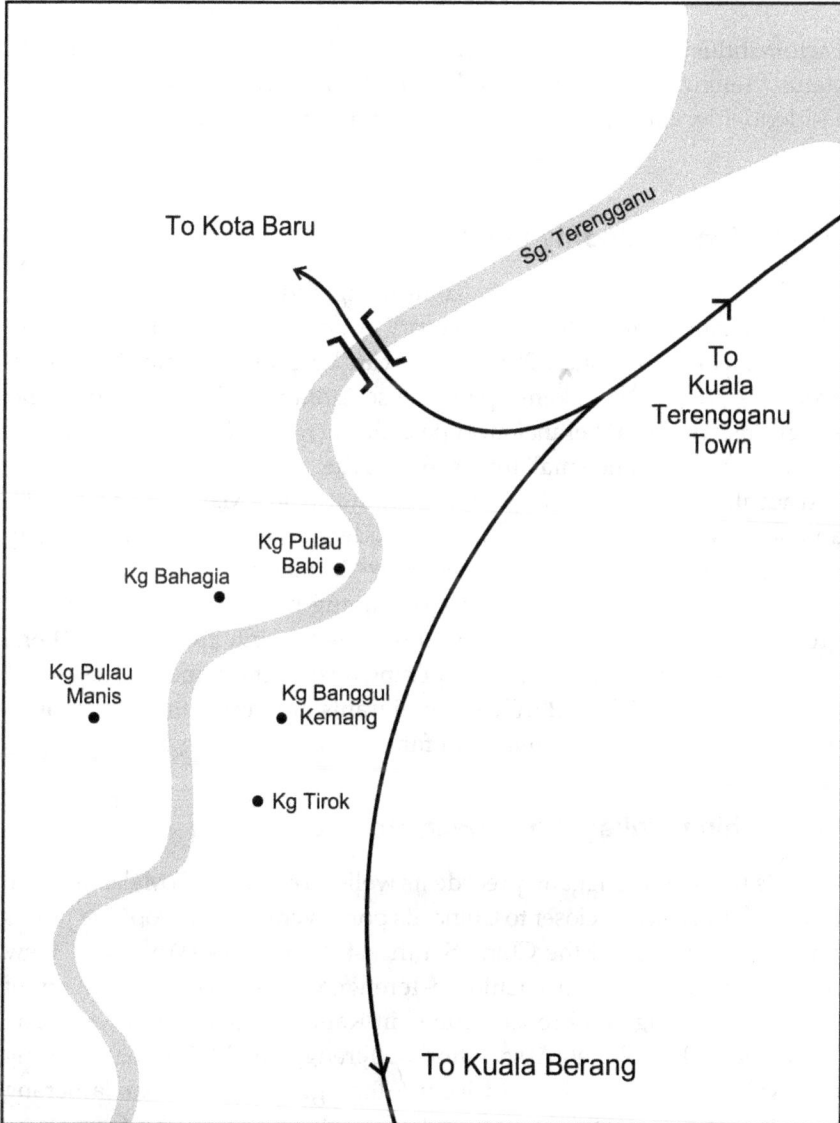

SHARED HISTORIES: FACTORS INFLUENCING CHINESE ACCULTURATION AND IDENTITY IN TERENGGANU

Factors influencing the acculturation of the Chinese include their minority status, Terengganu's ancient links to China, and similar occupations, residential locations, shared schools, and a common language with local Malays.

Population: A Minority in a Malay Muslim State

The Chinese are a tiny minority, comprising close to 27,000 or 3 per cent of Terengganu's Malay Muslim majority population of one million in 2013 (Department of Statistics, 2014). They can be classified into three main groups — rural Peranakan-type Chinese, urban localized Chinese, and emigrants. The rural Peranakan-type Chinese numbering over 10,000 live mainly in villages and small towns, where they still enjoy close interaction and acculturation with Malays. Being a minority in a Malay-majority state, and sharing similar occupations and residential locations as their Malay rural counterparts, they remain open to acculturation by Malays. The urban localized Chinese, who make up the remaining 15,000, comprises two sub-groups — a working-class segment descended mainly from rural settlers, and a small urban middle class comprising businessmen and professionals[5] (Lua, Interview, 12 June 2010). The emigrants are those who have moved interstate or overseas but maintain family links in Terengganu.

Early China Links: The "Cheng-Ho" Connection

China's links to Terengganu precede its well-known links to Malacca. Since it was geographically closer to China, its ports were natural stopping points for traders who plied the China-Southeast Asia routes (Wong and Liew n.d.). An evidence of early Chinese-Terengganu links is the discovery of two ancient Dong Son bronze drums[6] in Kampung Jeram and Kampung Tirok near KT (Hokkien Association of Terengganu 2005, p. 63).[7] During the twelfth to fourteenth centuries the Terengganu port of Kuala Berang was one of the regions busiest and was referred to by the Chinese as *Fo-Lo-Ann*. The Chinese historian Chau Ju-Kua wrote that Chinese traders visiting the port exchanged gold, silverware and food for local goods such as *kayu cendawan* (mushroom), elephant tusks and scented *kayu gaharu* (agar wood), which were exported to China and the Middle East. Another historian, Chau Chu Fei, described Kuala Berang as a great trading centre, similar to Kedah's Bujang Valley during Srivijaya rule (Mohamed Alias 2008). Kuala Berang is today better known for the famous Batu Bersurat, an inscribed stone slab with inscriptions similar to ancient Chinese writing, which has fuelled speculation that Islam was introduced to Peninsular Malaysia from China via Terengganu.[8] Chinese annals also show that Terengganu and Pahang were vassal states of Srivijaya, the powerful seventh to thirteenth century maritime trading kingdom which had close ties with China, while Javanese records of the Majapahit Kingdom in the fourteenth century specifically mention KT, Paka and Dungun as trading ports (Wong and Liew, n.d.).

While historians have long known of these ties, what is significant is the recent heightened interest among ordinary Terengganu Chinese about their state's ancient links to China. The story of Admiral Cheng Ho's (Zheng He's) supposed visit to Terengganu remained mired in local legend for centuries, and was part of oral and local history among not only the local Chinese, but also the Malay community. For many years his reported visit was merely acknowledged and symbolized in an ancient shrine, the "Keramat Sampokang", located below a large tree on the banks of the Sungai Nerus (Wong and Liew, n.d.). "Sampokang" is the religious label for Cheng Ho who, despite being a Muslim, is venerated as part of Chinese animistic beliefs.[9] Local Chinese philanthropists upgraded the shrine into a temple in the 1940s, and it was restored in the 1990s by local Chinese associations (Sam Poh Kong Temple Committee n.d., p. 60).

However in recent years new historical evidence of his visit was published and widely disseminated, adding credibility and currency to the story. In 2004 a Terengganu Chinese researcher announced that Cheng Ho's visit was documented in 1436 in annals called *Xing Cha Sheng Lan* written by one of his commanders, Fei Xin, and further substantiated in 1451 in another publication entitled *Ying Ya Sheng Lan* compiled by Ma Huan, also known as Mohd Fuad. The announcement received wide press coverage (Wong Alcoh, Researcher, Malaysian Chinese Historical Research Committee, quoted in *New Straits Times*, 1 December 2004). In 2005 Professor Kong Yuan Zhi of Beijing University said in a public talk organized by KT's Chinese Assembly Hall that a map of Cheng Ho's Southeast Asian voyages discovered in China clearly indicates he visited

Kampung Jeram (*New Straits Times*, 10 April 2005). Concurrently a booklet published by KT's Sam Poh Kong Temple Committee reported further historical evidence from China about the trip. It said Cheng Ho's original seafarer's map — currently displayed in China's Naval Survey Research Centre — indicates he stopped in Terengganu with a fleet of 200 vessels and 28,000 men during his fourth trip west. It also quoted another Chinese academic Professor Tang Wei Chee confirming that Cheng Ho did stop by trading posts in Kelantan, Terengganu, Pahang and Johore en route to Malacca (Sam Poh Kong Temple Committee, n.d. p. 60).

Cheng Ho's reported visit took on historical form and became accepted as fact after evidence of his stop-over was widely publicized in the mass media by the Assembly Hall and the Temple Committee, and subsequently through the Hokkien Association of Terengganu's sixtieth anniversary celebrations and souvenir publication (Hokkien Association of Terengganu 2005). These reports helped authenticate the widespread and long-standing belief among the Peranakan-type community that some of them are direct descendants of Cheng Ho's entourage (Fieldwork, March–April 2010). The news reports claimed that Cheng Ho travelled up the Sungai Nerus, docked at Kampung Jeram for food and water, and that eighty-five years later, descendants of his crewmen comprising Hokkien farmers from coastal Zhangzhau District settled along the river (*New Straits Times* 2004, 2005; Wong and Liew n.d.).

These events appear to point to a process of re-emphasizing "Chineseness" among the Terengganu Chinese. While a cultural resurgence among the Chinese worldwide is linked to a number of factors, including China's rise, in the case of the Terengganu Chinese, it also provides a long-settled minority in a Malay Muslim majority country and State an opportunity to harness fluid identities to advantage. The purported authentication of their early and direct ties to China allows them to tap dual "Malaysian" and "Chinese" identities. For the non-Peranakan Chinese, it can serve as a useful reminder of the Chinese community's early settlement and deep Malaysian roots. For the Peranakan-type Chinese, sometimes derided by "pure" Chinese for not being "Chinese" enough, these ancient links — particularly the claim that descendants of Cheng Ho's crewmen settled in Terengganu — can be utilized to restore and rejuvenate their "Chineseness". Though these claims require further historical verification, what is significant is that many Terengganu Chinese (and some Terengganu Malays) believe them to be true (Source: Fieldwork 2009–10).

Immigration Cohorts, Dialect Groups and Length of Stay

The degree of acculturation varies according to immigration cohorts and length of stay, which is in turn related to dialect groups. Most early settlers were Hokkiens from Fujian Province, who still comprise about 60–70 per cent of Terengganu Chinese today. The others include the Hainanese, Cantonese, Hakka and Teochew clans, all of whom are able to speak Hokkien.[10] The Hokkiens entered Terengganu from as early as the 1700s, worked in rural areas, interacted closely with the Malays and acquired Peranakan-type social features. The Chinese in Kampung Tirok are a good example of such people. (Kampung Tirok residents, Interviews, March–April 2010).

Others experienced step-migration from small port towns. For example Tan Teng Hong, a sixth-generation *kain songket* (hand-woven textile) trader, says his ancestors first immigrated to Marang port in 1778 and later moved to KT's Chinatown. In fact Tan still works and lives in his "great-great-great grandfather's" shophouse in Chinatown, where I met him. His 83-year-old mother sits nearby. She is dressed in a *sarong kebaya*, speaks crisp British English, and listens intently as we talk. "She is the best embroider in town — she still does embroidery for the *kain songket* and the *kebaya* for the royal family, including the (former) Queen," he whispers. Tan's family history reflects the diversity and complexity of Chinese migration to Southeast Asia:

> I am a sixth-generation Terengganu Chinese. My paternal great-grandfather's granddad immigrated during the Ching Dynasty; he was a fisherman in China, but came here to trade. His five brothers went to different parts of Southeast Asia, and so today we have relatives in Indonesia, Singapore, Thailand and the Philippines. He arrived at Marang Port in February 1778. In those days he had to travel by elephant for three days to get to KT for various festivals and ceremonies such as *cheng beng* (All Souls' Day). The second generation, that is, my great-grandfather's dad, was settled in Chinatown. He probably migrated from Marang. The third generation — my great grandfather — barter traded in local products like batik and tobacco with Singapore. Unfortunately he died young. My great grandmother took over the business.
>
> On my maternal side, we don't know much about the earliest immigrants. But we do know that the second generation, that is my great-great grandfather on my mother's side, was born in 1827 in Terengganu. The third generation on her side was quite wealthy; they owned five or six

large boats and bartered betel nut, wine, yarn and dyes for Thai salt. We
know the location of the graveyards of all our ancestors, except the first
generation on my father's and mother's side. We make it a point to visit
and pray at all the graveyards every year during *cheng beng*.

(*Source*: Tan Teng Hong, interviews by the author,
19 March and 4 April 2009, KT, Terengganu).

Unlike the Hokkiens, the Hainanese and the Hakka arrived later, in the
nineteenth century. Their shorter length of stay and relatively less inter-
ethnic interaction contributed to fewer Peranakan-type characteristics. A
number of Hainanese families live near KT town, especially in Kampung
Kemasek (in Kemaman District), which had a population of several
thousand people a few decades ago. In 1989, about 171 households with
900 people remained, but by early 2009 out-migration left only 20 families
comprising about 100 people (Interviews, Lua Yik Hor, head of Terengganu
Hokkien Association's Education Committee, 2 and 5 April 2009, KT).

Kemasek has a fascinating history. It was once a customs port serving
Hainanese junks plying the China-Terengganu route, with stops in Annam
(the ancient Chinese name for Vietnam). The junks brought rice, pigs
and ducks to Terengganu and took back areca nut and gambier to China.
Chinese immigrants in Kemasek first settled in the coast but later moved
inland in search of better agricultural land where they planted gambier;
today their descendants plant cash crops such as cocoa, oil palm and
rubber (Tan 2002, p. 22). Due to these early contacts, a few immigrants from
Vietnam and Cambodia, referred to as "Annam people", were engaged in
barter trade right up to the Second World War (Tan 2002, pp. 17–22). On
a field visit in early 2009, I befriended an air-conditioning technician in a
Chinese coffeeshop who said he was of "Annamese" origin. He said he
knew of his origins through his family's oral history and cuisine (Interview,
2 April 2009, KT).

Working and Living Together

When Chinese and Malays share similar or complementary occupations,
they are likely to live near each other; the closer Chinese live to Malays,
the greater the opportunities for interaction and acculturation. The
most acculturated Chinese in Terengganu today comprise smallholders,
fishermen and traders in small Malay-dominated villages and towns. Some
locations where acculturated Chinese can be found today are:[11]

- Kampung Tirok, the oldest Chinese settlement, where Malays and Chinese have worked and lived close to each other for centuries. The case of Kampung Tirok will be discussed later.
- Agricultural villages such as Wakaf Tapai where long-settled Peranakan-type Chinese own oil palm and rubber smallholdings.
- Fishing villages such as Batu Rakit (KT District) and Rhu Seulu (Setiu District), where Malay and Chinese fishermen work and live together.
- Sundry shop owners and petty traders living in isolated but more multi-ethnic villages such as Kampung Renek (Besut District) and the fishing village of Kampung Fikri (Setiu District) where there are Malays, Chinese and Thais. Here there is a high degree of Chinese interaction with Malays, and to a lesser extent, Thais, and it is common to meet Peranakan-type Chinese who are fluent in Terengganu Malay and Thai, in addition to a Chinese dialect.
- Smaller coastal towns such as Dungun and Marang and old riverside towns like Kuala Berang, where a number of Chinese families are engaged in the retail and wholesale trades. Since these towns are Malay-dominated there is a high degree of interaction with Malays, especially Malay customers, and some Peranakan elements still persist among long-settled Chinese.

KT, the state capital, began as a Chinese trading and urban settlement with few Malays, except for some petty traders. This has resulted in minimal acculturation among the Chinese in its Chinatown. The Chinese in KT include more recent immigrants who came in the twentieth century directly from China and other parts of the Peninsula. However those who still clearly display Peranakan-type characteristics comprise rural immigrants and a small trading class whose parents were educated in English or Malay and had close links to the Peranakan community in Singapore. The Chinese who first grew up in Terengganu's rural areas and interacted with Malays have more Peranakan-type cultural features in terms of attire, language and cuisine compared to those whose forefathers were rural Peranakan-type Chinese and others who migrated directly to urban areas from other parts of the Peninsula (Fieldwork, March–April 2010).

Wee Kwee Siew, 87, who lives in Jalan Bandar in KT's Chinatown with three sisters almost as old as her, has deep rural roots. When I visited, she emerged from her 200-year-old shophouse in a worn-out *sarong* and rice powder on her cheeks. Her house has a high ceiling, with an open centre courtyard. In the sitting area there is an old cupboard and a reception desk, once used for her tailoring business. The wall is adorned with photographs of her parents, grandparents, children and grandchildren, including a beautiful wedding photo of a grandson who married a Terengganu Malay-Muslim girl, who is clad in a headscarf (*tudung*). The home altar has statues and drawings of the deities Guan Yin and Cheng Ho. She recalls:

> My paternal grandfather came from China 150 to 200 years ago. He was a textile trader who imported cotton thread and made it into sarongs. My grandfather and father inherited the business, but diversified into more refined *sarong* cloth. My father later opened a sundry and barter business that traded in rice, *pinang* (betel nut), salt and salted fish in Singapore and Siam. My forefathers spoke good Malay and were fluent in the local Terengganu dialect because it was the language of trade. But I do not speak good Malay! I am a townsperson and interact mainly with the Chinese in Kampung Cina. But I wear the *kebaya*. This is because I was influenced by the Singapore *Nyonya*. You see I had an uncle there, and used to visit Singapore frequently. In my time all the women wore *sarong kebaya* after marriage. Before marriage we wore a shorter version. The earlier generation of Chinese women wore the *baju kurung*, just like the Malays. My father and grandfather sported a Manchu hairstyle, with a fringe in front and long hair at the back. It was the fashion then!"
>
> (*Source*: Wee Kwee Siew, Interview, 18 March 2009).

KT also has a small but influential Chinese urban middle class who are in business and the professions. Most are semi-retired and some are bilingual (English and Mandarin educated) and they manifest a degree of acculturation through their cuisine, and — in the case of older women — Malay-style dress. This is usually because at least one parent was Malay or English educated, or was acculturated through education in Singapore and later Penang, both of which once had thriving Peranakan Chinese communities.

"In the early days shipping and barter trading links were stronger with Singapore than the Peninsula's west coast because the Main Range impeded road links," recalls trader Tan Teng Hong, who studied at Penang's Chung Ling High School. "Some Terengganu people stayed back in Singapore for business and there was chain migration as their Terengganu relatives went to Singapore to study or work" (Interviews, 19 March and 4 April 2009). The historical links to Singapore persist to this day, with many young Terengganu Chinese heading to Singapore to study, work or settle down. One reason for this was that until recent years, Terengganu had poorly developed tertiary education facilities. Another reason is the lack of jobs in the state. "Most of our rural youths leave for education and jobs in towns in Terengganu while urban youths with post-school education leave for the Peninsula's west coast, Singapore or overseas," explains Lua Yik Hor of the Hokkien Association. "This situation is compounded because Terengganu remains a resource-rich state with very few jobs in manufacturing and services, while public sector jobs are mostly reserved for Malays" (Interviews, 2 and 5 April 2009).

SHARED SPACES: FACTORS FACILITATING ACCULTURATION IN KAMPUNG TIROK

The evolution of an acculturated Chinese community in Kampung Tirok was linked to their early emigration and long settlement, a similar farming occupation with Malays, their location adjacent to a rural Malay community, intermarriage, common schooling, and a shared Malay language. However the occurrence and degree of acculturation is now decreasing with Chinese primary education, out-migration to towns and a generational transition into urban trades.

Early Immigration and Long Settlement

Kampung Tirok, the oldest and largest remaining Peranakan-type settlement in Terengganu, is a riverside village 17 kilometres from KT town, on the main road to the ancient port of Kuala Berang. An adjacent Chinese village, Kampung Banggul Kemang, is part and parcel of the Tirok Chinese community. Acculturation has been fostered by the fact that the Tirok community is located in the centre of a cluster of Malay villages such as Pengadang Baru, Kampung Beladau, Kampung Banggul Chempedak, Kampung Baru Serada, Kampung Banggul Tok Ku and Kampung Banggul Mempelam.

The Chinese are known to have lived in Kampung Tirok since at least the eighteenth century, but local folklore has it that the first immigrants came much earlier. "Our people descended from the Chinese who visited with Admiral Cheng Ho when he stopped in Terengganu enroute to Malacca," claims Koo Ong Jin, the Chinese headman (Interviews, 18 and 20 March 2009). "We disembarked in Dungun, Marang and Pulau Babi, where we grew sugarcane and reared pigs. Later some settlers from Pulau

Babi crossed the river to Tirok, where we continued pig farming," he adds.[12] Tirok was an important early immigrant entry point from which there was rural-urban movement into KT. Eighty-seven year-old Mrs Wee Kwee Siew, who traces her ancestry to the village, recalls:

> I have lived in Kampung Cina all my life. My mother was born here. But my great-grandmother is from Kampung Tirok and used to travel to KT town regularly by boat. Tirok was then a bigger town than KT. It was a drop-off point for Chinese — mainly Hokkien — immigrants.
> (*Source*: Wee Kwee Siew, interview with author, 18 March 2009, KT).

With urbanization and emigration to towns, the Tirok community has shrunk. In 2006 it was reported to have 315 residents (*Bernama* 2006) but by mid-2010 there were 73 residents comprising 26 families living in 23 houses. Most are rubber and palm oil smallholders owning less than 2 hectares of land, and although land ownership and the high price of commodities have ensured increased incomes and reduced poverty, many youths have moved to towns for education and employment. "A lot of people maintain homes here, work outstation, but return on weekends," observes Koo.[13] (Interview, 11 June 2010).

Working and Living with Malays

Within the Tirok community there has been long and intimate interaction, initially between Malay and Chinese farmers, and later oil palm and rubber smallholders. This has contributed to close bonds and the adoption of the Malay language, dress, food, and house designs among Chinese settlers. The Chinese community in Tirok live adjacent to Malay villages, and until a road was built some years back they had to traverse footpaths across these Malay villages daily to get to work, school or visit Chinese friends. This geographical layout facilitated social interaction. Even today as one takes the return road trip from the village to KT town, one notices a cluster of Chinese houses around a Chinese temple in Kampung Tirok, followed by Malay homes, interspersed again by Chinese houses in the adjacent Kampung Banggul Kemang (Fieldwork, March–April 2010).

Mr Koo the village headman says that unlike his own generation, his school-going nieces and grandnieces living in the village today have secondary, reciprocal ties with Malays. But he says this is due to circumstantial and practical reasons rather than choice. The construction of a road through the village has encouraged the use of cars and motorbikes and reduced opportunities for interaction between Malay and Chinese villagers. Moreover the Chinese youngsters now attend urban Chinese-medium primary schools, not the neighbourhood village schools which their parents and grandparents once shared with Malays. "Parents send children to Chinese schools to master Mandarin and also because they feel these schools offer better quality teaching and discipline. Some Malays choose Chinese schools for the same reasons. Proximity to their homes is an additional factor for some urban Malays," he adds (Interview, 18 and 20 March 2009). Chinese children now do not speak the Terengganu Malay dialect which used to be an important means of inter-ethnic communication. Also, since the majority of the Chinese villagers today work, live and study apart from their Malay neighbours, there is less inter-ethnic interaction, especially among the young.

Intermarriage and Intra-marriage

Intermarriage with Malays was not a key factor in acculturation; the main factors were close interaction between Malays and Chinese linked to trade, occupation and common residence. One scholar has pointed out that it is misleading to portray Malaysian Peranakan Chinese as people of "mixed-blood" because intermarriage was not widespread and occurred mainly among relatively wealthier single male immigrants who entered more than a century ago, before Chinese women arrived (Tan 2010, pp. 28, 37). In Terengganu some early Hokkien immigrants did in a few cases marry Malay women due to the lack of local Chinese women, their close interaction with Malays, and the fact that religious conversion was not compulsory then, though children were usually assimilated into Malay society (Tan 2002, p. 129). Among a few Tirok villagers and KT residents with Peranakan-type ancestry, the physical manifestations of such intermarriages appear to express themselves in non-stereotypical Chinese features such as larger eyes, curly hair and darker complexion (Fieldwork, March–April 2010). As with the Indian-Muslims, Peranakan Indians and Portuguese Eurasians, Malay-speaking mothers were a catalyst in the acculturation process because children of these inter-marriages began to speak Malay; it was literally their "mother-tongue".

Intra-marriage between Terengganu and Kelantan Chinese began in the early twentieth century and was fostered by geographical isolation, close trading links and the tiny size of the community in both states.

Today geographical isolation has been reduced by modern communication, the old trading links no longer exist, and due to high out-migration for education and work the east coast Chinese have ample opportunities to meet potential partners from other states. Yet some intra-marriage persists. Though the number of Peranakan-type Chinese is decreasing, the rural Chinese community in Terengganu and Kelantan remains a relatively cohesive group due to such intra-marriage. This is linked to the fact that irrespective of their degree of acculturation, many east coast Chinese share some common features, including speaking fluent Malay, wearing Malay-type attire and eating Malay cuisine.

"It's common for young Chinese from Terengganu and Kelantan to marry spouses from either state", says Lua Yik Hor, 40, who met his Terengganu-born wife at the University of Malaya. "We east coast Chinese are all still 'Peranakan' to different degrees and we feel more comfortable with our own kind," explains Lua, a manager who now runs his own business (Interviews, 5 April 2009). Tirok smallholder Chia Ban Hock, sixty-eight, popularly called "Awang", provides interesting insights into migration and marriage. A rotund man, he appeared in a *sarong* and flowered shirt in the veranda of his Malay-style house. His wife, also dressed in a *sarong*, joins us. He says:

> My wife is from Pasir Mas, Kelantan. It was a "recommended" marriage and today we have seven children, four of whom are married. Two married Kelantan Chinese, the other two married Terengganu Hokkiens; they met their spouses on their own, at work. I am a fourth-generation immigrant. So I guess my children and grandchildren are fifth and sixth generation. My wife is half-Siamese and she is fourth generation, like me, but Kelantanese. Our house was built in 1953. Most women leave this village to find work or to marry. That's why there are men in this village who seek brides in Kelantan. Do you know that there are about fifty small Chinese settlements in Kelantan? My own mum is a Chinese from Kelantan.... For young people there are not many jobs in Terengganu, except perhaps teaching. There are also few higher educational opportunities compared to Kuala Lumpur, Singapore and Penang.
>
> (*Source*: Chia Ban Hock and family, interview with author,
> 20 March 2009, KT).

Common Schooling and Shared Malay Language

Education and language fluency is another key factor explaining varying acculturation levels between rural settlers, their children, and the urban middle class. In Kampung Tirok the earliest Chinese farmer-settlers were so keen to learn Malay that before a school was established, they had hired a Malay tutor from Negeri Sembilan (Tan 2002, p. 83). In later years Chinese and Malay village children attended the same village school — Sekolah Dewasa Banggul Kemang — where both groups learnt the Malay and Arabic script. Today there are still a few old Chinese medicine men in the village who can read the Arabic script; they are deeply respected by the local Malay-Muslim community for this ability. Due to frequent interaction with Malays, both the early settlers and their children speak the Terengganu-Malay dialect as eloquently as local Malays (Koo, Interviews, 18 and 20 March 2009). Thus common schooling and a common language has fostered interethnic interaction and acculturation among the early settlers.

However the 1980s marked an important turning point as the children and grandchildren of these Chinese settlers began switching from rural Malay-medium State-run schools to urban-based Mandarin-medium primary schools. The experience of the Kampung Tirok villagers indicates that the drift to Chinese education was not merely due to a cultural resurgence, but to a variety of push and pull factors. Among push factors reported were peer group pressure and student-bullying in the State-run village school (Tan 2002, p. 32). The pull factors — which have also attracted some Malay parents to send their children to Chinese schools — include a desire to teach children Mandarin (in addition to Malay and English), and a perception that Chinese schools are better at teaching maths and science and instilling student discipline. Compared to the past, attendance at Chinese primary schools in town is also facilitated today by improved road access, better transport and higher income.[14] (Fieldwork, March–April 2010).

Terengganu State has ten Chinese schools where Chinese is the medium of instruction at primary level, but the two schools which are important to the Peranakan-type Chinese are Chong Hwa Wei Sin in KT, which also caters to secondary students, and Chong Hwa Primary School in Wakaf Tapai in the Marang District (Tan 2002, p. 38). "About 90 per cent of Chinese send their children to these schools despite overcrowding; there's an average of 1,000 students per school, compared to only 300 in fully-assisted government schools," laments Lua Yik Hor, who heads the Hokkien Association of Terengganu's Education Committee (Telephone interview, 12 June 2010).

The current trend is for children from Peranakan-type families in rural areas to attend urban-based Chinese schools, live with relatives in town and return to their villages on weekends. After completing their studies most of them obtain jobs and continue staying in towns. Working and living in urban non-Malay environments dilutes their Peranakan-type characteristics. Few of these rural children pursue post-school training due to the relatively poor education levels of parents, the lower quality of rural schools, and the lack of private tuition. Most are apprenticed into trades or run small businesses in towns, marking a key transition in their cultural journey from rural Peranakan-type to urban, localized Chinese. The younger generation does not display Peranakan-type features in terms of dress or food, although some are still able to speak the Terengganu Malay dialect and all can converse in standard Bahasa Malaysia (Fieldwork, March–April 2010).

IDENTITIES AND CULTURES: MANIFESTATIONS OF ACCULTURATION IN TERENGGANU

Embracing Malay Language and Cultural Life

The role of language varies with age, education, occupation and location. In contrast to the older Peranakan-type rural Chinese, among whom the Malay language developed organically as a means of inter-ethnic communication, younger non-Peranakan "Chinese-educated" urban-based traders use Malay mainly for commercial transactions. The children of the educated middle class use multilingual skills to pursue overseas education and employment, and they tend to embrace transnational identities. In addition to Hokkien, the Peranakan-type Chinese, especially rural smallholders, speak the local Terengganu Malay dialect among themselves and to Malays, thus fostering interaction and enabling acculturation and meaningful participation in Malay cultural life.

Long and deep inter-ethnic interaction between both communities over centuries resulted in the inter-flow of Malay words into Terengganu Hokkien and Hokkien words into the Terengganu Malay dialect. Malay words used in Terengganu Hokkien include *belik* (mislead), *jugok* (also), *masok* (earn some money), *lok ie* (let it be) and *buuduu* (or *budu*, a fermented fish sauce). Hokkien words said to be used in Terengganu Malay include *cinchai* (not fussy, easy), *kueh tiow* (noodle), *tauke* (boss), *tauge* (bean sprout), and *kueh* (cake, local delicacy) (Hokkien Association of Terengganu 2005, pp. 65–66). One Chinese-based word peculiar to Terengganu Malay is *paong*, a slightly sweet baked bun toasted and served with margarine, *kaya* (coconut jam), and half-boiled eggs. It is a popular breakfast in Chinatown. According to eighty-three-year-old Peranakan Wee Kim Beng, early Arab traders — whom she refers to as *"Syeds"* — first popularized the bread (Interview, 19 March 2009).

Another example of acculturation is Malay-assigned names and nicknames. For example, "Awang" is a common Terengganu nickname for a man, and so a Chinese man called "Kia" or "Peh" may be called "Awang Kia" or "Awang Peh". Similarly, "Mek" is a nickname for women, and so a woman may be called "Mek Wong" (Madam Wong) or "Mek Merang" (that is, woman from Merang). "Mok Ngoh" may be a nickname for an older woman and "Pak Ngoh" for an older man (Hokkien Association of Terengganu 2005, pp. 65–66). "We use nicknames for convenience," says Lua. "Malays are fond of using such names to identify us."[15] (Lua, Interviews, 2 and 5 April 2009).

Fluency in Malay also enabled Peranakan-type Chinese to appreciate and enjoy cultural performances traditionally enjoyed by Malays. For example, instead of Chinese operas which are the staple during religious festivals of most other Hokkien Chinese, the acculturated Chinese in Terengganu staged Javanese-Indian *wayang kulit*[16] shadow plays and *menorah* (Thai dance drama). This was due to Kelantan and Thai cultural influences, and the fact that some Peranakan-type Chinese understood Malay and Thai better than standard Hokkien. In addition, there were cross-cultural influences emanating from Singapore. Mrs Wee, eighty-seven, lights up when she recalls enjoying Peranakan-type performances brought to Terengganu by Singapore Malays:

> Singapore-Malay performers provided live entertainment during the Sultan's birthday celebrations in those days. I used to attend violin, *dondang sayang, pantun, bangsawan, mak yong* and *joget* shows. Chinese from other states were also invited to attend. We people used to mix with these performers!
>
> (*Source*: Mrs Wee Kwee Siew, interview with author, 18 March 2009, KT).

While older Peranakan-types still speak both Hokkien and the Malay dialect within the family and community, youths are today more fluent in

Mandarin and Bahasa Malaysia than the local Malay dialect. Unlike their forefathers their ties to Malays are therefore less intimate; their command of the local Terengganu Malay dialect is sufficient for exchanging simple greetings but not for close conversations and friendships[17] (Lua and Koo, Discussion, 18 March 2009). However, in towns Chinese use standard Malay when communicating with Malay customers and tend to see it more as a language of trade rather than social communication. As a young Chinese KT trader puts it: "Those of us who go to Chinese primary schools (followed by Malay-medium secondary schools) are still practising Malay culture; we can accept it. There is nothing bad in it. Malay is the language we use to *cari makan* (earn a living). Without Malay, how can we *cari makan*?"[18] (Interview, 18 March 2009).

Unlike Malay-speaking rural Peranakan-type Chinese and Mandarin-speaking urban Chinese, the older English-educated, urban middle-class Peranakan-type Chinese and their children tend to be multilingual. This prepares them for education, work, immigration and settlement in the Chinese diaspora, particularly Singapore. "I only speak English, Malay, and Hokkien," says manager Tan Teng Liang, 65. "But my 'Chinese-educated' children (Mandarin-medium primary, Malay-medium Chinese-dominated secondary schools) now speak virtually five languages — Bahasa Malaysia, the Terengganu dialect, Mandarin, English and Hokkien," he says proudly (Interview, 5 April 2009). It is also not uncommon for some Terengganu Chinese to also speak Thai. This is usually the result of intermarriage to a Thai spouse or residence in multi-ethnic Malay-Thai villages such as Kampung Renek or Kampung Pak Kiang in Besut District in northern Terengganu. These Thai immigrants entered Terengganu in search of jobs in the 1950s, just before independence in 1957.[19]

Malay-Style Attire and Cuisine

Malay-style attire is an identity marker among Kampung Tirok's Peranakan-type Chinese. At home older men often wear the *sarong* and singlet, and women the *sarong kebaya*, while older folk often use a Malay-style head cloth or *semutar* when out in the sun. The *semutar* is usually made of batik *sarong* cloth, with two drooping "ears" on either side, and is common among Terengganu and Kelantan Malay peasants.

I observed some interesting differences in attire between various generations when I joined the villagers at the main Kampung Tirok

graveyard during *cheng beng* (All Souls' Day) in 2009. Three generations —
grandparents, parents and children — were busy cleaning the graves and
offering food and prayers. The three generations displayed varying degrees
of acculturation. The grandparents and parents were Malay-educated
and the grandchildren were Chinese-educated, but all three generations
communicated to each other in Malay. Some older women were wearing
sarong kebaya and a head-dress. At the graveyard, I met a Mr Tan, 61,
who was there to visit his ancestral graves. He was English-educated and
had studied in Singapore, and chose to wear a *semutar* rather than a hat
to protect himself from the afternoon heat. (Fieldwork, Kampung Tirok,
4 April 2009).

Malay influences often remain among Peranakan-types even after
they move to urban areas, particularly small towns. One woman from
Kuala Berang, who was in her 30s, told me she wore the *sarong kebaya* at
home and ate Malay food. Many old women in KT town also wear the
sarong kebaya at home[20] (Fieldwork, 4 April 2009). Some elderly Peranakan-
type women still grow their hair long and tie it up in a *sanggor* (a bun).
For functions these older women dress in a formal *sarong kebaya* with
three *keronsangs* (brooches which serve as blouse buttons), and wear
a metal belt made of gold, silver or bronze called a *tali pening*, with a
buckle called *kepala pening*. Tan Teng Hong, the *kain songket* trader, says
that in the late 1800s and early 1900s women wore dark blue Malay-
style *baju kurung* and *sarong*, while men wore Western-style suites to
official events, visits to government departments, and palace functions.
"My grandfather used to wear *kain pelikat*[21] imported from India," he
says. (Interview, 4 April 2009).

The cuisine of the Peranakan-type Terengganu Chinese is heavily
influenced by Malay cooking, including liberal use of spices, chilli and
curry, but there are also Thai, Vietnamese and even Arabic influences (See
Appendix 4.2). "The older generation ate Malay-style food — *pucuk* (wild
vegetables) and *kunyit* (turmeric), curry, fish and chicken," says Mrs Wee
Kwee Siew, 87 (Interview, 18 March 2009). Tirok villagers enjoy typical
local Terengganu Malay favourites and eat with their fingers like Malays.
They love *budu* (fermented fish sauce), *asam pedas* (sour and hot) dishes,
and *pucuk paku* (fern shoots). Another popular dish is a *kicap* (soy sauce)
dip. This is made from *ikan bilis* (anchovies), *budu*, *gula melaka* (coconut
sugar), *serai* (lemon grass), *lengkuas* (also known as galangal, a rhizome
with culinary and medical uses), *daun laksa* (Vietnamese mint) and pomelo

leaves. The Terengganu garlic appetizer *bawang jeruk,* and preserved durian paste *tempoyak,* are also popular.[22]

Tirok Chinese, like the *Baba* and the Peranakan Chinese in Kelantan, do not normally drink Chinese tea, having dropped this traditional Chinese practice in favour of local coffee enjoyed by East Coast Malays. Older folk smoke a self-rolled cigarette called *rokok daun* which is popular among Malays (Tan 2002, p. 76). Some Chinese, especially those who grew up in Muslim-Malay neighbourhoods, also abstain from pork (Koo, Interview, 18 March 2009).

Traditional Malay Housing and Architecture

Except for a few cement bungalows, most Chinese in the village still live in traditional Malay-style wooden houses built on stilts. These are on individual plots averaging 0.6 hectares. These houses use timber from nearby forests and are designed to adapt to the hot, wet, flood-prone delta of the Terengganu River. Some houses have a sharp pointed shaft called a *buah buton,* a stupa to protect or disguise exposed ends of columns and posts. These were installed by Malay carpenters as part of the overall Malay-style architecture (Noor and Khoo 2003, p. 55). Like many Malay houses, most Chinese homes here have a veranda where guests are entertained.

Many Chinese houses are virtually identical to Malay homes, but are distinguished by greetings painted on red posters at the main entrance. The use of these Chinese posters, referred to as *lian,* with Mandarin words signifying luck or prosperity, is a traditional practice that has died out among other Chinese. However it is maintained by the Peranakan-type Chinese in Terengganu (and by the Baba-Nyonya) even though most of them cannot read Mandarin. This is clearly a social boundary marker to distinguish Chinese homes in a Malay-dominated neighbourhood. Chinese houses are also identifiable by the presence of small red altars of deities at the entrance (Tan 2002, pp. 77–79). A few pre-war houses still have roofs made of small, curved Siamese tiles. Unfortunately wear and tear has forced most owners to replace these quaint tiles with zinc or asbestos.

Acculturated but Not Assimilated: Religion and Identity

As with other Peranakan in the region, Terengganu's Peranakan–type Chinese freely adopted Malay customs but retained their religious beliefs.

Virtually any practice which proved practical, useful, aesthetic or "tasty" was adopted, so long as it did not contradict Chinese religious or cultural norms. Thus the Chinese became acculturated but not assimilated (Tan 1984, pp. 144–45).

Despite their acculturation to Malay ways, it is reported that about 90 per cent of the Tirok villagers still practise Chinese deity worship and Buddhism, 5 per cent are Christians and only 5 per cent have converted to Islam[23] (Koo, Interview, 18 March 2009). Legal requirements in Malaysia oblige non-Muslims who marry Malays to convert to Islam, while societal norms tend to encourage assimilation into Malay society. According to scholar Tan Chee Beng (Tan 1984, p. 201), it is this "religious barrier" that accounts for the persistence of Peranakan Chinese communities. "No matter how acculturated they are, they remain Chinese as long as they retain the Chinese religion and do not embrace Islam."[24]

Being a Taoist-Buddhist minority amidst a Muslim majority, Chinese parents are protective of their children and there are strong pressures against conversion. "There were strong objections when my sister wanted to marry a Malay, but eventually my parents came round to it," a young villager recalls. "We had no choice; she could not marry a Malay without changing her religion," he adds (Villager, Interview, 19 March 2009). When such marriages do occur in rural areas, they usually involve a Chinese man marrying a Malay woman whom he meets at work. The man usually settles in the wife's village and assimilates into the Malay community.

Tirok villagers observe all major Chinese and Hokkien festivals, including Chinese New Year, the Mid-Autumn Festival, Hungry Ghosts and *cheng beng*, says Koo Ong Jin, the village leader.[25] (Koo, Interview, 18 March 2009). Unlike other Chinese who emphasize the patrilineal line, Peranakan ancestral altars represent both patrilineal and matrilineal lines. This is due to the small size of the community, the shortage and significance of women, and matrilocal marriages (Tan 2002, pp. 103–105).[26]

Deity worship is also part of their lives. The whole village celebrates an annual festival dedicated to the local village deity, Kong Teck Choon Ong.[27] For many years *wayang kulit* performances were staged at the Tirok Temple as part of the entertainment during the deity's annual religious festival. It was stopped partly because the urban Chinese dominating the temple management committee after the late 1980s were not keen on *wayang kulit*, perhaps due to their lack of acculturation. "We are still keen on these performances but are held back by a lack of funds and Kelantan performers; it costs too much to employ Terengganu performers," says village headman Koo.[28] (Koo, Interview, 11 June 2010).

HARNESSING MULTIPLE IDENTITIES: BETWEEN "CINA-KAMPUNG" AND "CHENG HO" CHINESE[29]

We will conclude by analysing likely future identity trends. To do this it is necessary to resort to typologies again. While these typologies are useful for analysis, it should be remembered that identities are fluid, and can overlap or change either within a lifetime or between generations, often due to social and geographical mobility.

As noted, the Terengganu Chinese are not homogenous and can be broadly classified into three main groups — rural Peranakan-types, urban localized Chinese and inter-state and overseas emigrants. Due to Mandarin education and rural-urban migration, younger rural Peranakan-types tend to morph into urban localized Chinese if they remain within the state. Yet, as mentioned earlier, both rural and urban Chinese can harness dual identities. Depending on the context, Terengganu Chinese can thus claim to be acculturated "Cina-Kampung" with deep roots in Malaysia, and/or exotic "Cheng Ho" Chinese with ancestral links to Admiral Cheng Ho's men. However if they emigrate from the state, their identities are likely to take different routes — they enter the Malaysian-Chinese-Mandarin mainstream if they move to other parts of Malaysia, and take on trans-national identities if they relocate overseas (Fieldwork, March–April 2010).

The Rural Peranakan-type Chinese

As mentioned earlier, the Peranakan-type Chinese number about 10,000 and live mainly in villages and small towns. Since many share similar occupations, residential locations and close interaction with Malays, they remain open to acculturation by Malays and see themselves as culturally distinct from non-Peranakan Chinese.

Interestingly, perceptions of State discrimination appear least evident among these rural Peranakan-type Chinese compared to the urban localized Terengganu Chinese. The main reason for this is that as smallholders with independent means whose children usually enter urban trades after school, they are less dependent on the State and are less likely to compete with Malays for educational access, public sector jobs and contracts. The situation parallels that in Penang, where Indian Muslim petty traders are by and large economically independent of the State, and — unlike the Indian Muslim middle class — are less likely to compete with Malays. In contrast to the Peranakan-type Chinese however, many Indian Muslims qualify as Malays and are therefore eligible for State assistance.

It is also interesting to note that Terengganu's rural Chinese use the term *Tanah Melayu* (literally "Land of the Malays") when referring to the emigration of their ancestors into early Malaya. *Tanah Melayu* is the correct term for the Malaya of that period, particularly when speaking in Malay, but it could also signify their understanding that Malaysia was once a Malay nation.[30] (Lua and Koo, Discussion, 18 March 2009).

Urban Localized Chinese

The urban localized Terengganu Chinese, numbering about 15,000, comprises two sub-groups, one made up of petty traders and workers and the other a middle-class segment.

The first segment, the larger group, comprises mostly descendants of Peranakan-type rural settlers who migrated to towns in search of jobs. "Many men work in KT for a while and once they have got enough experience, they open their own business," says Tirok smallholder Chia Ban Hock (Interview, 20 March 2009). They operate or work for small businesses catering to the local Malay population and thus maintain close commercial rather than social links to local Malays. Despite their "Chinese-educated" school backgrounds (Mandarin-medium primary and Malay-medium secondary), most are fluent in Bahasa Malaysia. Intra-marriage to Terengganu and Kelantan Chinese and local Thais reinforces a degree of localization in cultural practices and outlook within this group. For example, while smallerholder Chia Ban Hock lives in a Malay milieu and retains his Peranakan-type cultural features, his daughter who lives in Kuala Berang, a small riverside town, perceives herself as different, and is acutely aware of the varying degrees of acculturation within her family. Without much prompting his daughter, who is in her mid-thirties, explains:

> I am married to a Hokkien (Peranakan-type) Chinese, and I help him run a Bata shoe shop. The food we eat at home is more Malay, stuff like *ikan*

goreng kunyit and curry. Our vegetables are usually stir-fried, Chinese-style. We also eat Peranakan cakes like *akhoh, kuih lapis* and *kueh kochi*. I wear the *sarong kebaya* at home but Western dress at the shop or when I go out. As far as I am concerned I am Chinese, but my customers are often confused, and ask me whether I am Malay! I studied at the Malay school in this village, unlike those born after 1980, most of whom went to Chinese primary schools. For example my younger sister who is twenty-two went to a Chinese school, does not wear the *kebaya* and does not speak the local Malay dialect. But she speaks Bahasa Malaysia, which she learnt in school.

(*Source*: Chia Ban Hock's daughter, interview with author, 20 March 2009, KT, Terengganu).

The second urban localized group comprises middle-class businessmen and professionals. They include both English and Mandarin-educated types who remain partly acculturated because their parents had a Peranakan-type background within Terengganu or were exposed to education and acculturation in once Peranakan-dominated Penang and Singapore.

However not all appear comfortable discussing their Peranakan roots. Interviews with three — a lawyer, a businessman and a retired civil servant — indicated a reluctance to acknowledge the acculturation of their parents or themselves to Malay language and culture. The reasons appeared to be linked to two related factors. One was a desire to meld into the Malaysian Chinese mainstream and identify with East Asia's economic and cultural resurgence. The other was their alienation from the Malay-dominated establishment by a perception — rightly or wrongly — that the Federal Government's affirmative action policies are unfairly implemented. While they did not question the constitutional Malay special position, they sought more transparent public procurements and contract systems, and need- and merit-based criteria for university entry, scholarships, and poverty alleviation. (Conversations/interviews, March–April 2010).

Thus all three men did not perceive fair career prospects for their children in Malaysia. Two of them, whose children are settled overseas, made frequent references to East Asia's economic success, and talked, with sadness tinged with pride, of how their children were "forced" to seek education and employment in Singapore, Hong Kong, Australia, New Zealand or the United States due to (perceived) discrimination in education and employment in Malaysia (Fieldwork Interviews, KT, March–April 2010). [It should be noted however that the "brain drain" from Malaysia is due not just to perceived "push" factors, but also "pull" factors such as higher pay and perceived superior work, political and living standards overseas. Thus one is not surprised to hear of Malaysian Malays emigrating as well].

Interstate and Overseas Emigrants

The third group involves those who migrate to other parts of Malaysia or overseas. Those who have moved interstate over the last few decades have been incorporated into the Malaysian Chinese-Mandarin mainstream through education, work, marriage and settlement in Chinese-dominated urban spaces in Penang, Perak and the Klang Valley in the west coast.

Younger Terengganu Chinese who emigrated for education and work to places such as Singapore, Hong Kong and Australia have developed transnational identities. They are emigrants but still maintain their Malaysian and Terengganu links, particularly through their Terengganu-based parents.

CONCLUSION

Perceptions of ethnic, political and regional discrimination exist to varying degrees among all Malaysian ethnic groups, partly because ethnic-based politics engenders a deep sense of insecurity among all communities. However perceptions of ethnic discrimination appear particularly strong among segments of the urban Chinese of Terengganu. There are several possible reasons for this. For one, the Terengganu Chinese comprise a non-Malay, non-Muslim minority with a relatively weak political voice in a conservative Malay-Muslim majority state. Secondly, given their early immigration to Peninsular Malaysia and deep acculturation to Malay customs, many Terengganu Chinese feel deeply rooted to Terengganu and to the Malaysian nation; yet some, particularly the urban Peranakan-type, are alienated by what they perceive to be a "Malay-non-Malay" and a "Muslim-non-Muslim" dichotomy in policy implementation.

This alienation requires them to negotiate and navigate multiple identities, retaining their deep-rooted Malaysian identity (as long-settled, acculturated, loyal citizens), maintaining their long-standing ties to Malays (as neighbours, customers and officials who govern the State and the country), while cultivating and emphasizing their "Chineseness", particularly to non-Peranakan Chinese (to maintain access to the politically and culturally influential Malaysian Mandarin-educated Chinese mainstream).

For the Peranakan-type Chinese in particular, the recent verification of the community's long settlement and supposed ties to Cheng Ho's crewmen are powerful tools in such negotiation since they can simultaneously restore both their "old Malaysian" and their "direct Chinese" identities — as both "Cina-Kampung" and "Cheng Ho" Chinese.

Despite these dilemmas, the acculturation process of the Peranakan-type Chinese of Terengganu provides interesting insights into possibilities for improving ethnic relations in Malaysia.

Firstly it illustrates the preconditions for acculturation. These include working, living and schooling together, and the critical importance of Bahasa Malaysia as a bridge between communities. Both development planning and citizens groups should therefore foster such preconditions — for example, through better quality multi-ethnic public and private Bahasa Malaysia schools which attract both Malay and Chinese students, and through civic programmes which emphasize the shared histories, cultures and common values of both communities.

Secondly, it illustrates that acculturation is by itself an important but insufficient factor in fostering inter-ethnic harmony, as the experience of the urban middle class in Terengganu illustrates. What is equally important, as I argue in the concluding chapter, is that public policy should be, and be seen to be, inclusive — without affecting the constitutional position of the Malay community.

APPENDIX 4.1
KUALA TERENGGANU'S CHINATOWN

Though some Chinese settlers to Kuala Terengganu (KT) came from the Peranakan-type settlements in the rural areas of Pulau Babi and Kampung Tirok, it was Hokkien immigrant traders from China who first established its Chinatown (Kampung Cina). These early traders were also acculturated through long stay and interaction. The scholar and travel writer Munshi Abdullah who visited KT in 1836 noted that the Chinese headman's family dressed, behaved and spoke like Malays (Tan 2002, p. 7). Unlike the first rural immigrants and the early Hokkien traders, the majority of the Chinese in KT arrived much later and are thus less acculturated.

KT town was a thriving business and residential area before rent controls were removed by the late 1990s. "Higher rents forced the closure of many small businesses and traditional trades, and poorer workers and youths had no choice but to immigrate to other states in search of jobs," recalls a trader (Interview, 19 March 2009, KT). Today, about 1,000 people work in Chinatown, but only half of them actually live there; the first floors of many shophouses are now used for breeding swiftlets (Fieldwork March–April 2010). KT is now a popular overnight stopping point for island-bound tourists, many of whom have dinner in restaurants located among 200 heritage shophouses in Chinatown.

Terengganu Chinese have lived in these houses for over 200 years, and most houses are well preserved, thanks to joint restoration efforts between the state government and local Chinese clan groups. Some riverside homes have beautifully crafted facades with motifs of flowers and creeping plants, similar to those used in Terengganu's traditional Malay batik designs. The main doors are of one-piece timber, while the high roofs and open wooden windows ensure good ventilation. Chinese posters ("*lian*") are pasted on doors. Above the main door there are usually two Chinese characters representing the owner's surname (Wong and Liew, n.d.). As is the case with other heritage towns in the country, higher rents have led to gentrification, renovations and restorations, not all of which have preserved the original character of the shophouses. Higher-end tourist-related businesses now dominate, though some old retail and wholesale businesses still survive (Fieldwork March–April 2010).

The Chinese penchant for citizens' groups, common in Southeast Asia and Malaysia, is amplified in Terengganu where they are a minority. KT alone has more than thirty Chinese-based associations, including dialect, clan, guild, alumni, recreational, sporting and youth groups, in addition to a chamber of commerce. These associations assist the community to be self-reliant, but also complement the weak political voice of the Chinese by acting as an alternative channel for negotiating with the State (Tan 2002, pp. 40–52). This was especially so during the rule of the opposition Islamic PAS party, when there were no elected Chinese representatives in the State government.

An important house of prayer is the Sam Poh Kong (Cheng Ho) Temple in Kampung Jeram on the Sungei Nerus, where Admiral Cheng Ho landed. The local Chinese venerated him at a shrine below a tree for centuries until a temple was built on the site in 1943. The Hokkien Association of Terengganu later received permission from the State to own the land and preserve the temple, which is still popular despite its isolated location. Two KT town temples, the Ho Ann Kiong (1801) and Tien Hou Kong (1869), double up as the Hokkien and Hainanese community centres (Wong and Liew, undated). The first has a China-made bell dated 1801, and residents say the temple was relocated to KT from Pulau Babi in 1918. Unfortunately, an accidental fire destroyed the entire temple, except its altar, in early 2010 (Noor 2010). The second temple is linked by local folklore to the Qing Dynasty; construction at its current site in Kedai Payan was completed in 1895. Mazu, the Goddess of Sailors, a deity of indigenous Chinese origin, is worshipped in both temples (Tan 2002, pp. 25–32).

APPENDIX 4.2
TERENGGANU PERANAKAN CHINESE FOOD

The Peranakan-types have a number of unique delicacies which are a hybrid of (Terengganu) Malay and (Terengganu) Hokkien ingredients, flavours and skills. They include:

- *Moho*: a Terengganu specialty containing potato, sugar and corn flour steamed in a bowl (Penang Babas make a similarly shaped cake, without the potato).
- *Paong*: a Terengganu Peranakan-type specialty. This was originally a small, round, baked bun. These days it is more convenient to bake it as a square bun with four serrations. It is a popular breakfast in Chinese coffee shops in KT and is usually eaten with margarine and *kaya* (coconut jam). Oral history records this as an Arab influence. "We learnt this from the *Syeds*," recalls 83-year-old Mrs Wee Kim Beng.
- *Caitao kueh*: a Hokkien Peranakan-type specialty. Made from radish, steamed rice flour, and sugar, with groundnuts and onions.
- *Putu pisang*: a Terengganu specialty similar to *putu piring* but with sliced banana inside, rice flour, and *pulut* (glutinous rice).
- *Tamansari*: green bean cake (Siamese influence), yellow, diamond-shaped.
- *Kueh bakul*: although not unique to Terengganu, was very popular with Terengganu Malays, who obtained it from the Chinese.
- *Cimkueh*: originates from Malacca or Singapore. A crab dish mixed with lard and pork mince, small onions, pepper and eggs, steamed in crab shell. Many tourists travel all the way to Kemaman, where some restaurants serve it.
- *Bangi kueh*: white glutinous rice stuffed with green bean paste.
- *Chalwan*: fish paste shaped into biscuits or fish balls in *lemak* or coconut-based gravy.
- *Banteng*: a three-layered cake popular among the *Babas*.
- *Ahkok*: a diagonal-shaped Malay cake made from egg, coconut milk, and rice flour.
- *Sekaya pulut*: a yellow diamond-shaped layer cake made of *kaya* and *pulut*.

(*Source*: Mrs Wee Kim Beng, 83, interview with author,
19 March 2009, KT, Terengganu).

Notes

1. A pseudonym.
2. Little has been published about them. An exception is a monograph by Tan Chee Beng (2002). In contrast, there are a number of number of publications on the Chinese in Kelantan, including Sharon Carstens' *Cultural Identity in Northern Peninsular Malaysia* (1986) and Teo Kok Seong's *The Peranakan Chinese of Kelantan: A Study of the Culture, Language and Communication of an Assimilated Group in Malaysia* (2003).
3. The Terengganu Hokkien Chinese refer to themselves as *"Teng-lang"* or "people of the Tang Dynasty" in the local Hokkien dialect (Tan 2002, pp. V, 1–3).
4. Lua Yik Hor (head of the Terengganu Hokkien Association's Education Committee), interviews with author, 2 and 5 April 2009, Kuala Terengganu.
5. Lua Yik Hor, interview with the author, 12 June 2010.
6. These drums were produced by the Dong Son culture in the Red River Delta of northern Vietnam and are found in many parts of Southeast Asia (The Metropolitan Museum of Art n.d.).
7. Further clarification by Lua Yik Hor, interviews with author, 2 and 5 April 2009, Kuala Terengganu.
8. A definite link to Muslims in China however, is the immigration of six Chinese Muslim families in the early twentieth century. They came from Guangzhou but were popularly referred to as "Orang Yunnan", or "people of Yunnan", which has a significant Muslim population. Today these families have fully assimilated into the local Malay population (Wang Ma n.d.).
9. There are temples, cave shrines and monuments devoted to him in Malacca and Perak in the Peninsula, Indonesia, the Philippines, Sri Lanka, India, and Somalia and Kenya, which he visited (Sam Poh Kong Temple Committee n.d., p. 60).
10. A clan comprises of a group of people who can often trace their ancestry through the male side of the family (daughters are usually encouraged to join the grooms' family after marriage). Most clans often have a common surname and may even share a mutual ancestor. In southern China, clan ties are usually strong due to the sharing of a common ancestral village, property and specific dialect.
11. Lua Yik Hor, interviews with author, 2 and 5 April 2009, Kuala Terengganu, and author's fieldwork, March–April 2010.
12. Pulau Babi is Malay for "Pig Island". (In Hokkien *"ti"* means pig and *"rok"* means pig-pen, hence "Tirok"). Pulau Babi — since renamed Pulau Bahagia — was among the first and most important immigrant settlements in Terengganu, a location from which the Chinese also dispersed to other rural areas such as Kuala Som, Pok Pili, Batu Besar, Marang, Dungun, and Kuala Terengganu's Chinatown (Tan 2001, pp. 10–12).

13. Koo Ong Jin, telephone interview with author, 11 June 2010.

14. Interviews with Kampung Tirok residents during author's fieldwork, March–April 2010.

15. Lua Yik Hor (head of the Terengganu Hokkien Association's Education Committee), interviews with author, 2 and 5 April 2009, Kuala Terengganu.

16. *Wayang kulit*, performed in the Malay archipelago, traces its origins to India. Derived from a Javanese Hindu-Buddhist tradition, it involves handcrafted leather puppets depicting epic stories of gods. A gamelan orchestra accompanies story-telling (Salleh 1999).

17. Lua Yik Hor and Koo Ong Jin, discussion with author, 18 March 2009, Kampung Tirok, Terengganu.

18. Anonymous Kuala Terengganu-based trader, interview with author, 18 March 2009, coffee shop in Kampung Tirok, Terengganu.

19. Lua Yik Hor, interview with the author, 20 March 2009, Kampung Tirok, Terengganu.

20. Author's fieldwork in Kampung Tirok, Terengganu, 4 April 2009.

21. *Kain pelikat*, a *sarong* for men, often worn with the Malay costume, *baju Melayu*.

22. This description of Kampung Tirok cuisine is summarized from Tan 2002, p. 76.

23. Koo Ong Jin, interview with author, 18 March, 2009, Kampung Tirok, Terengganu.

24. According to Tan (Tan 1984, p. 201), converts are often discriminated by other Chinese who see them as Malays or "nominal Chinese". This encourages them to identify with Malays and be assimilated into Malay society. "If Chinese Muslims remain Chinese and are accepted as such by Malays and Chinese, this will certainly encourage more Chinese to embrace Islam, and indirectly promote inter-marriage with Malays. Chinese will then not see Islam in communal terms and will regard it as one of the religions they have access to, like Buddhism, Christianity, Bahai and many others. This will remove much of the prejudice and conflict surrounding religion and identity in Malaysia." (Tan 1984, p. 201).

25. Koo Ong Jin, interview with author, 18 March 2009, Kampung Tirok, Terengganu. The Mid-Autumn Celebration, more popularly known as the Mooncake Festival, is a harvest festival remembered by baking moon-shaped cakes (journeymalaysia.com n.d). Ancestor-worship is a Chinese tradition dating thousands of years. It includes the Hungry Ghost Festival, held on the seventh month of the lunar new year to remember deceased family members (journeymalaysia.com n.d), and *cheng beng* or All Souls' Day, involving cleaning and the offering of food and prayers at ancestral graveyards (My Malaysia Books n.d.).

26. Matrilocal refers to living patterns or customs where a married couple lives with or near the wife's parents.

27. Most households have domestic altars dedicated to the deities Toa Peh Kong or Kuan Teh Yah, the former being particularly popular among Hokkiens. During the festival, the deity is carried on a sedan chair to each household altar. According to village oral history, the deity's statue was brought from China by an immigrant family several hundred years ago and was installed in a temple at a nearby river. However, flooding forced a relocation of the temple to a hillside in the vicinity. The temple is today run by committee members from Kampung Tirok and Kuala Terengganu. Interestingly, the temple committee meetings were once conducted in both Malay and Chinese for villagers who did not understand Chinese (Tan 2002, pp. 102–105). It is still not uncommon for some local Chinese to refer to their temple as *mesjid* (mosque).

28. Koo Ong Jin, telephone interview with author, 11 June 2010.

29. Except where stated, observations in this section are drawn from off-the-record conversations with other residents in casual settings in the Kuala Terengganu and Tirok areas during the author's fieldwork, March–April 2010.

30. Lua Yik Hor and Koo Ong Jin, discussion with author, 18 March 2009, Kampung Tirok, Terengganu.

5

"MEREKA SAYANG KITA"
The Malay Journey of the Baweanese

INTRODUCTION: BAWEAN AND THE CULTURAL REPRODUCTION[1] OF MALAY ETHNICITY

The Baweanese, popularly referred to as *Orang Boyan*,[2] are a little-known people from the tiny island of Bawean, located in the Java Sea. The island has a population of only 65,000 but a diaspora at least ten times larger spanning the Asia-Pacific region, particularly Malaysia and Singapore, where they form an important component of the Malay community (Ali 1996, p. 3). Malaysia and Singapore are so well known on the isolated island that two roads on it are named after their ex-prime ministers Dr Mahathir Mohamad and Mr Goh Chok Tong (Abd Rahman and Omar 2007). Baweanese immigration, a small but unique stream of the broader Indonesian flow into Malaysia, is important in terms of its long history, sustainability, and its acculturation and assimilation strategies.

According to one scholar, in the mid-1990s Malaysia had an estimated 500,000 and Singapore between 50,000 and 80,000 "Malays" of Baweanese descent, whose forefathers had entered during colonial times (Ali 1996, p. 2). A smaller cohort of about 4,000 Baweanese entered Malaysia in 1975–85, arriving initially as single, male, temporary foreign workers, followed by full family formations. By 2010 these post-colonial immigrants, together with their children and grandchildren, were estimated to total 50,000 and were among the largest and most settled of the new Indonesian communities in squatter settlements in the Peninsula's west coast towns of Johor Bahru, Seremban, Kuala Lumpur, Klang, Rawang and Ipoh (Group Discussion, Baweanese Community Leaders, Gombak, 14 July 2010).[3]

Unlike the other ethnic minorities described in this book who arrived and evolved as communities before the British colonial period, most Baweanese — like most Chinese and Indians — entered and settled during the British period. Despite being relatively recent immigrants, the Baweanese have not merely acculturated but have assimilated into the Malay community. The scholar Wang Gungwu refers to Malays of Indonesian ancestry and recent Indonesian foreign workers as "migrants of similarity", who share a common religion, language (Malay) and customs with Malays. This is in contrast to Chinese and Indians whom he refers to as "migrants of difference", with different cultural backgrounds (verbal comments, quoted in Miyazaki 2000, p. 77).

Given their similarities with Malays, the Baweanese experience of acculturation is different from that of non-Muslim ethnic minorities. Firstly, for the Baweanese there is no religious barrier to intermarriage and social assimilation into the Malay community. Secondly, since the Baweanese are Muslims, speak Malay and eventually practise Malay customs, they meet three of the four constitutional requirements of being Malay (see note 1 in Preface) and the State eventually reclassifies them as "Malay Muslims". However, as with some Indian Muslims, for most Baweanese it takes several generations before they are able to replace their own ethnic label with "Malay" in their identity card.

In 2014 Malaysia employed 2.5 million documented foreign workers (Department of Statistics, 2014), mostly Indonesians. The number of undocumented workers is not known, although one press report estimated the numbers at 1.8 million in 2011 (*The Star*, 19 February 2011), prior to an amnesty and registration exercise. Though the majority comprise single males — and increasingly single females — full-family formations are growing, and with it increased Indonesian settlement, with long-term implications for Malaysia's demography, labour market and ethnic composition (Hugo, Graeme 1993). Given their large numbers and future growth potential, it is important and useful to understand the process through which Indonesians become acculturated and eventually assimilated into the majority Malay community. Focusing on a little-known group also underlines the wide diversity of the Indonesian entry into Malaysia and the heterogeneity of the Malays as a community.

The Baweanese are just one of 300 ethnic sub-groups in Indonesia. They are an economically marginalized island-community and are culturally distinct from "Malays", who within Indonesia are an ethnic minority associated with the Riau Islands and parts of Sumatra and Kalimantan. Yet Baweanese immigrants have managed to change their ethnic identity, become "Malays", and belong to the Malay-majority in Malaysia. This chapter examines the process through which a relatively obscure ethnic sub-group within Indonesia immigrated, acculturated, assimilated, and eventually obtained social and State recognition as "Malays" in Malaysia.

The chapter begins by briefly tracing the history of pre-colonial and colonial Indonesian immigration to the Peninsula. It then discusses Baweanese immigration into Malaysia and Singapore during the colonial period and in the years 1975–85. This is followed by an analysis of the cultural factors facilitating Baweanese immigration, acculturation and assimilation, and the process through which they strive to acquire a Malay identity. The chapter ends with life-history interviews of six individuals; the aim is to place individual immigrant experiences and perceptions in the context of broader historical and social forces. These life-histories provide the reader with a peek into the lives of Indonesians — the newest, fastest-growing and largest group of new immigrants into Malaysia.

Information in this chapter is drawn from the author's PhD thesis (Pillai 2005), based on in-depth interviews with Baweanese community leaders and individuals, life-history profiles (Appendix 5.2), and a 1999 survey of 100 mainly Baweanese immigrants in Kampung Sungai Kayu Ara (Kaska), a Baweanese-dominated squatter settlement in Petaling Jaya, Selangor, Malaysia. Fieldwork was conducted in 1998–2000, before the settlement was demolished. Updated information on the Baweanese community in Malaysia was obtained in mid-2010 through discussions with a group of ten community leaders in another Baweanese-dominated settlement, namely Taman Harmonis in Gombak, Kuala Lumpur. Further insights were obtained in late 2011 through follow-up interviews with former Kaska residents who are also community leaders — religious teacher Alim and businessman Azmi — who had relocated to other parts of the Klang Valley.[4]

FLOW AND FLUX: PRE-COLONIAL AND COLONIAL MIGRATION TO THE PENINSULA

Islands, accessible waterways and maritime cultures formed the basis of early social organization, regional mobility and diversity that characterized the Malay-Indonesian archipelago. As part of this flow and flux, streams of "Malays" entered the Peninsula, beginning with Melaka's fifteenth-century founder Parameswara, a Muslim convert whose lineage was linked to Sumatra's great Srivijaya Empire. Melaka's cosmopolitan immigrant-based multi-ethnic community, a microcosm of present-day Malaysia, had an important impact on Malay perceptions of immigrants and on Malay-Muslim identity (Andaya and Andaya 1982, pp. 39–54).

Islam transformed Melaka after it was spread by Indian traders in the early fifteenth century. Throughout the fifteenth century it was seen as a model commercial and religious centre by other Muslim kingdoms in the archipelago, which imitated its distinctive literature, statecraft, music, dance, dress, games, titles and *pantun* (two-part stanza). Malay eventually became the lingua franca of the region, and language was so closely identified with culture that the word *bahasa* (language) meant correct behaviour and knowledge of Malay customs. Melaka's main contribution to Malay court culture was the incorporation of Islamic ideas, which became so intimately associated with Malay society that to become Muslim was to *masuk Melayu*, or "to enter the fold of the Malay" (Andaya and Andaya 1982, pp. 54–55). Scholars today generally agree that the term "Malayu", associated with a river in Sumatra, refers to a Srivijaya raja-centred polity whose followers moved to Melaka, embraced Islam, and ushered an age of archipelago sultanates in which "Malay" was correlated with Melaka (Milner 2011, pp. 19, 230).

In the mid-seventeenth century circular migration by the Minangkabaus of Sumatra led to the entry and settlement of a large immigrant community, particularly in the nine districts of what is now Negeri Sembilan in Peninsular Malaysia. Another large group of immigrants in the last quarter of the seventeenth century were the Bugis, who settled in Selangor after fleeing civil war in Sulawesi (Andaya and Andaya 1982, pp. 80, 94–96).

Population mobility persisted until colonialism divided the archipelago into territories, imposed borders and introduced immigration controls. Though colonialism reduced free and spontaneous mobility, it facilitated the large-scale and systematic entry of labour to serve colonial economic interests. While the Dutch encouraged Javanese out-migration to less populated parts of Indonesia, the British allowed the entry of Chinese, Javanese and Indian labour for Malaya's tin mines and plantations, creating a multi-ethnic society (Pillai 2005, p. 69).

There were three main Indonesian immigration sources and streams in the period 1850–1957 (See Appendix 5.1). Firstly, the British encouraged the recruitment of Javanese contract workers for rubber plantations. Secondly, Indonesian immigrant farmers were offered rent remissions and loans to increase food production, particularly in Selangor; by 1886 two-thirds of the Malay population of Selangor comprised Indonesians (Sadka, 1968, pp. 327–28). A third channel comprised pilgrim brokers who facilitated the entry of independent Indonesian immigrants via Singapore. The early Baweanese immigrants possibly included such pilgrims who stopped to work and save in Singapore on the way to Mecca; the pilgrimage may even have had an "emancipating function" (Vredenbregt 1964, p. 117) in breaking the island's isolation. In 1957 these three sources contributed to Indonesians comprising a third of Selangor's and a quarter of Johore's total population, and 8.7 per cent of the total Malayan population (Table 5.1). However Indonesian immigration was relatively small compared to Chinese and Indian entry, and was confined to the Federated Malay States.

SAILORS AND TAPPERS: COLONIAL BAWEANESE IMMIGRATION, 1850–1957

Bawean: The Place and Its People

The tiny 20,000-hectare island of Bawean lies in the Java Sea, and the Baweanese speak a dialect which is a variation of Madurese. The island is mountainous and though the soil was fertile it was insufficient to feed the population. Poverty was rife. Moreover fishermen from nearby Madura, Kalimantan and Sulawesi exploited the island's rich fishing grounds. Bawean was also neglected by the Dutch. The roots of Baweanese emigration go back to the early twentieth century when poverty drove many to emigrate to Java, the Riau Islands (south of Singapore) and even to Sumatra. Geographical mobility was aided by the fact that the Baweanese were seafarers who frequented neighbouring islands to fish and trade (Baginda 1967, pp. 18–26). This fishing and trading route eventually mutated

TABLE 5.1
Malaya: Percentage of Indonesians in Total Malayan Population 1911–57

State	1911	1921	1931	1947	1957
Singapore	42.4	39.9	42.1	38.2	31.7
Penang	4.5	3.1	2.4	2.2	1.7
Melaka	4.0	3.2	3.3	4.5	3.6
Perak	16.6	18.8	21.4	17.1	10.5
Selangor	27.3	28.4	45.6	43.9	32.3
Negeri Sembilan	4.5	3.9	6.5	5.9	4.7
Pahang	1.2	4.2	5.8	3.0	2.6
Johore	34.2	42.5	51.5	31.5	25.6
Kedah	1.0	1.2	1.2	1.0	1.1
Kelantan	0.01	0.3	0.3	0.1	0.1
Terengganu	0.02	0.1	0.1	0.2	0.2
Perlis	0.1	0.1	0.1	0.1	0.2
MALAYA	8.6	10.8	14.5	12.3	8.7

Source: Malayan Census Reports, 1911 to 1957, as quoted in Shamsul, "The Growth and Distribution of the Indonesian Population in Malaysia", Bijdragen, Deel 123 Martin Nijhoff, 1967.

into a labour circuit, with implications on emigration today. Businessman Azmi, 39, a second-generation Baweanese now living in Malaysia, recalls the stories told by his elders:

> ….my maternal grandmother immigrated to Malaysia during the Dutch period. She came in a *perahu* (small boat) sometime in the 1920s. I think she came to join her husband and relatives. Most of the men worked as syces, tending to the horses in Kuala Lumpur's Turf Club …my grandmother used to move between Bawean and Singapore. I was told that in those days the *perahu's* took forty days and nights for the trip. There were no engines until the 1970s. Everyone travelled via Singapore, and then took the train to Malaysia. The old Baweanese folk referred to Malaysia as *Selat* (The Straits).
>
> (Azmi, Interviews, August/September 1999).

The Baweanese "Invasion" of Singapore

The Baweanese first visited Singapore with Bugis seafarers in the early days of British rule, and reports of Singapore's prosperity later attracted streams of Baweanese immigrants. It is reported that the earliest Baweanese arrived in Singapore in or before 1828, though they were not separately identified in the census data at that time (Baginda 1967, pp. 18–26). Up to 1934 when passports were not yet introduced the Baweanese moved freely in and out of Singapore. Before the Second World War the Dutch shipping firm KPM ran a direct fortnightly service between Singapore and Bawean, facilitating emigration (Vredenbregt 1964, p. 10) and short visits.

However the Second World War contributed to famine in Bawean, forcing large numbers of Baweanese to enter Singapore to avert starvation (Baginda 1967, p. 28). Sometime in 1947 or 1948 "thousands of Baweanese invaded Singapore by *perahu* (small boats)" (Haji Fadzal 1967, p. 12). They sailed towards the Immigration Department at East Wharf at dawn, resulting in panicked officials detaining them on their overcrowded boats. The Colonial Secretary granted landing permits only after the Baweanese Association of Singapore (Persatuan Bawean Singapura, or 'PBS') intervened to guarantee their employment as labourers in Singapore and rubber tappers in Johor's plantations (Haji Fadzal 1967, p. 12).

The Baweanese community at that time had 138 communal migrant dwelling houses or *pondoks* in Singapore and two in Johor Bahru, and the *pondok* headmen found jobs for these new arrivals. Many worked as syces and drivers (Haji Fadzal 1967, p. 12), occupational niches they virtually monopolized through mutual recommendations. The number of Baweanese entering Singapore rose steadily after 1849, with the male-female ratio becoming more balanced over the years. By 1957 there were about 22,000 Baweanese in Singapore (Table 5.2).

Baweanese Immigration to Malaya

Singapore was the main centre for Baweanese migrants but from there they worked their way up the Peninsula, settling in *pondoks* in the more prosperous Straits Settlements of Penang and Melaka and later in Taiping, Ipoh, Kuala Lumpur, Seremban and Johor Bahru (Baginda 1967, p. 28). The proportion of Baweanese among Indonesian immigrants in Malaya rose steadily in 1911–47 to reach 20,000 or 7 per cent (Shamsul 1964, p. 134) (Table 5.3). The PBS was registered in 1947 but its network extended through the Peninsula right up to Penang, with almost all states having associations and *pondoks*. To mobilize themselves to play a more active role in Malayan society, a Congress of Baweanese Pondoks and Associations of Malaya and Singapore was organized in Kuala Lumpur in 1956, officially opened by the then Crown Prince (*Raja Muda*) of Selangor. Two other

TABLE 5.2
The Baweanese Population In Singapore 1849–1957

Year	Males	Females	Total	Number of Females per 1,000 Males	Number of Males per 1,000 Females
1849	720	43	763	60	16,744
1871	1,377	257	1,634	187	5,338
1881	1,504	607	2,111	404	2,478
1891	1,808	869	2,677	481	2,081
1901	1,701	1,011	2,712	594	1,682
1911	3,028	2,058	5,086	680	1,471
1921	3,765	2,824	6,589	750	1,333
1931	5,338	4,075	9,413	763	1,309
1947	8,237	7,197	15,434	874	1,144
1957	11,580	10,587	22,167	914	1,102

Source: Vredenbregt, 1964, p. 115. Vredenbregt obtained this data from the following sources: The Census of the Colony of Singapore, 1849; Journal of the Indian Archipelago and Eastern Asia 4 (10); Walter Makepeace, One Hundred Years of Singapore, vol. 1 (London 1921), pp. 355–62; Census Report of British Malaya, 1921; C.A. Vlieland, British Malaya, Report of the 1931 Census; M.V. DelTufo, Malaya, Report on 1947 Census of Population; and the Census of Population, Singapore 1957.

TABLE 5.3
Indonesians by Ethnic Sub-Group, Malaya, 1911–47

Ethnic Sub-Group	1911		1921		1931		1947	
	No.	%	No.	%	No.	%	No.	%
Java	79,200	67	112,800	66	169,200	60	187,700	61
Banjar	21,300	18	37,800	22	45,400	16	62,400	20
Sumatra	2,900*	2	2,400*	1	40,100	14	26,300	8
Bawean	7,600	6	9,800	6	14,000	5	20,400	7
Bugis	6,500	6	8,400	5	10,000	3	7,000	2
Others	200	–	–	–	2,000	2	5,400	2
Total	117,800	100	170,200	100	280,600	100	309,100	100

* Most immigrants from Sumatra were classified as Malays.
Source: Shamsul, 1964, p. 134; cf., Malayan Census Reports, 1911–47.

gatherings were organized later, one in Singapore and the other in Kuala Lumpur in 1962 (Haji Fadzal 1967, pp. 12–13).

After the war, immigration rules were tightened and only those who had previously been in Singapore and Malaya were allowed re-entry. To overcome this barrier Tanjong Pinang in Riau became a Baweanese transit point for entry into Singapore, its proximity enabling many Baweanese to enter camouflaged as boatmen. Another factor that encouraged Indonesian workers to seek employment in Tanjung Pinang was that the legal tender in Riau was the Straits Dollar, which was higher in value than the Indonesian Rupiah (Baginda 1967, p. 28). Till today both Bawean and the Riau Islands, especially Tanjong Pinang and Batam, continue to be important transit points for undocumented immigrant entry into Singapore and Malaysia (Spaan 1994, p. 97). The persistence of these geographical points of entry indicates the sustainability of traditional sea routes despite the advent of State immigration controls, extensive law enforcement and the alternative of air travel.

POVERTY AND PIETY: FACTORS FACILITATING BAWEANESE IMMIGRATION

Marginalization and *Merantau* among Baweanese

Indonesia, with 17,000 islands, is the world's largest archipelago. It has hundreds of ethnic groups and languages and with 250 million people in 2014 (worldpopulationreview.com), it is also the world's fourth-most populous country, with the largest Muslim population. The small size of Bawean and its location in an isolated periphery of a huge archipelago contributed to its economic neglect by the colonial and post-colonial State, and poverty forced many to leave. The Baweanese, being a marginalized but mobile minority, view the entire region as an "ethnic-hinterland", much like the Sumatra Minangkabau people's *rantau* (area of circular migration) (Ali 1996, pp. 29–30).

The Baweanese traditionally used the term *alajer ke selat* (set sail to the Straits) to describe their journeys to Singapore and Riau, but in later years the Malay term *merantau* was commonly used to refer to return and circular migration within the region (Ali 1996, p. 5). *Merantau* is an important indigenous concept which captures the migratory spirit and culture of the Malay, or more specifically, the Minangkabau of Sumatra. The term can be stretched over many nuances, and has been defined and translated as:

> To leave one's home, one's relatives, one's home village or country either temporarily, for a very long time, or forever. The *rantau*, that place outside, or a foreign country, is the place where you work hard, seeking knowledge

and skills and gaining experience, and your success there would add greatly to your security and happiness and that of your relatives and your own home village or country.

(M.D. Mansoer et al. 1970, p. 3 as translated in Wang 1992, p. 169).

Merantau is sparked by economic factors but is buttressed by a shared identity among people in an open and borderless maritime Malay world who consider themselves *orang serumpun*, that is, people of a common cluster, stock or group. This same identity is drawn upon by Indonesian immigrants today to rationalize *merantau*, entry, settlement and acculturation (Pillai 2005).

The Baweanese were for centuries fishermen and traders in a maritime trading network stretching to Java, Kalimantan, Riau, Singapore and Malaya. However with the advent of colonialism in the mid-twentieth century, this trading link mutated into an active labour network, with the largest flows into Singapore and Malaya. Malaysian Baweanese religious teacher Alim reflects on his people's migration history and links it to his own family experience:

> The Baweanese have a long history of migration. Most of them were fishermen and seafarers, brave men who travelled far in small *perahu's* to earn their living. That is how they came to know Singapore and Malaysia. At first they went to Singapore — which during colonial days was quite open — and only later, after Singapore was closed to them and Malaysia more developed did they move here. In the same way, many of our relatives had migrated to this region years ago. My mother's family all migrated to Batam and Malaysia years ago, just like my father's siblings, who moved to Malaysia and Singapore. My father first migrated here in the 1970s, and I came many years later. He was a very poor farmer in Bawean before coming here. We were so poor that I remember he could not pay my school fees and we could not even afford a radio in the house.
>
> (Interview, Alim, Kampung Sungei Kayu Ara (Kaska),
> Petaling Jaya, Selangor, 6 May 1998, in Pillai 2005, p. 212).

Foreign Labour Demand in Malaysia

After Malaya's independence in 1957, immigration restrictions were imposed, initially due to tighter border controls by the new nation-state, and later because of Indonesian hostility towards Malaysia. However in the 1970s, given Malaysia's high growth rates and segmented internal labour markets, workers were imported even before an absolute local shortage occurred. In the early 1970s several hundred Indonesian immigrants were already working in rubber and oil palm plantations in Johor, south of the Peninsula. Additionally, sugar plantations in Perlis and padi farms in Kedah and Kelantan in the north employed Thai seasonal workers. Indonesians began entering the construction sector, particularly during the construction boom of the late 1970s and early 1980s. The Indonesian inflow gained momentum in the early 1980s when the plantation and construction sectors lost Malaysian workers to the fast growing manufacturing and services industries (Pillai 1992, pp. 2–13).

The first large wave of Indonesian immigration in the 1980s was encouraged by high growth and greater labour demand after foreign manufacturers took advantage of liberalization and deregulation to relocate and invest in Malaysia (Pillai 1992, p. 3). Indonesians gradually began replacing Malaysian Chinese construction workers, many of whom were semi-skilled and skilled workers who moved to Singapore and East Asia, particularly after the 1985 recession.[5] With economy-wide labour shortages, foreign worker employment spread from plantations and construction into services (mainly domestic maids). Indonesians entering the construction sector in the late 1970s and early 1980s comprised both new entrants and those who had earlier entered as plantation workers. The Baweanese interviewed in Kaska in Selangor, Malaysia, who entered in the 1970s and 1980s, were among these new entrants.

For example Lokman entered Malaysia in 1978 as a tourist via Tanjung Pinang and Singapore. His uncle helped him to find work in Malaysia as a construction worker at RM13 per day, equivalent to three days wages in Indonesia then. He moved jobs, eventually settling down permanently in Malaysia as a *bomoh* (medicine man/mystic) (Interview 30 September 1999). Similarly, businessman Azmi entered in the late 1970s to join his father who was a construction worker in Malaysia. Azmi recalls:

> I specialized in steel fabrication (*tukang besi*). I was a worker helping build Damansara Jaya housing estate, which was just being opened up then. I earned only RM10 per day ....After three months, friends told me I will not progress (*tidak akan maju*) in that job, so I switched to being a carpenter, working with my father. My wage jumped to RM22 per day. I did this for five months, helping construct houses in Taman Tun Dr Ismail, which was also being developed then....My next work location was Taman Seraya in Cheras, but this time as a sub-contractor, working

with my dad. I was in my early twenties then. From then onward I was never an *orang makan gaji* (employee) again; I have always been a sub-contractor (he says this with a glint of pride).

(Interviews, August/September 1999).

Islam and the Baweanese Migration Tradition

In addition to economic factors, Islam plays a powerful facilitating and ideological role in Baweanese immigration. The Baweanese share the cultural and social history of other groups on the north coast of East Java, where the trading community was associated with the respected *santri* tradition. This is a tradition which claims Islamic purity traced to the *wali songo* or the nine Islamic saints of Java, who spread the religion in Indonesia. Islamic organizations such as Nahdlatul Ulama (NU) have been established on the island since 1934 (Ali 1996, p. 4, p. 18). The NU is the world's largest Muslim organization, once led by the late Indonesian President Abdurrahman Wahid (Gus Dur). Interestingly, some Baweanese have maintained their NU affiliations in Malaysia; in 2000 a few immigrants reported being members of a "Selangor State branch" of NU (Pillai 2005, p. 384).

These strong religious traditions and affiliations have contributed to the growth of many religious boarding schools or *pesantren* on the island. Children are socialized into the culture of immigration in these *pesantren*, where they are cared for from an early age, before and after their parents immigrate. Bawean's strong religious institutions have ensured the cultural reproduction of a migration tradition which involves the weakening of emotional ties between parents and children, the care of immigrants in *pesantren*, and the support of these schools through immigrant remittances. As a result many immigration decisions are made in *pesantrens* and *suraus* (prayer house), and most journeys made with school and *surau* companions[6] (Vredenbregt 1964, p. 122).

The *pesantren* developed mainly to look after the children of these emigrants. More such boarding schools appeared in the 1970s, and they multiplied in the 1980s as immigration to Singapore and Malaysia increased. These schools are financed by ex-students who become immigrant workers in the region, resulting in a co-dependence between the religious infrastructure and the immigration network (Ali 1998, pp. 25–34, 47). In addition to boarding schools, prayer houses and mosques began to mushroom over the years through support from the diaspora; by 1996 there were 575 places of worship on the island (Ali 1998, p. 18). This social and religious "umbilical cord" (Vredenbregt 1964, p. 132) has deep historical roots and goes back to the early twentieth century, when *pondoks* in Singapore gave financial support to places of worship in Bawean.

The practice continues to this day in Malaysia. Money raised by Baweanese religious leaders in Malaysia is sent to their counterparts on the island to build mosques and *suraus* and to run *pesantrens*. Students on the island are often sponsored by immigrants. For example Alim, a Baweanese religious teacher and community leader in Selangor, has organized a system where a group of Baweanese immigrants in Malaysia sponsor 300 students in a *pesantren* on the island (Alim, Community Leader, 24 October 2011). Surplus funds in Malaysia are also repatriated. When a *surau* in a Baweanese squatter settlement in Malaysia was demolished, the community donated its RM13,000 collection to support *suraus* and *pesantrens* in Bawean (Pillai 2005, p. 379).

In the past money was also raised through social enterprises involving group tours of the island for immigrants and their children. Azmi, the Baweanese businessman, recalls:

> In both 1994 and 1997, I was one of the first people to organize group tours to Bawean. The first time a return trip was RM900, the second time RM1,000 per person. There was a good response for both tours. Many people cannot afford to pay a lump sum so I arranged for them to repay in instalments of RM100 a month. Profits were re-channelled to the Yayasan Al'amin (Al'amin Foundation), which does welfare work on the island. The foundation receives a lot of support from Baweanese migrants, including those working within Indonesia.
>
> (Interview, Azmi, Businessman, August/September 1999).

In addition to caring for children and socializing them into immigration, the *pesantren* emphasize character-building. This reinforces the Malay image of the Baweanese as religious, honest, humble, and hardworking, a positive stereotype which eases entry and settlement into Malaysia and acculturation and assimilation into the Malay community. The Baweanese themselves are fully aware of their image as people who are regarded as trustworthy and law-abiding. A resident of Kaska, the Selangor Baweanese settlement, says proudly:

> Do you know there is a very low crime rate here compared to other kampungs in the Klang Valley? This is because we have many respected Baweanese migrants here — and they help organize and give good guidance to villagers. You know all these years I have never had any serious problems with my four kids. One particular year we even invited the Indonesian Consul here to address us during *Maulud Nabi* (Prophet Muhammad's Birthday) celebrations. He advised us to take care, and asked the village head to look after our interests too. Among all the villages in Kuala Lumpur, Kaska has four *suraus* — the largest number of *suraus* [prior to the mid-1999 demolishments]. There are three Indonesian-controlled *suraus*, one Malay *surau*, and one *masjid* (mosque).
>
> Baharuddin, Security Guard (Interviews, June 1998, March, May 1999), Kaska, Petaling Jaya.

The *pesantren* also trains a core of people with religious knowledge who perform a critical role as religious teachers within the Malay community. Baweanese businessman Azmi puts it this way:

> The Baweanese *pesantren* are like informal universities! It has produced lots of ordinary people who have a deep knowledge of Islam. Malay religious officials themselves have said that "native Malays" ("Melayu Asli") can learn a lot about Islam from we Baweanese.
>
> (Interview, Azmi, 19 October 2011, Taman Harmonis, Gombak, Kuala Lumpur).

The belief that Baweanese have deep Islamic knowledge creates a role for them as religious teachers, increasing their interaction with Malays, gaining their respect, and eventually easing their claims to Malayness. Interestingly, Azmi uses the term "Melayu Asli" to refer to native Malays, implying that there are also non-native Malays, including people of Baweanese origin.

Just as the *pesantren* play a strong facilitating role, immigrants also display an acute awareness of the strong ideological link between Islam and immigration. A quote from the Malaysian Baweanese religious teacher Alim, which he says is inspired by Surat An-Nahl, verses 68–69 of the Holy Qur'an, beautifully captures a view of the moral, legal and material justification for immigration:

> I am different only in name — I am from Indonesia, but my ideal is the same — to develop the human being. (*Nama saja lain — daripada Indonesia*

— *tetapi wawasan-nya sama* — *untuk membangunkan manusia!*) I can serve mankind anywhere. In Islam the world is one. For me the migrant is like a bee. It travels far and wide and does not disrupt but nurtures the environment. The plants and flowers need the bee. It does not eat any impure, defiled matter, but only the cleanest things and it produces clean, pure honey. Bees are also very cooperative, and won't disturb others. But they will attack if provoked.

(Interview, Alim, 6 May 1999, in Pillai 2005 p. 216).

In these few deeply symbolic words, Alim has captured a wide variety of meanings — the concept of universal values ("in Islam the world is one"), the free, roving spirit of the migrant ("bee"; "travels far and wide"); the migrant's search for harmony ("does not disrupt"); and their important contribution ("nurtures the environment") — so important, in fact, that some societies and economies are dependent on them ("the plants and flowers need the bee"). But it goes further. The commoditization of immigrant labour is made sublime because the bee "does not eat any impure, defiled matter, but only the cleanest things and it produces clean, pure honey". We are also reminded of immigrant solidarity and networks ("cooperative") and given a warning ("they will attack if provoked").

HELPFUL "MALAY" NEIGHBOURS: FACTORS FACILITATING ACCULTURATION AND ASSIMILATION

Geographical and Ethnic "Rerouting" via Riau

When colonialism ended, new nation-state boundaries threatened to severe the Baweanese labour flow into Singapore and Malaysia, which was part of their long-held social space (Ali 1996, p. 27). To sustain their social space and labour network, the Baweanese resorted to a process of geographical and ethnic "rerouting".

Geographically they rerouted their emigration destinations from Singapore and Malaysia to other parts of Indonesia, particularly the Riau Archipelago (especially its provincial capital, Tanjung Pinang, on Bintan Island). This confetti of islands lies forty-five minutes by boat south of Singapore and historically served as a transit point for entry into Singapore, and in recent years, Malaysia.[7] The Riau Islands have been a trading and transit point for Baweanese immigrants for almost 200 years.

Its proximity to Singapore and Malaysia makes it a convenient stopover location; even today potential Baweanese immigrants rely on a network of relatives, friends and agents there for accommodation and assistance while awaiting for an opportune time for transport, entry, documentation and employment (Ali 1998, pp. 10–12). Thus historically there has been a process of geographical step-migration from Bawean to Riau, then Singapore and finally into the Malay Peninsula.

The case of Malaysian Baweanese immigrant Baharuddin, for example, is not untypical. He was Singapore-born but returned to Pulau Bawean with his parents. He initially worked in Pulau Belitong near Java before moving to Tanjung Pinang in 1974, from where he unsuccessfully applied for a passport to re-enter Singapore. "....I lost all hope of entering Singapore. So I said to myself: 'OK! Let's enter Malaysia." (*Jom! Mari masuk Malaysia!*). He entered Malaysia by train as a tourist, worked as a construction labourer, and obtained Permanent Residence (PR) status within two years. (Interview, 22 June 1998, in Pillai 2005, pp. 207–208).

Another is the case of Lokman the *bomoh* (mystic). His father worked in Java for decades; later Lokman himself moved to Java for work and Madura for studies, before heading to the Rhiau Islands, Singapore, and finally Malaysia, where he found work, obtained PR status, and established a family (Interview, 30 September 1999 in Pillai 2005, p. 262).

The journey via Riau involves not merely geographical but also "ethnic" re-routing. In a fascinating case of "ethnic reinvention" illustrating the fluidity and flexibility of the category "Malay", the Baweanese are initiated into Malay cultural mores on these islands, which are regarded as the Malay heartland of Indonesia. "Riau is a very Malay place; I would say it's the only Malay place in Indonesia!" claims Baweanese businessman Azmi, who entered Malaysia via Singapore after first travelling by boat to Java and then to Tanjung Pinang in the Rhiau Islands (Interview, 19 October 2011).

Alim, the Baweanese religious teacher who also entered Malaysia after spending some time in the Riau Islands, explains how the process of "becoming Malay" works. He says those who arrive in Riau stay with other long-settled Baweanese who are already familiar with Malay customs, and this helps socialize them to Malay ways. "Moreover there are many opportunities to learn Malay customs from Riau Malays who work in Singapore, and from Singapore Malays who visit the Riau Islands to shop or holiday." He gives some examples of these customs:

The Malays are more refined than us. For example most Malays say "*Jemput makan*" (We invite you to eat) while we say "*Sila makan*" (Please help yourself). When it comes to dressing, the Malay woman's *tudung* (headdress) is different from ours both in terms of type and style (*bentuk dan cara*). The Malay *tudung* is made to fit and is usually of better material than ours, which is just a simple scarf loosely tied around the head and neck.

(Interview, Alim, Religious Teacher/Community Leader, 25 October 2011).

Alim's comment about Malays being "more refined" in speech and dress than the Baweanese reflects a long perceived notion of the "civilizing process" of Malayness, as noted by Milner (2011, p. 200) in the case of the "Orang Laut" in the Riau (Wee 2005, p. 6, 1988) and the Muslims in Sabah (Yamamoto 2004, p. 248).

Given their familiarity with Malay customs, it is thus not surprising that many Baweanese, including those who enter via Riau, blend easily into the Malay community. "They are very good at imitating Malay ways (*Mereka pandai tiru cara orang Melayu*)", marvels a KL Malay taxi driver. "I can spot Indonesian passengers immediately, but not the Baweanese; even if they are newly arrived they speak just like us Malays!" (Interview, 19 October 2011).

Language, Ethnicity and Inter-marriage

In addition to geographical and ethnic rerouting via Riau, other key factors which assist Baweanese acculturation and assimilation are a common language, the broad and flexible State definition of Malay, and intermarriage.

A common language fosters acculturation. While the immigrant generation speaks the Baweanese dialect at home and within their community, they use Malay at the workplace and to communicate with Malays. Their children, who attend Malay-dominated Malay-medium national schools, also speak Malay with family and friends. Most children understand but do not speak their community dialect. Thus socialization in school and fluency in Malay are additional factors fostering Baweanese acculturation into Malay society (Pillai 2005, pp. 167–96).

The broad and flexible nature of the concept "Malay", which captures a whole range of ethnic groups, also facilitates Indonesian settlement in Malaysia. The concept has its roots in colonialism since "the very simplicity of British categorisation of Malayan society served to extend the boundaries of Melayu" (Andaya and Andaya 1982, p. 180).

Another factor contributing to assimilation is intermarriage. Most immigrants and the locally born first generation marry within the Baweanese community due to shared residential locations, social interaction, and arranged marriages. However, among the second generation, that is, the grandchildren of immigrant settlers, intermarriage with Malays is contributing to assimilation into the Malay community. It is estimated that about 75 per cent of the second generation today marry Malays they meet in school, university and the workplace. Most of the second generation speak only Malay and hardly any of them speak Baweanese, though a few can understand it. All members of the second generation possess Malaysian citizenship, are fully recognized by the State as Malays, and therefore see themselves as Malays. "Unlike the earlier generations they are very confident, and are not ashamed to say they are of Baweanese background. Even their Malay spouses are exposed to Baweanese culture!" explains Azmi. (Interview, Azmi, 19 October 2011, Gombak).

"Mereka Sayang Kita": Occupying Malay Spaces

The Baweanese successfully harnessed their cultural resources to emigrate from their peripheral rural, subsistence-based Baweanese ethnic space in Indonesia (Ali 1996, pp. 29–30) into a core industrial-urban wage-earning Malay ethnic space within Malaysia. This was achieved by positioning themselves in occupational and residential spaces vacated by Malays, and creating co-dependency rather than competition with them.

Occupationally, they first took up unskilled low-wage jobs shunned by Malaysians. A 1999–2000 study showed that more than two-thirds of a sample of immigrants who entered in 1975–85 began their lives in Malaysia as unskilled construction workers before graduating into skilled workers or sub-contractors (Pillai, 2005). However subsequent generations — depending on their nationality status and education — have been more occupationally mobile. Those who were Malaysian-born, domiciled and educated have enjoyed relatively better education and careers. In contrast, the Baweanese-born often experienced disruptions in their schooling and careers due to family mobility and delays in obtaining PR and citizenship. As a result most foreign-born males hold unskilled jobs in offices, factories and workshops, while females usually work in the services sector — as sales staff in supermarkets, for example (Group Discussion, Community Leaders, 14 July 2010).

In terms of residential locations newly-arrived Baweanese immigrants usually rent squatter homes from Malays, who tend to gradually relocate from squatter areas to low-cost public housing as immigrant numbers increase. Unlike other Indonesian immigrants who usually live in ethnic clusters, the Baweanese prefer to live within Malay squatter settlements upon initial entry. A community leader explains:

> We seldom stay with other Indonesians. We either live in mixed Malay-Baweanese settlements or in pure Baweanese villages, which are common in Balakong and Gombak. Our long and virtually unbroken immigration link during both the colonial and post-colonial period has resulted in strong networks and group solidarity, which makes it easier for us to be settled here. We are settlers! We have families and homes here, unlike recent Indonesian Javanese and Minangkabau immigrants. They are sojourners! They have no links with the Malays of Javanese and Minangkabau ancestry. We however have very close links with Malays of Baweanese origin, especially those who came in 1975–85, and those who have been here for generations, most of whom are happy to acknowledge our common ancestry. They are fond of us (*Mereka sayang kita*)! In addition, compared to other Indonesians, we have much better ties with Malays because of our religious connections with them.
>
> (Community Leader, Group Discussion, 14 July 2010).

In contrast to certain Indonesian sub-groups that are sometimes unfairly portrayed as trouble-makers, the Baweanese are generally regarded by Malays as religious, law abiding, trustworthy and helpful. The Baweanese themselves are aware of their favourable image, and therefore seek to harness these positive stereotypes to cultivate close links with Malays, especially influential Malays who can assist them with residence status, housing and jobs (Pillai 2005). In some cases they also look to the Malays to protect them, as another Baweanese leader confirms:

> Unlike other Indonesians, we Baweanese choose to live with Malays. We seek protection (*minta perlindungan*) from them. For example, when I first arrived my father introduced me to the Malay village chief, an influential man who could help me in case I got into any kind of trouble, especially with the police.
>
> (Community Leader, Group Discussion, 14 July 2010).

Within the Klang Valley many newly settled Baweanese live in Kuala Lumpur's sprawling Malay-dominated suburban districts of Gombak, Ulu Klang and Sungei Chinchin in the north, Balakong in the south and Kuala Selangor in the west. In Gombak they are mostly settled in Baweanese or mixed Malay-Baweanese settlements, while in Balakong alone there are an estimated three to four thousand Baweanese individuals, including one village, Taman Setia, which is completely Baweanese (Group Discussion, Community Leaders, 14 July 2010).

Up to half the Baweanese are said to own the land and houses where they live. These mostly comprise self-built spacious two-storey terrace houses on both lease and freehold Malay reserve land bought from Malays. "Those who have not obtained their citizenship yet purchase the land from Malays thorough Baweanese relatives who are citizens. They later transfer the property to children or grandchildren who are citizens," said businessman Azmi, who owns a double-story terrace in Taman Harmonis, Gombak (Interview, Azmi, 19 October 2011).

Creating Symbiotic Ties with Malays

Two studies have shown that the Baweanese — especially those living in mixed Malay-Baweanese villages — recognize the critical role of Malays as power-brokers and therefore strive to cultivate symbiotic economic, political and religious relationships with them (Pillai 2005, pp. 359–63 and Ali 1998, p. 30).

Economically the Baweanese are important as tenants, customers, and workers to Malay landowners, house-owners and businessmen. Some long-settled Malay squatters rent or sell houses built illegally on government land to Baweanese, and provide extensions of electricity and water supplies to them (Ali 1998, p. 30). These Malay squatters had in earlier years harnessed their political strength as citizens to negotiate with local authorities to obtain electricity and water for themselves. Other Malays, who have licences to run businesses, find that Indonesians not only make reliable workers but form an important customer base in their villages (Pillai, 2005, pp. 359–63). Baharuddin, a Baweanese immigrant in Kaska, explains how they also cultivated ties with Malay leaders to secure their future:

> When I first arrived here in 1975 I came with three new migrant families, in addition to ten other migrant families with blue identity cards. A

Baweanese named Pak Ali started an UMNO branch and competed for the loyalty of villagers against Pak Razak, the Malay community head and the leader of another (the original) UMNO branch. Pak Ali, who was an office worker, had the advantage of speaking the Baweanese language, which was useful in making him close to the Baweanese migrants. He helped the Baweanese community organize their weddings, funerals, and build their *surau*. He was also the head of the *surau*. But most of us Indonesians followed Pak Razak because he was the village head (*ketua kampung*) and was recognized by the government as such. He could help us.

Baharuddin, Security Guard (Interviews, June 1998, March, May 1999).

The Baweanese make themselves indispensable to Malays by performing a number of critical roles — as religious tutors to their children, *bomoh*, and construction workers who readily help repair or renovate Malay houses (Pillai 2005). By far the most influential of these are the religious tutors, as noted by a number of scholars. While Shamsul (1964, p. 181) and Junipa (1992, p. 93) emphasize the common religious bond between Indonesians and Malays, others note that the Baweanese role as religious teachers gains them respect and facilitates their integration into the Malay community (Ali 1996, p. 40; Pillai 2005, p. 432). In addition, Jamilah Ariffin (1995, pp. 130–33) observes that Baweanese are perceived by Malays as religious and law-abiding, while Mariam Ali (1998, p. 24) says the Baweanese harness Islam to facilitate "entry into Malayness".

A clear example is Alim, the Baweanese religious teacher in Kaska who has a degree in religious studies and gave free religious classes as a "service" to thirty Malay children living nearby to his house soon after immigrating to Malaysia. He also taught voluntarily at a *surau*, with the students and parents only paying for electricity costs. He gained deep respect among the Malays through these efforts (Pillai 2005, p. 215).

In addition to tutoring Malay children, the Baweanese in Kaska consolidated their ties to the Malay community by electing influential Malays to head the *suraus* in the immigrant quarter of the village (Pillai 2005, pp. 359–63). Though the majority — about 70 per cent — who frequent the *suraus* were Baweanese, the chairman of the *surau* committee was almost always Malay. Alim, the religious teacher, explains why:

We always elect Malay chairmen because the Malays are influential. They can help us. For example, if we want water or electricity we always go via the Malays. There are very few Malays in our area (of the village), but those who are here are also squatters and like us they too need water and electricity. So we apply for these utilities under their name. While they help us this way, the Malays, on the other hand, look up to us Baweanese for Islamic education, or for help with various chores like organizing a feast (*kenduri*).

(Interview, Alim, Kaska, Petaling Jaya, Selangor,
6 May 1998, in Pillai 2005, p. 360).

In 1998 there were five such private Indonesian prayer houses or *suraus*, four built and managed by the Baweanese community in Kaska. Since the Baweanese have no formal organizational structure or community centres of their own, these *suraus* perform a variety of functions. In addition to being places of worship, they are symbols of religiosity, venues for weddings and funerals, centres for children's religious education, a site for various religious celebrations and a centre for information exchange, particularly on employment. Each *surau* has a committee which organizes social and religious events, but they also have the ability to mobilize immigrants on wider issues related to the State, such as housing (Pillai 2005, pp. 300–302).

FROM BAWEANESE TO MALAY: THE LONG JOURNEY

The mobility of the Baweanese is facilitated by a long history of emigration, religious institutions such as boarding schools, step-migration, and ethnic rerouting via the Riau Islands. Their settlement and acculturation has been hastened by their ability to fill jobs and residential spaces vacated by Malays, and their symbiotic relationships with them. Despite these efforts the Baweanese take several generations to reach their ultimate goal: to be Malaysian citizens classified as Malays.

In terms of nationality status, recent Baweanese immigrants can be classified into three groups. The first is the 1975–85 cohorts comprising the estimated 4,000 immigrant settlers. The second group — the largest — comprises the Indonesian and Malaysian-born children and grandchildren of these immigrants. The Indonesian-born children had to endure a long wait for Permanent Residence (PR) and citizenship, while the locally born obtained Malaysian citizenship upon birth. The third group are post-1990 immigrants who entered as temporary foreign workers with work permits; most comprise relatives and friends of the 1975–85 cohorts. We will now examine the process through which the first and second groups — the immigrant settlers, and their children and grandchildren — became

Permanent Residents (PRs), Malaysian citizens, and were finally recognized as Malays.

Immigrant Settlers: Malaysian PR's, Indonesian citizens

The 1975–85 cohorts of Baweanese immigrants entered and obtained Malaysian PR status with ease, but remained Indonesian citizens. A 1999 sample survey of 100 Indonesian immigrants in Kaska shows that ease of entry and settlement was related to high economic growth, labour demand and lax State policy during that period (Pillai 2005, pp. 167–96).[8]

A total of 92 per cent of the sample held Malaysian PR status, and two-thirds had entered Malaysia and obtained PR status in the period 1976–85, often within months of applying. For example, Baharuddin, a Baweanese security guard said: "After working for a year as a construction worker I applied for a red identity card. I obtained it within six months" (Interview, 22 June 1998 in Pillai 2005, p. 208). Another immigrant, Bohari, a Baweanese construction worker, reported: "In 1984, within two years of first immigrating, I applied for and obtained my red identity card" (Interview, 15 December 1998, in Pillai 2005, p. 221) (A red identity card is provided to PRs to distinguish them from citizens, who hold blue cards).

Within five years of obtaining their PR most of these immigrants applied for Malaysian citizenship, but for almost two decades until 2008 very few applications were processed. Without citizenship — a prerequisite to buying or renting affordable public housing — many are forced to live in the squatter settlements. Non-citizens also face problems getting their children into public schools and obtaining textbook loans[9] for them. A young man explains:

> There are many advantages in becoming a citizen; unlike a PR you are not barred from buying houses costing below RM250,000, buying land, or end up paying higher medical fees (RM2,000 maternity fees in the University Hospital compared to RM500 for Malaysians, for example). In education, the chances of getting a university place or a scholarship are less if you are a PR compared to (being) a citizen.
>
> (Hamzah, Office Administrator, Interviews, 8, 15, 17 May 1999).

The lack of housing and education access discouraged many from establishing deeper social roots in Malaysia. They therefore maintained transnational economic and political links — working and living in Malaysia, owning property in Indonesia and voting in elections there — while retaining a strong Baweanese identity (Pillai 2005, pp. 167–96). Despite their transnational links, a chain migration pattern and full family formations occurred, with single males entering first, joined later by wives and children. More than 80 per cent of those surveyed had Baweanese-born spouses, three quarters with Malaysian PR (Pillai 2005, pp. 172–74).

According to community leaders many of these 1975–85 immigrant settlers reapplied for citizenship after 2008, and by September 2011 about half of the surviving 4,000 original immigrant settlers had been granted citizenship (Group Discussion, Community Leaders, 14 July 2010. This information was cross-checked and reconfirmed with Alim, a religious teacher and community leader interviewed on 24 and 25 October 2011 in Sungei Buloh, and with Azmi, a respected and well-informed Baweanese businessman, interviewed on 19 October 2011 in Gombak, Kuala Lumpur).

"Citizenship for PRs was 'part-open' during (Prime Minister) Mahathir's time (1981–2003), shut during Badawi's time (2003–09), and is now open again during Najib's premiership," states a Baweanese community leader (Community Leader, Group Discussion, 14 July 2010). He was referring to the Najib Administration's policy of processing long-outstanding applications for citizenship, particularly for long-settled foreigners with families here. Under the programme, identity cards were also issued to long-settled Malays, Chinese, Indians and East Malaysians who did not possess these documents due to improper application, ignorance or remote residence (*The Star*, 7 April 2008 and MySinchew, 28 September 2009).[10]

First Generation: Malaysian Citizens "Of Indonesian Descent"

The first generation comprise the children of the immigrant settlers, and are mostly locally-born persons who became citizens upon birth. The key problem faced by this group is that despite their relative poverty they are not eligible for affirmative assistance aimed at Malays. This is because while their identity cards identify them as Malay Muslims, their birth certificates identify them differently — as people of Indonesian descent (*keturunan Indonesia*). Only the children of the first generation — namely the grandchildren of the immigrant settlers — are recognized as Malays. As one community leader puts it:

> Only the grandchildren of the immigrant generation will be able to remove the label *Keturunan Indonesia* (of Indonesian descent) from their birth certificates. It takes two generations! In the meantime we are not considered *bumiputeras* and are not entitled to benefits given to *bumiputeras*. Our children often have problems related to public university entry, choice of courses and eligibility for scholarships and loans.
>
> (Community Leader, Group Discussion, 14 July 2010).

A Baweanese businessman recalls a case of a group of *Baweanese* students who qualified and were accepted into a MARA (Majlis Amanah Rakyat) college in Malacca, but upon arrival were told they were not eligible due to their Indonesian parentage. However he concedes that this may not be the norm:

> One of my employees sons obtained 'A' grade passes in all his subjects for his school-leaving certificate and managed to get accepted into a MARA college. When the college authorities discovered his background they tried to withdraw the offer. But the boy pleaded. "It's me not my father who needs an education. Please don't discriminate against me," he told the authorities. They allowed him to stay.
>
> (Interview, businessman Azmi, Gombak, 19 October 2011).

Given the dominance of ethnicity in Malaysian life and the difficulties they face in being recognized as Malays eligible for affirmative action, it is not surprising that immigrant settlers and the first generation harness their multiple identities to gain social acceptance by the Malay community and official recognition by the State. Socially the Baweanese are fully conscious of the fact that they are respected by Malays, and always identify themselves to Malays as "Indonesians of Baweanese origin". As one middle-aged first-generation Baweanese puts it:

> If I enter a Baweanese-dominated settlement I identify myself as Baweanese. If I meet other Indonesians I say I am Baweanese, and if it's Malays I say I am an Indonesian of Baweanese origin. But when I meet non-Malays I just say I am Indonesian.
>
> (Community Leader, Group Discussion, 14 July 2010).

Relations with the State are complicated for both the immigrant and first generation, both of whom are classified as "Malay-Muslims" in their identity cards but of "Indonesian descent" in their birth certificates. It can be especially tricky when the State requires information on their ethnic background. For example Hamzah, aged twenty-seven, a Baweanese office assistant who is Indonesian-born and has Malaysian PR, says:

> In forms, when they ask me to classify my ethnicity i.e. whether I am a *bumiputera* or come under "Others", I mark myself as *bumiputera*. But it's when they ask for *keturunan* (descent) that I get confused. I usually write "Indonesian".
>
> (Interview, 15 May 1999, in Pillai 2005, p. 252).

Lokman, the Baweanese *bomoh* said he has five different "identities", and chose one depending on choices provided in official application forms. He considers himself having Bawean ethnicity and Indonesian citizenship, but marks either *Melayu* or Malaysian on application forms, depending on the choices available. Asked to explain, he said: "I have multiple identities. I am Baweanese, Indonesian, Muslim, *Orang Jawa Timur* (Eastern Javanese) and from Perkalongan in Bawean!" (Interview, 30 September 1999, in Pillai 2005 p. 267).[11]

The Second Generation: Malaysian and "Malay"

The second generation — the grandchildren of the immigrant settlers — are local-born Malaysian citizens who have studied, lived and worked locally. Since their parents are citizens identified as Malays in their identity cards, the second generation is recognized by the State as Malays in both their identity cards and birth certificates. Being settled in Malaysia and secure in both their nationality status and social identity, they tend to perform better at school and at work and enjoy higher self-confidence and occupational and social mobility. Many meet Malays at university or the workplace, and inter-marry and assimilate fully into the Malay community. They become, for all intents and purposes, Malay. For this generation the journey from Baweanese to Malay is finally complete. Hamzah, the young Baweanese, responds thoughtfully when asked how different his generation is from his parents:

> I think our culture, like the Malay and Chinese culture, is undergoing change and the process of *modenasasi* (modernization). The mentality of teenage Baweanese today is so different. When I was younger, I was very aloof with friends, and shy. But the Baweanese teenagers today are very "advanced". They look just like the Malay youths. The "Pan-Asian" looks

are fashionable. If you look at their fashion and music, you will not guess
they are Baweanese. They look more *Malaysian* [his emphasis] rather than
Baweanese or Malays. They can wear the *cheongsam* (Chinese dress), the
baju kurung, go to the disco (and yes, eat at McDonald's!)

Hamzah, 27, Office Administrator (Life History Interviews:
15 May 1999. Meetings: 8 May 1999 and 17 May 1999).

Hamzah's statement that the new generation has changed, and that
"....the Baweanese teenagers today are very 'advanced'....They look just
like the Malay youths," is again a clear expression of the "civilizing"
influence of Malayness noted earlier in the case of Baweanese and
Orang Laut in the Riau Islands and Muslims in Sabah. His comments
about Baweanese looking "Pan-Asian" and "Malaysian" reflect his
consciousness of cultural influences emanating from a globalizing
multi-ethnic society.

CONCLUSION

Compared to the four other ethnic minorities discussed in this book, the
Baweanese have had a different experience of immigration, acculturation
and assimilation. Unlike the other groups, most of whom arrived in the
pre-colonial period, the Baweanese first entered the Peninsula during
the colonial period. Despite being relative late-comers, their immigration
was facilitated by maritime links, open boundaries and free movement
during that period, while the broad legal and cultural definition of Malay
enabled them to subsume a Malay identity. Though closed borders in the
post-colonial period reduced Indonesian entry, the Baweanese flow has
persisted, with many eventually settling in Malaysia.

Various factors explain the persistence of Baweanese immigration.
Within tiny Bawean Island out-migration continued due to the island's
ethnic, geographical, and economic marginalization in the huge Indonesian
archipelago. The Baweanese overcame post-colonial borders through
geographical and ethnic rerouting via the strategically located "Malay"
Riau Islands. The concept of *merantau* (circular migration) and their strong
Islamic beliefs serve as powerful ideological justifications for mobility.
The placement of children of immigrants in religious boarding schools
on the island has also served to culturally reproduce the social tradition
of migration in each succeeding generation.

Within Malaysia, their assimilation into Malay society has been aided by their astute use of cultural resources. Upon entry they successfully occupied vacant occupational niches in Malaysia and residential and cultural spaces in Malay areas. They also created symbiotic links with Malays by presenting themselves as devout and trustworthy Muslim workers and religious teachers.

Unlike recent Indonesian temporary foreign workers, most of whom are non-Baweanese single males (and increasingly, females) many Baweanese immigrants are permanent settlers, with full family formations. Being relatively poor working-class immigrants, they strive to change their citizenship from "Indonesian" to "Malaysian", and their ethnic status from "Baweanese" to "*bumiputera*" ("Malay") to gain access to State-linked educational, occupational and economic opportunities. Thus while ethnicity is defined and delineated by the State, at the individual level it is also a personal political and economic choice.

However their ethnic journey from "Indonesian" to "Malay" is a long and difficult one. Both the post-colonial immigrant settlers and their children are regarded by the State as people of Indonesian ancestry; only the second generation — the grandchildren of immigrant-settlers — are able to register as Malays in both their birth certificates and identity cards. This gives them access to State-linked educational and occupational opportunities, improves their social and geographical mobility, and increases their prospects of assimilating into the Malay community.

For the Baweanese, as with other Muslim groups in Malaysia, the process of becoming Malay clearly illustrates the fluidity of the concept of ethnicity, particularly Malay ethnicity. In Indonesia "Malay" is categorized as a "*suku bangsa*" or ethnic group, which is less inclusive than the broader term "*bangsa*" or "people" used in Malaysia.

"The category Malay brings together many peoples, many histories", states Anthony Milner, a leading historian, who prefers the term "civilization" rather than ethnicity to describe "Malay" because the category is so open and broad (Milner 2011, pp. 10–11, 196, 12–13). While the legal definition of "Malay" in Malaysia is clear, in the region as a whole the concept of "Malay" is highly contested, its meaning varying over time, place and situations. Moreover the process of "becoming Malay" continues, encompassing Malay-speaking Muslims such as Orang Asli in the Peninsula, the native peoples of Sabah and Sarawak, and Bugis,

Minangkabau, Javanese, Baweanese, Bataks and Achehnese in the region (Milner 2011, pp. 10–11, 12–13, 196).

Perhaps the heterogenous nature of Malay ethnicity is most beautifully captured in a poem by the respected Malaysian poet Usman Awang:

> Melayu di tanah Semanjung luas maknanya:
> Jawa itu Melayu,
> Bugis itu Melayu,
> Banjar juga desebut Melayu,
> Minangkabau memang Melayu,
> Keturunan Acheh adalah Melayu,
> Jakun dan Sakai asli Melayu,
> Arab dan Pakistani, semua Melayu,
> Mamak dan Malbari serap ke Melayu,
> Malah mualaf bertakrif Melayu
>   (Excerpt from "Melayu", by Usman Awang,
>   in Muhriz, 2013, p. 245)

APPENDIX 5.1
SOURCES OF INDONESIAN IMMIGRATION,
COLONIAL PERIOD 1850–1957

Contract Workers

Contract labour was probably the single largest source of Indonesian migrant labour in colonial times. After 1870 recruiters sent Javanese contract workers abroad, particularly to the Peninsula and Surinam, but also to New Caledonia, Thailand (Siam), Sabah (North Borneo), Sarawak, Vietnam (Cocin China) and Australia (Hugo 1993, p. 37). In the early stages of the rubber industry's development in the late nineteenth and early twentieth century, these Javanese contract workers were recruited through European firms in Java. Although regarded as hardworking and compatible with Malays, not many were recruited compared to Indian plantation labour because the Dutch imposed strict controls on Javanese labour recruitment. In addition to long delays, the recruitment of Javanese cost two or three times more than Indians (Sandhu 1969, p. 56).

Migrant Farmers/Settlers

In a bid to increase the peasant population and food supply in Selangor, the British also encouraged the entry of land settlers from present day Indonesia. Thousands of Javanese, Sumatrans and Outer Islanders arrived in groups and applied for State land. The British provided rent remissions and small loans to encourage settlement in the coastal districts of Selangor. By 1886, two-thirds of the Malay population of Selangor comprised immigrants from Indonesia (Sadka, 1968, pp. 327–28).

Independent Migrants via Singapore Pilgrim Brokers

A third source of Indonesian entry comprised individual, independent migrants who came via Singapore-based pilgrim brokers. Dutch restrictions on the Mecca pilgrimage led to between 2,000–7,000 Javanese per year taking an alternative route via Singapore between the mid-nineteenth century and 1910. In addition to assisting direct migrants, these pilgrim brokers also recruited bonded labourers (known as *orang tebusan*), who cleared land in neighbouring Johor for Malay or Javanese employers. Between 1886 and 1890, an estimated 21,000 Javanese labourers signed contracts with the Singapore Chinese Protectorate to work on rubber estates. After 1910 many stayed on to open up land and settle in Johor (Roff 1967, pp. 36–39).

The Number of Indonesian Migrants

As a result of contract movements, by 1931 there were almost 90,000 Java-born persons in Malaya (Shamsul 1967, p. 280) and 170,000 ethnic Javanese (Volkstelling, Population Census, 1936 pp. VIII, 45 as quoted in Hugo 1993, p. 70). This was in addition to the movement of Minangkabau, Batak, Bugis, Banjarese and Baweanese. The 1931 census estimated that 244,000 of the 594,000 Malays in the Federated Malay States were either first-generation Indonesian immigrants or descendants of immigrants who entered Malaya between 1891 and 1931 (Ooi 1963, p. 119).

However, Shamsul (1967, p. 284) has cautioned that although Indonesian migration occurred from ancient times it was not numerically significant until British rule, and even then was relatively small compared to Chinese and Indian entry. In addition, it was mainly confined to the Federated Malay States (FMS) as well as Johor, Selangor and Singapore, but not to the whole of Malaya. The northern and eastern coast of the Peninsula comprising the Unfederated Malay States — where Malays were most numerous — was little affected by Indonesian migration (Shamsul 1967, p. 284).

Between 1911 and 1957 the Indonesian population never exceeded 15 per cent of the total Malayan population and was more than 50 per cent in one state (Johor) only once, in 1931. Elsewhere and at other times the Malays remained the majority (Shamsul 1967, pp. 284–85).

The rate of increase of the Indonesian population in Peninsular Malaysia in 1947–57 was only 5.8 per cent. This was partly due to government immigration restrictions and also because children of Indonesian parentage were enumerated as Malays (Shamsul 1967, p. 279).

APPENDIX 5.2
BAWEANESE LIFE-HISTORIES

No. 1: Baharuddin, 49, Security Guard[1]

Baharuddin, who claims he is forty-nine, is a thin, wily, fast-talking and fast-moving man who now works as a security guard. It was difficult to fix an appointment to meet him, mainly because of his long twelve-hour workdays, except Saturdays, when he had family chores. With his metal-rimmed spectacles he looks more like an intellectual than a security guard; he does not give himself away easily. Indeed, I got the feeling that he was always in "control" of our discussion. He was also quietly determined that I reciprocate his help by being of service to his community. He was especially interested in my being an advocate in persuading the authorities to cater to the housing needs of migrants; I did later mention his request to the local State Assemblyman. He was very cooperative and courteous, but despite several inquiries, there were inconsistencies in key dates in his life history. I did not press too hard; I assumed this was because, like many in his time, he had possibly under-stated his age (to postpone retirement), or just could not remember.

Early life: I have been here for twenty-five years, and have four kids aged twenty and below. And one wife! I was actually born in Singapore but I followed my parents back to Bawean after the war. [If he was correct about being born before the war he would have to be more than 49 years old.] My father inherited land from my grandfather who had passed away, and so my father decided to return to Bawean to take care of the land.

I then grew up in a *pondok pesantren* in Kediri in Java Timor. While I was still studying there, poverty forced my father to migrate to Pulau Belitong in search of work. I had to stop schooling because there was no money for fees, and had to find work. I had a sister and brother-in-law in Surabaya, and so managed to find work in a glass factory there.

However, I lost my job in 1963 because of the economic crisis during Soekarno's rule, and returned to Bawean for one or two years. Then I went to Pulau Belitong to meet my dad and find work. In Bawean I held three jobs in succession. One was in an Indian shop called Bombay selling textiles, another as a security guard in a tin-mine, and a finally as a worker in a kaolin factory.

Migration to Malaysia: By working and saving, I managed to save enough to go to Tanjung Pinang in 1974, from where I applied for a passport to try to my luck in Singapore. In Singapore, I had my grandmother and many uncles and aunts who had settled there since the war. I had lived in Pasir Panjang where I helped a relative run a business. I then tried to trace my birth certificate through an Indian man who said he could help. But then I discovered that I was over-aged. My records were with the Registration Department, but it was no use. I was too old. So I lost all hope of settling in Singapore. So I said to myself, *Jom! Mari masuk Malaysia!* (OK I'll enter Malaysia!).

I came by train, and entered on a tourist visa for three or six months, I cannot remember. On arrival, I contacted a Pak Nazri and his son Encik Ahmad. Pak Nazri is also a Baweanese who came to Malaysia before the war. He had worked in Shell in Malaysia, and retired in Kaska in his son's home. My friends who came to Malaysia from Singapore recommended him; he was their contact. He told us to live in Kaska if we were coming to Malaysia.

Employment: When we arrived in 1975 this entire area was either rubber plantation or jungle being cleared for housing, so I realized I could get a job nearby. After working for a year as a construction worker I applied for a red identity card. I obtained it within six months.

I then worked as a security guard but lost my job after two or three years because they had a new rule which disallowed permanent residents from working as security guards — now the rule does not apply I think, since I see all sorts of foreign workers working as guards. Then for more than ten years I worked as a construction worker, helping to build Taman Tun Dr Ismail (an upmarket middle-class housing area). I specialized in steel reinforcement. Due to my age, I left the construction sector and went back to being a guard.

Village life in Malaysia: In the early years I was the unofficial head of the Indonesian community in the village. We had no problems with the Malays here. I worked well with the Malay village chief, and even helped out in his son's wedding. On two occasions we had a *gotong-royong* (cooperative venture) with the Malays to help them clear the Muslim graveyards. This was with a view towards our future. Even the police joined us in the *gotong-royong*. In this way we got to know the *bumiputera* community better.

When I first arrived here in 1975 I came with three new migrant families, in addition to ten other migrant families with blue identity cards. A Baweanese named Pak Ali started an UMNO branch and competed for the loyalty of villagers against Pak Razak, the Malay community head and the leader of another (the original) UMNO branch.

Pak Ali, who was an office worker, had the advantage of speaking the Baweanese language, which was useful in making him close to the Baweanese migrants. He helped the Baweanese community organize their weddings, funerals and build their *surau*. He was also the head of the *surau*.

But most of us Indonesians followed Pak Razak because he was the *ketua kampung* (village head) and was recognized by the government as such. He could help us. Pak Ali's UMNO branch, on the other hand, was not recognized by the government. So we used to follow Pak Razak in activities like *gotong-royong*. Pak Ali got upset by all this.

Do you know there is a very low crime rate here compared to other *kampungs* in the Klang Valley? This is because we have many respected Baweanese migrants here — and they help organize and give good guidance to villagers. You know, all these years I have never had any serious problems with my four kids. One particular year we even invited the Indonesian Consul here to address us during *Maulud Nabi* (Prophet Muhammad's Birthday) celebrations. He advised us to take care, and asked the village head to look after our interests too. Among all the villages in Kuala Lumpur, Kaska has four *suraus* — the largest number of *suraus* [prior to the mid-1999 demolishments]. There are three Indonesian-controlled *suraus*, one Malay surau, and one *masjid* (mosque).

Housing: Indonesians who are PRs are almost all squatters here, and eviction from their illegal homes poses a very serious problem. This is because they get very little compensation (RM500, compared to citizens who get RM7,500), no alternative housing like longhouses as in the case of Malaysians, and no eligibility for the low-cost houses which the private housing company is building on State land where our houses are currently located.

Relocating is problematic for many of us because our kids go to nearby schools and we work nearby. But we're red IC (PR) holders, so we have no choice but to move. Housing is our biggest worry. Many appeals have been made. Pak Razak the village head said in his speech during the *Maulud Nabi* celebrations: *"Sedangkan ayam pun ada rebannya"* (even chickens have their coops). Yet nothing has been done.

Reflection: Looking back at my experience of migration, the happiest part is that I was never unemployed. My biggest fear was the constant threat of eviction. Its harder finding alternative accommodation when you have two kids schooling nearby and your job requires you to live here. What really saddened me during the demolishment was that there was no one around to support us — we had no *persatuan* (association) to defend us, no one from the *Konsul Indonesia* (Indonesian Embassy), no one.........we were all alone.

No. 2: Alim, 36, Religious Teacher[2]

Alim, 36, a freelance religious teacher from Bawean, is urbane, articulate, and intellectual. His educational background (degree in Islamic Studies), occupation and dignified bearing make him stand out in the village. He is highly reflective, being conscious of his role and contribution to village life and community development. He sees himself as a person who expounds the role of Islam, knowledge and education in helping migrants adapt to their new environment. Being intellectual, he is probing and cautious, only consenting to narrate his own life history after first observing and inquiring about my interviews with other villagers, many of whom he had personally introduced to me. He was also a man of many parts; despite our friendship and many informal conversations he only revealed to me what he thought I should know, and that too after what appeared to be thorough preparation, an example of how respondents can be better prepared than researchers! Coming from a family background of religious teachers, he is deeply involved in religious affairs, is respected and liked by villagers, many of whose children he teaches, but at the same time he is discrete in socializing with the village folk. A handsome bachelor, he is now engaged to a Malay university student, but his world still remains essentially Indonesian, more specifically, Baweanese. Like most other Indonesians his interaction with local Malays appears to be limited, his closest friends being Indonesians.

My own background: I was born in Kg. Sukaoneng, Bawean. I come from a poor farming community. We used traditional farming methods, and received no subsidies. Most farmers had their own land, but many leased land from landowners. My father was landless, and so he worked for others living from hand to mouth (*kais pagi makan pagi, kais petang makan petang*). This was common; many in our village were poor — they needed the equivalent of RM5 per day, but they only earned RM1 or RM2.

My family's migration history: The Baweanese have a long history of migration. Most of them were fishermen and seafarers, brave men who travelled far in small *perahus* to earn their living. That is how they came to know Singapore and Malaysia. At first they went to Singapore — which during colonial days was quite open — and only later, after Singapore was closed to them and Malaysia more developed did they move here.

In the same way, many of our relatives had migrated to this region years ago. My mother's family all migrated to Batam and Malaysia years ago, just like my father's siblings, who moved to Malaysia and Singapore. My father first migrated here in the 1970s, and I came many years later. He was a very poor farmer in Bawean before coming here. We were so poor that I remember he could not pay my school fees and we could not even afford a radio in the house. He began life here as a construction worker, but also served as the *imam* of a Malay *surau* located near the tin-mining pool in Kaska, where he lived. My dad's father and brothers were also *imams* in Bawean. He had a younger brother who was a *kyai*, that is, a spiritual leader/guardian. His elder brother was a Sufi follower. This uncle was said to be so holy that he got a fever whenever he did not fast (*kena demam kalau tak puasa*).

My decision to migrate: Up to 1990, I had never thought of migrating. There were three reasons. Firstly, as we say, even if it rains gold in another country and it rains stones in our country, it is better to be at home (*hujan emas di-negeri orang, hujan batu di-negeri sendiri, lebih baik di-negeri sendiri*). Secondly, I realized that as a migrant, my individual freedom would be curtailed; I cannot vote, and must go through a whole set of new legal procedures. Thirdly, I felt my experience and expertise would not be fully utilized in the new environment.

Why then did you migrate? Family poverty, no other reason. My aging parents needed me, and I also needed to look after my sister's education. I had these two powerful, contradictory pressures on me — on the one hand to migrate for the reasons stated, on the other hand to stay and fulfil my dream to serve my *kampung* and community.

My grandfather runs a religious boarding school (*pondok pesantren*) and has established a foundation in our village which supports children's education and runs a mosque. The people there really need me. But in the end I decided I had to leave aside my own dreams for the sake of my family. It was hard at first, but maybe one day — though it's unlikely — I may go back. My dreams and hopes have changed since I came here. It is because of exposure and knowledge. Even though I am not there, from a long distance I still keep in touch with my people and occasionally send money to help. The money, including that collected from friends, is to help build or repair mosques, for example.

I first came here in 1991, with plans to study at the International Islamic University, not to settle in Malaysia. Moreover, I had not seen my dad for fifteen years because he had migrated (*merantau*) and I had been in the *pesantren* during that time. (I was studying at the Pesantren Lumajang in East Java from the age of 12, away from my family. My father too had studied at this same place when he was a boy).

I decided to join them because I had been away from my family for so long and I missed them. I realized that my parents had been working hard all these years to support me. From the age of 16, I had been teaching part-time to support my family and myself. I used to teach part-time right up till I was in university, despite having a Saudi government scholarship.

Entry into Malaysia: When I first arrived here to visit my parents in 1991, I had a shock. Over the years I had gazed at photos my parents had sent me. I saw photos of very nice, luxurious, big houses, with televisions and other amenities.

But I was quite shocked to discover how dirty it was in the squatter area where my father lived. I was not used to such squalour. In Jakarta I had always lived in neat, clean hostels and regularly visited the homes of middle-class people to give religious lessons to their children.

I had entered Malaysia in 1991 on a twenty-five-day tourist visa, and realized that as a visiting foreigner it was difficult for me to apply to the International Islamic University (IIU). So after only twenty-five days here I was forced to return to Jakarta. I decided to pursue my studies in Jakarta instead.

I returned to Malaysia in 1993 after graduating from the Ibn Al Saud University, an Arab-supported university in Jakarta. This time I came to Malaysia with a proper visa and decided to stay. Again, I wanted to further my studies at UIA, but by then my younger sister, who is a Malaysian citizen (having been born here), had obtained a place in the Mara Institute of Technology (a large government educational institution established to train *Bumiputeras*). She was not able to obtain a student loan to support herself. Since I already had a tertiary education in Indonesia, we decided that her studies took priority and my parents and I would support her education instead.

What work did you do when you arrived? The *surau* (village prayer house) then was very old. I had a vision of making it the centre of community activities, and I felt a good way to start would be to organize religious classes for Baweanese children in the village. So I arranged a timetable and began classes. Once the villagers saw that the *surau* had a number of activities going, they had a stake in its development and future and supported the idea of rebuilding it. So we managed to collect RM50 per family (a total of RM7,000 to 8,000) to rebuild the *surau*. Since we had so many construction workers with us, it was no problem at all — we rebuilt it with our own hands, in *gotong-royong* style. [He is referring here to a beautiful, small, blue and white tiled *surau*, which was demolished in May 1999 in the first phase of the privatized housing project.]

How did you feel when this *surau* you had helped build was demolished recently? I was emotionally ready for it. I didn't cry, though others did. God's will (*Takdir Tuhan*). The *surau* is just a material thing. Like I often tell the parents of my students, "it (the building) is only a material thing. Knowledge and skill are more important; it is ignorance that will imprison us" (*Benda sahaja. Ilmu dan pakaran lebih penting; kekurangan ilmu-lah yang akan penjarakan diri-sendiri*).

Aspirations/Hopes: I am already able to supplement my family's income and help my father. I hope to further my education and do more. Now I give religious lessons to schoolchildren in addition to a few adults, but in future I hope to teach at higher levels such as pre-university or even have students from the government and private sector. My aim is to contribute to human development in this country. Vision 2020 (Malaysia's aim of becoming a developed nation by 2020) cannot be achieved unless human beings are developed first. No matter how strong the institutions, if humans are dishonest or corrupt, the society will never develop.

What nationality do you consider yourself? [He answers immediately] I am different only in name — I am from Indonesia, but my ideal is the same — to develop the human being (*Nama saja lain — daripada Indonesia — tetapi wawasan-nya sama — untuk membangunkan manusia!*). I can serve mankind anywhere. In Islam the world is one. For me the migrant is like a bee. It travels far and wide and does not disrupt, but nurtures the environment. The plants and flowers need the bee. It does not eat any impure, defiled matter but only the cleanest things, and it produces clean, pure honey. Bees are also very cooperative, and won't disturb others, but will attack if provoked. (The idea for this illustration, he informs me, is drawn from The Holy Koran, Surat Annahal, Ayat 68–69).

I am never shy about my origins and background though I know many people have prejudices about us (Indonesians). As long as we serve society well we will always be accepted. But there are many other Indonesians I know who are very shy to reveal their background and identity. The reason? They are afraid they will be attacked (*"diserang"*) by the many prejudices people have about Indonesians.

Social/Political life compared: Both are not very different from home. We manage to get along with Malays, even though some of them may have prejudices about us. [His short response to this important question was untypical of his usually longer, more reflective answers, but I did not press him further.]

Working life compared: Big difference! More money here, about four or five times more after considering the exchange rate differential. For giving tuition twice a week I can earn RM150 per month here; three or four times more than what I earned for the same work in Jakarta ten years ago.

Lowest point in migration experience: When I got a warning from the Immigration Department during my second visit in 1992. My visa expired after three months; I had already got a two-week extension, and it could not be extended further. I was therefore forced to leave for Singapore and then to Batam, where I lived with my maternal grandma for a month.

Contact/Communication with home: The phone is faster and more direct. There's even a direct line to my *kampung* now. We call each other once a month or so. We talk about health, money, things like that. Those days I used to write once a month, not now though. In terms of keeping up with home news, I do read Indonesian magazines like *Tempo*, *Panji Mashyarakat*, and *Gatra*, which I buy from the Chow Kit area of Kuala Lumpur.

Any interest by others in migrating here too? I do get inquiries off and on from relatives and friends who know I am here, and who know I have a car. [Again, a brief response.]

No. 3: Hamzah, 27, Office Administrator[3]

A 27-year-old bachelor, Hamzah was born in Bawean but brought up and educated in Malaysia since the age of seven. He works as an administrator in a small insurance agency, where he also acts as accounts clerk and office boy. A quiet, unassuming youth with a Diploma in Graphic Design and considerable computer skills, he is over-qualified for the current job, but says he sticks to it because of family circumstances. Regarded by some villagers as among the more educated youths with a white-collar job, he was one of the informal leaders who helped the community take their house eviction issue to the courts, a task he found challenging. He now seeks to improve his own career and life prospects and support his aged, poor parents. A helpful informant about village activities, we had known each other for almost a year, meeting often in coffeeshops or chatting on the phone. His life history was compiled in two interviews.

Family migration history: My father migrated with his friends, first to Singapore by boat and then to Malaysia. He came in 1969 and I came a decade later. I entered Malaysia with my mum and a group from our *kampung*. We came on a cargo ship called *Tempoh Mas* — I still remember its name — from Surabaya. Close to shore we shifted to a smaller boat and reached Singapore, where we lived at my grandmother's house. My grandmother had been in Singapore for many years. From Singapore in July 1999 I entered Malaysia legally, since my father was a PR by that time.

Childhood in Malaysia: I had a normal childhood. I used to bathe in the mining pool, which was present in our village in the early days. I had many friends who were Malaysians. We played kites, I schooled with Malays. But I was late in school and entered Standard One (the first year of primary school) at the end of the year because I had lost my travel documents.

Schooling: My mum encouraged us to work hard. She said we had suffered a lot, and we had to work hard to have a better life. In school I was a prefect, and a class monitor. By the time I was in Standard Two or Three, I overcame my shyness about my background. My parents were uneducated and could not advise us on our career or which education stream — science or arts — to take. In secondary school I felt like any other boy — I mixed with everyone — even my girlfriend was Malay. I studied until Form Five in the Taman Tun Dr Ismail Secondary School [a relatively good school in a Malay upper middle-class residential area]. Later I went on to do my Form Six (pre-university) in Victoria Institution [a long established elite school in Kuala Lumpur].

Further education and employment: But my Form Six results were not good enough for university. I was in a dilemma about what course to do and where to go. I just followed everyone else, and managed to complete a Diploma in Graphic Design in a private college. Over the years, in addition to short stints within the advertising industry, I have worked as a temporary teacher, a salesman and a lawyer's clerk. I have been in thirteen jobs since school! I think what I lacked most was proper guidance in training and career choice. But I've stayed in my current job in the insurance industry for two years.

I want very much to further my education and get a better job, but family responsibilities make it necessary for me to have a job near home and help in the family business. My father is getting old, and I help him in his food stall every morning before I go to work.

[Information below is from a follow-up interview, July 1999]

As a boy of migrant origins, did you feel at home in school here? In school I felt it [as a migrant] a bit, especially when I was not eligible for textbook aid. In the early years, I did not want to say who I was because there used to be many prejudices against us. Nowadays I am proud to stay I am a Baweanese of Indonesian origin. This is because I realize that all human beings should be judged by their values and actions, not their background. Also, the image of Baweanese has improved. Previously, we were regarded only as construction workers; now many of us have improved professionally and some are doing even better than locals. Academically many got a number of A's in the Malaysian secondary school-leaving certificate (*Sijil Pelajaran Malaysia*) (SPM).

But it seems as if each ethnic sub-group or *suku* keeps very much to itself: We are like the Malaysians when they go overseas — they have the Kelantanese, Negri Sembilan and Johor Malays — each with their own groups. Baweanese tend to speak Baweanese dialect to each other, just like those from Madura would speak their own dialect, but we use Bahasa Malaysia to speak "across" to all Indonesians.

How did you get the job you hold now? There was an advertisement for an office boy in *The Malay Mail* (a daily English tabloid). When I applied I was very confident of getting the job because I had a lot of experience already.

Will you switch jobs if you could? Of course I would, but I remain in this job because it's five minutes from home. Also, this job is quite easy, so I have peace of mind; I do not bring work problems home.

Is it possible to tell me how much you earn, and how do you spend it? I earn RM1,000 per month; RM600 goes to my car loan, RM100 I save, and the rest for "rock and roll" (transport, petrol, eating out occasionally, incidental expenses).

Have you applied for citizenship? Yes, in 1998. I have to wait at least two years.

Why did you apply for citizenship? There are many advantages in becoming a citizen; unlike a PR you are not barred from buying houses costing below RM250,000, buying land, or end up paying higher medical fees (RM2,000 maternity fees in the University Hospital compared to RM500 for Malaysians, for example.) In education, the chances of getting a university place or a scholarship are less if you are a PR compared to a citizen [In Malaysia there is high demand and limited places in local public universities, and applications are processed using a points system; in addition to qualifications, ethnicity (and citizenship status) counts].

What race (bangsa) do you consider yourself? Bangsa Melayu. In forms, when they ask me to classify my ethnicity, that is, whether I am a Bumiputera or come under "Others", I mark myself as "Bumiputera". But it's when they ask for keturunan (descent) that I get confused. I usually write "Indonesian".

What is your biggest current problem? I can't leave my house, business, and kampung. I have to remain nearby to help my family.

[Asked how different his generation is, and whether he felt the same links to Bawean as his parents' generation, he responded with many thoughtful comments] Our culture is changing all the time. Our intentions are the same but our culture evolves. For example our weddings are the same, but the music is now very different from traditional Baweanese music. And instead of giving the bunga telor (traditionally a symbol of fertility) we now give a glass or a bar of soap. I think this is because people are competing to show how rich they are, what they can afford to give. An egg costs only 20 sen but a bar of Lux soap costs more. In many years' time, I think the gifts will become even more expensive.

I think our culture, like the Malay and Chinese culture, is undergoing change and the process of modenasasi (modernization). The mentality of teenage Baweanese today is so different. When I was younger, I was very aloof with friends, and shy. But the Baweanese teenagers today are very "advanced". They look just like the Malay youths. The "Pan-Asian" looks are fashionable. If you look at their fashion and music, you will not guess they are Baweanese. They look more *Malaysian* [his emphasis] rather than Baweanese or Malays. They can wear the *cheongsam*, the *baju kurung*, go to the disco, and yes, eat at McDonald's!

No. 4: Dzulkifli, 43, Despatch Clerk[4]

I first met Dzulkifli at a wedding in September 1998, where he was the chief cook. A stout, jolly man, he was quite proud of his role, and was always joking and laughing with guests. During the casual chat at the wedding feast he showed himself to be an articulate and amusing story-teller, as befits an ex-sailor. I managed to meet him again months after the wedding, but a subsequent interview was not possible because he was busy finding alternative accommodation after his squatter home was demolished.

Background: I am from Bawean. I am the eldest of four children, the only boy. I used to help supplement my family's income by fishing — but we earned just enough for subsistence (*kais pagi makan pagi*). From my younger days there were already many people in my village who had migrated to the region in search of jobs. As a teenager I had chatted with many elders, listening to their stories, to their advice. I was told even then about the importance of working hard, mixing well and choosing friends carefully.

Migration: I got married when I was about twenty years old and when I was about twenty-two, that is, in 1979, I decided to work in Singapore. By that time, most of my friends and relatives were working abroad in ships, and I was the only one at home; I didn't want to be left out. So I borrowed money from my mother-in-law to finance my travels. I followed a friend to Singapore. He had been there before. He advised me to pack just a few things — no cigarettes or drugs. We travelled to Jakarta, and from there flew to Singapore.

Relatives, including my father-in-law who was already settled in Singapore where he worked as a ferry driver, met me. I had no problems with immigration officials — when I told them I was there to visit relatives, they merely gave some advice about sticking to immigration rules. The very next day I was out looking for work at the seaside place where workers gather in search of employment. I helped a relative for the first month when I could not get a regular job.

Do you know we had migrant associations to help us? They ran *"perkalongan"* or migrant communal houses, each for people of a particular village. You got free board and lodging until you could repay. We still have such places at Datuk Keramat in Kuala Lumpur. The problem is those who stay in these places nowadays actually have relatives here; originally these places were meant for those without any relatives.

First job: After one month I managed to get a job as a deck hand on a tugboat. This was OK with me because I was used to working at sea. My workmates were Indonesians, not just Baweanese, but they were very helpful. It was good I mixed with others, because I learnt a lot.

However, we were unfortunate. After six months with the tugboat, we were stranded in Semarang after an accident en route to Kalimantan. I was penniless. We almost starved. My savings were all used up and I even had to cannibalize parts of the boat to get money. I managed to earn the trust of another boat-owner, and worked for a few weeks for him until my salary arrived from Singapore.

By the time I made my way back to Singapore via Tanjung Pinang, I was down to a shirt and a pair of trousers — I had sold off everything to finance the trip to Singapore. I told the Singapore Immigration my tale of woe, and after getting details of my Singapore address they gave me a one-month visa.

As soon as I reached home, my father-in-law — who did not know what happened — scolded me! I then related my ordeal to him — including how I lived on dried fish (no fisherman lives on dried fish!), and he understood. I cried when I read my desperate wife's letters to me. She asked if I had broken my promises. "Why had I not sent money or kept in touch with her and my two kids?" she asked.

Second job: I could not get another job for almost a month. I used to sit by the seaside crying, dreaming sometimes of working on a big ship. A fellow Baweanese helped with food and money then. Finally, I managed to get a job with a ship owned by Pacific International (PIL). It was a 12,000-tonne ship called the *Kota Rakyat*. My employer (*towkay*) applied for my work permit. I worked on this ship for six years, travelling to Penang, Calcutta, Colombo, Bombay, ports in Saudi Arabia and to Aden, South Africa, China and Taiwan. I send money home regularly, and got along with my workmates. I always remembered my father's advice: "If you want to be a migrant, always remember to keep your voice down, and never show off, even if you know more."

After six years on this ship, the boredom and homesickness drove me home. I had only returned home once during the six years and really missed my family. I returned to Bawean with 1.5 million rupiah in 1982–83. There was no work (there was little fish left in our seas), no entertainment, so I wanted to *merantau* again. I discussed it with my wife, who agreed, provided I was not away too long.

Eventually I took another loan and returned to Singapore, this time working for a tugboat collecting soil from Johor for reclamation work in Singapore. For six months I worked day and night, without any overtime pay, till I was — forgive me — "as dark as an Indian", as my father-in-law put it. When I wanted to quit, they promised more money and asked me to stay, but I bargained and instead got a free open-air ticket to Kuala Lumpur.

In Malaysia: I then entered Kuala Lumpur via Subang Airport on a tourist visa, and came straight to my niece's home here in Kampung Sungai Kayu Ara. When I mentioned the village, even the Malay taxi driver from the airport said: "Oh, the place where the Baweanese live."

No. 5: Lokman, 45, *Bomoh* (Mystic)[5]

Lokman, 45, was one of the first people I met in Kaska, and one of the first of the many Kaska residents I knew who had "graduated" from a squatter house in the village to his own house and land in Gombak, Kuala Lumpur. His role as the village mystic (bomoh), medicine man and counsellor, and his reputed access to VIP clients made him an unofficial village leader. He was a very busy man. I tried to interview him several times in 1998 when he was living in a large, old and dank squatter house in Kaska, but we were constantly interrupted by his five young children and his clients. They ranged from a sobbing Datin who telephoned with marital problems, an Indian worker collecting *ayer suci* (holy water), to a desperate looking red-eyed Chinese couple who arrived in a van. It was difficult to talk at length, but we managed to break the ice and build up a friendship. His "practice" was obviously successful, and by early 1999 he was busy supervising the construction of his own house. By mid-1999 when his squatter home was demolished he had moved to a concrete terrace house deep in Gombak, a sprawling semi-rural Malay-dominated Kuala Lumpur suburb. It had tiled floors, chandeliers, an air-conditioned hall and a leather sofa set. When I visited one rainy night in late 1999, his children were glued to a Chinese drama on TV; except for a brief visit from a neighbour reporting problems with a relatives' work permit, we were left alone. Only shrills from his pet birds, including the mystical merboks, punctuated our chit-chat about his life, Indonesian immigrants, and mysticism.

Background: I come from a family of five; I have four sisters, and am the only son. We were all-dependent on the land, and were not poor in the sense that we all had enough to eat. My father was always away from Bawean. He was a mystic and spent thirty-five years travelling in Madura and Java. He was mastering mysticism all those years. We never needed to send him money. He was self-sufficient.

Family migration history: When I was fifteen years old, being the second eldest and the only boy, I decided to lead the family by migrating to find work. I had six years of schooling by then. I moved to Jakarta and became apprenticed to a Minangkabau tailor. I worked for seven years and saved enough to support my family. I never once met my dad all those years. Then I moved to Surabaya in Java Timor, again working as a tailor. Here I finally met my father. On his advice

I decided to further my studies. He arranged for me to attend the Pondok Sabani in Madura under a *kyai* (religious scholar) named Haji Thabrani Abdul Aziz. I was already twenty-four then. I was chief cleaner of the *pondok* and always asked for permission to clean the graves of powerful individuals because I wanted to follow the tradition of my forefathers.

Migrating to Malaysia: After one year of study my mother urged me to help the family out by migrating to work in Malaysia. I had heard of people working in Malaysia, but had not planned to go there myself until she suggested it. So in 1978 I took the ship *Tempoh Mas* from Tanjung Priok near Jakarta to Tanjung Pinang in the Riau Islands, and from there travelled by ferry to Singapore. From Singapore I took the train to Malaysia. I entered as a tourist. At first I lived in Datuk Keramat with a friend (he was a neighbour in our *kampung* back home) but later my uncle (mother's younger brother) asked me to live in Kaska with him. He had come here a year or two earlier.

Employment History: My uncle was a leader of a team of construction workers — a *kepala* — and he took me on as a construction worker. I earned RM13 per day. That was equal to three days' wages at home then. Moreover things were cheap then. After three years as a construction worker I switched to working for a Chinese businessman. My job was to maintain potted plants in offices. I moved around to various offices on my motorbike doing this. But I found the pay too low, so I went back to construction, but did tailoring part-time to earn extra money. I even learnt to read building plans. I learnt this through my own efforts, not any kind of formal course or education.

In 1982 I married a girl from Bawean. In 1989 when I already had five children, I had an *ilhan* (a calling); I was not to do ordinary work but to take up the struggle of my ancestors....*saya di-perintah* (I had a calling). I listened to the prompting and subsequently meditated for two months at a *keramat* (holy place, one endowed with supernatural powers) in Pulau Besar, an island off Malacca. I had been on holiday there once in the 1980s and knew of it. This time I spent two months alone there, fasting and praying. Though it is crowded on weekends, it was quiet and I was alone on weekdays.

When I returned home people accused me of dabbling in black magic, but I was patient. I proved to them this was not true. I am a mystic and I practise mysticism. I have certain powers, which I use to help people. I don't know where I get it from, but there have been mystics in my family for fourteen generations. One of my children will inherit my powers.

Today I have many people who come to see me for help and advice and they range from ordinary people to VIPs like top police officers, and even a minister (whom he named). Some I meet here, others in Kaska, and some in top hotels, depending on who they are. I don't impose any fees. People just give me what they want. It could be anything from RM10 onwards. I never ask or specify the amount, but I have always had enough to feed, house and educate my children. I already own three houses now, which I have bought for my children.

Working here compared to Indonesia: Here you can earn and save more, build a house, buy a car. Like many migrants I came not to just survive but to do better/be successful (*bukan untuk cari makan tapi untuk cari kelebihan*).

Experiences that made you happy/sad here: I feel happy when I realize that in Malaysia you can work hard, earn money and succeed. But sad when I hear stories of family members back home, those ailing or dying, without us being there for them.

Hopes/Aspirations: To look after my children and educate them so that they will not have bitter experiences like me (*menjagakan anak-anak saya supaya mereka jangan ada pengalaman pahit seperti saya*). Life was hard for me in Jakarta.

How do you maintain contact with Bawean: Via the telephone once a month. They call us on reverse charge. They let go of their worries (by talking about it) (*mereka melepaskan rindu*).

What nationality (*bangsa*) do you consider yourself? Bawean, from *Kampung* Perkalongan.

Citizenship — *Warnanegara*? Indonesian.

How do you identify yourself when you fill up forms? Melayu or Malaysian, depending on what the form states (that is, the choices to tick).

How come you tick "Malay" when you say you are "Baweanese"? [Glaring at me, he asks, "do you know what the term 'Malay' constitutes"? "Yes," I reply, "I just wanted to hear your response — if you have more than one identity."] Yes, I understand what you mean. When you telephoned earlier and identified yourself, my five-year-old son who took the phone asked me if you were Christian! I have multiple identities. I am Baweanese, Indonesian, Muslim, *Orang Jawa Timur* (Eastern Javanese) and from Perkalongan in Bawean!

Life in Kaska village: When I first came here in 1978 there was no water or electricity. There was no electricity and lots of unemployment among Malays. The perception that we have a problem with the Malays stems from several factors. One is cultural. Just different ways of life. In the early years for example, we used to bathe in the mining pool here because there was no water. The Malays got upset. Many newly arrived Indonesians often drive motorbikes bare-bodied. In *kongsis* (communal houses in construction sites) it is common to see Indonesian women bathing with men. The men just wear suspenders. That's because the facilities are such that we have no choice. There is no other way to bathe. The Malays should show us how we should behave and we should follow…they say our dress and behaviour is bad, we bathe naked, etc. but they too did this before. The second reason is jealousy (of the success of the Indonesians). Some Malays say *kita bermaharajalela* (do as we like), operate unchecked — but this too is not true. Whatever we earn is *kerana hasil berdikari sendiri* (due to our own efforts).

You know, we Baweanese, like the Madurese and Javanese, are very closely knit, while those from Lombok and the Bugis are less so. The Baweanese built the RM15,000 *surau* in Kaska (the one later demolished) with our own hands, *gotong-royong* style, in just two weeks. Unlike many Baweanese settled here most Madurese come just to work, without their families, so they live in *kongsis*.

No. 6: Azmi, 39, Businessman[6]

I had heard so much about Azmi even before I met him. He seemed to be everything to everyone in the village. He was variously described as entrepreneur, community leader, role model, village historian and housing advisor. But it was next to impossible to catch him. He was reported living both in Kaska and in a newly constructed house in Gombak. Telephone calls to both homes went unanswered. Finally, someone gave me his mobile-phone number, and I managed to contact him. Even then, it took weeks before he was free to meet me; he was working day and night. He began his day at 4 a.m., buying fish at the wholesale market for his wife's stall. Then, from 6 a.m. to 7.45 a.m. he ran a school bus. After a quick breakfast, he was a building sub-contractor, between which he made two more school runs, at mid-day and in the late evening. As if three jobs were not enough, he worked as a video cameraman at weekends, covering weddings and religious ceremonies. I managed to meet him at 10 p.m. one night and was surprised to see how he had moved from a riverside squatter hut to a tastefully furnished semi-detached brick house. I expected to see another tired, prematurely aged migrant, but instead found a cool, calm and youngish looking man of thirty-nine who was happy to talk about himself.

Family Background: We had a bit of land, which we inherited. My father was a farmer. My paternal grandfather had migrated to Singapore in the early 1940s to escape the suffering of the Japanese Occupation. He got to Singapore on a boat and worked as a driver there. Some years later he divorced my grandmother and remarried. My father was actually keen on migrating to Singapore, but after the divorce he decided to go to Malaysia instead. My father first came here in 1974 as a construction worker. He lived in Kaska. Three years later my mum joined him. I was fifteen or sixteen years old then, and in school, but was forced to stop because we did not have enough money.

In fact my family's migration history goes back even further. You know, my maternal grandmother migrated to Malaysia during Indonesia's Dutch period. She came in a *perahu* (small boat) sometime in the 1920s. I think she came to join her husband and relatives. Most of the men worked as syces, tending to the horses in Kuala Lumpur's Turf Club, where the Twin Towers are now located. (Since horses were domesticated in Bawean, many early Bawenese migrants to Singapore and Malaysia worked in race-courses, and later as horse-carriage drivers and car drivers). My grandmother moved between Bawean and Singapore. I was told that in those days the *perahus* took forty days and nights for the trip. There were no engines until the 1970s. Everyone travelled via Singapore, and then took the train to Malaysia. The old Baweanese folk referred to Malaysia as *Selat* (The Straits).

When did you first think about migrating to Malaysia? I did not think about migrating at all until I was aged twenty. I married at nineteen and had planned to further my studies. Seven of us children were living with my grandma while my parents were working in Malaysia. I worked the land after marriage but I felt I would not *maju* (progress) as a farmer. So I decided to visit my parents in Malaysia, who had not been back for the last five years. I came with my wife. We did not have plans to stay — we just came to visit, but after a month here they advised us to stay on in Kaska.

What job did you first take up? Construction worker. I specialized in *tukang besi* (steel fabrication). I was a worker helping build Damansara Jaya housing estate, which was just being opened up then. I earned only RM10 per day. Things were cheap then; a Coke was only 20 sen I think. After three months friends told me I will not progress (*tidak akan maju*) in that job, so I switched to being a carpenter, working with my father. My wage jumped to RM22 per day. I did this for five months, helping construct houses in Taman Tun Dr Ismail, which was also being developed.

I did not have an identity card (IC) then, and so I had to be very careful because illegal workers were hunted by the police (*diburu oleh polis*). I was never arrested though. It was then that I decided to learn about building plans. My next work location was Taman Seraya in Cheras, but this time as a sub-contractor, working with my dad. I was in my early twenties then. From then onwards I was never an *orang makan gaji* (employee) but a sub-contractor [he says this with a glint of pride].

When the economic crisis hit in the mid-1980s it was tough but I maintained my sub-contracting work while diversifying into the fish business. I got a trading licence for a provision shop, bought fish at wholesale prices and sold it at this shop. One day I realized that since I was ferrying my kids to school daily, I might as well make some money from it by ferrying others too. I saw a notice inviting applications for bus licences. The notice stated that permanent residents were eligible too. I applied three times before I got a permit. Now I operate a school bus. So for the last few years I've been doing these three jobs daily, and on weekends I do video recordings for weddings and religious ceremonies.

Do you remember how you first entered Malaysia? The usual route from Bawean to Surabaya by boat, then from Jakarta I took a ship, *Tempoh Mas*, to Tanjung Pinang (Rhiau), off Singapore. [Many Baweanese migrants to Malaysia have travelled from Surabaya to Tanjung Pinang on this ship; some years ago the ship sank and people went down with it.] From Tanjung Pinang I went into Singapore where I lived with my uncle for ten days before taking the train to Malaysia.

What kind of contacts do you maintain with Bawean? I've been back four times since coming here, the first time in 1984, once with the family. In both 1994 and 1997, I was one of the first people to organize group tours to Bawean. The first time a return trip was RM900, the second time RM1,000 per person. There was a good response for both tours. Many people cannot afford to pay a lump sum so I arranged for them to repay in instalments of RM100 a month. Profits were rechannelled to the *Yayasan* Al'amin (Al'amin Foundation), which does welfare work on the island. The foundation receives a lot of support from Baweanese migrants, including those working within Indonesia. Our foundation was a model for channelling money home; now there are many other similar set-ups. On our first trip we helped construct a library in our village of Desa Sukaoneng. On the second trip we fenced up and tiled a school.

Do the villages in Bawean depend a lot on remittances? Bawean used to be a very poor place, but now it's much better because eight out of every ten families have members who have migrated to work in Malaysia or Singapore! Most of them send money back regularly through couriers or relatives. It is very safe; no one ever cheats. We have had to develop our own system because till this day there is no bank on Bawean Island.

Notes (Appendix 5.2)

1. Main interview: 22 June 1998. Subsequent meetings: 6 March 1999, and May 1999.

2. Main interviews: 6, 8 and 14 May 1999. Prior meetings and discussions, including 6 December and 19 December 1998, and March 1999.
3. Life History Interview: 15 May 1999. Meetings: 8 May 1999 and 17 May 1999.
4. Life History Interviews: February 1999.
5. Life History Interview: 30 September 1999.
6. Interviews/Meetings: Early August/September 1999.

Notes (Chapter 5)

1. Defined as "the perpetuation of existing cultural forms, values and ideas". (Jary and Jary 1995, p. 138).
2. *Orang Boyan* is a British corruption of the word Bawean (Abd Rahman and Omar 2007). The *Orang Boyan* were in the past stereotyped as exponents of pre-Islamic Hindu shamanistic practices once prevalent in Java and the island (The Baweanese Corner, 2009).
3. Ten Baweanese community leaders, Group Discussion with author in Kampung Harmonis, Gombak, 14 July 2010.
4. To respect privacy, pseudonyms are used for all informants.
5. The construction sector found it difficult to attract Malaysian workers at the wage rates prevailing during the construction boom of the late 1970s and early 1980s. As a result cheaper immigrant labour, which was paid about RM14–16 per day, compared to RM20–25 for Malaysian Malays and RM25–35 for Malaysian Chinese, was employed during that period (Pillai 1992, p. 10).
6. A 1964 study found that *merantau* was not done individually but was part of a social tradition in Bawean. More than 64 per cent came with friends or *surau* companions, 29 per cent with parents or relatives and only 6 per cent came alone. Interestingly, immigrants were very young then, with 70 per cent emigrating before age twenty and 30 per cent between twenty and thirty years of age. No one in the sample undertook his first *merantau* after the age of thirty (Vredenbregt 1964, p. 122).
7. Other Baweanese moved to Jakarta, Belitung and Bangka (Ali 1996, pp. 4–6).
8. The data in this 1999 survey reconfirmed and reinforced the findings of two earlier studies of the same village, namely a local council survey (MPPJ 1997) and a qualitative study by an academic (Ariffin 1995).
9. In 2010 the Malaysian government announced plans to assist non-citizen children with education (*The Star*, 20 July 2010).
10. In January 2009 there were 32,927 citizenship, 16,812 PR and 93,360 late registrations of birth certificate applications pending, but by early September 2009 a Home Affairs Ministry taskforce had processed more than half these cases (Gabriel 2009). There have also been long-standing allegations of citizenship being traded for political loyalty, initially in Sabah and in recent years in Peninsular Malaysia (Hafiz, 18 May 2011).
11. In a discussion with the author on 19 September 1999, a group of Javanese immigrant settlers said they relied on three sub-identities. They saw themselves as *Orang Jawa* (Javanese) in terms of *suku bangsa* (ethnic sub-group); Indonesian in terms of *warganegara* (citizenship); and also as Malaysians, since they possessed PR.

6

CONCLUSION

HYBRID GROUPS AND HARMONY: LESSONS FROM THE PAST

The acculturation experiences of ethnic minorities covered in this book provide interesting insights into possibilities for improving ethnic relations in Malaysia. Firstly, their experiences demonstrate that Malaysians should not fear acculturation; it is possible to acculturate without being assimilated, without losing one's core religious beliefs, values and identities. These groups freely absorbed elements of language, cuisine, dress, music, performing arts and architecture from the Malay community and from each other. Today the hybrid heritage resulting from such inter-cultural fertilization remains, though the consciousness of its shared elements has been virtually forgotten. This book recalled some shared elements which have made these ethnic minorities an epitome of cross-cultural influences. Secondly, it illustrates the preconditions for acculturation. These include working, living, and schooling together, and the critical importance of Malay as a truly Malaysian language belonging to all communities.

However the experiences of these minorities indicate that acculturation is by itself an important but insufficient factor in fostering inter-ethnic harmony; a sense of belonging is equally essential. In the course of fieldwork for this book I was struck by the fact that despite their long settlement and deep acculturation, some among these minorities feel left out by an ethnic-based political party system where they are inhibited by the lack of a clear-cut identity and numerical strength. Believing that *bumiputeras* gain the most from affirmative action, they harness multiple identities, including an indigenous identity, hoping this will give them greater State cultural recognition and economic opportunity. They see this as an effective way to protect their land and housing, gain better educational, occupational and economic opportunities, and bolster their cultural pride. This yearning for an indigenous identity was an unexpected finding of my research, but it requires some elaboration since it is a recurring theme, with implications for ethnic relations.

YEARNING TO BELONG:
HARNESSING MULTIPLE IDENTITIES

Unlike larger groups with more defined State categories, hybrid groups are able to develop new ethnic routes by drawing upon their multiple identities. All ethnic groups utilize multiple identities, but in a complex multi-ethnic society the pressure to harness such identities is often more intense among minorities, particularly if they perceive marginalization.

At the State level, most of these minorities are classified as "Indian", "Portuguese Eurasian", or "Indonesian" on their birth certificates and identity card computer records. However unlike Malays, Chinese and Indians whose categories are fixed and non-negotiable, for most ethnic minorities discussed in this book these classifications are open to contestation. For example, Indian and Indonesian Muslims can potentially be considered for Malay-*bumiputera* status because of the broad constitutional definition of Malay. Similarly in Malacca the Portuguese Eurasians harnessed their hybrid origins to gain part-recognition as *bumiputeras*, while Peranakan Indians have begun publicly articulating a desire for indigenous status. The exception is Terengganu's Peranakan Chinese, who, though conscious of their long settlement and deep acculturation, have not sought the *bumiputera* route.

These contestations, while revealing the fluid nature of ethnicity, also indicate that ethnic minorities are engaged in a process of "ethnic rerouting", redefining themselves as *bumiputeras*, with various degrees of success. Even at the community and individual levels, these minorities are better able to present and harness multiple identities. This is because their hybridity — embedded in the diverse but shared histories and cultures of Malaysia and the region — confers them numerous identity niches as shown in Table 6.1.

While at first glance these wide choices — to bid for *bumiputera* status at State level and exploit a range of other identities at community and individual level — appear advantageous, in practice it involves a constant struggle to assert minority identities in an ethnic-based political system dominated by larger groups.

At State level the fastest way out of this dilemma is to mobilize for *bumiputera* status, with the enticing prospect of obtaining both an indigenous social identity and State support in one stroke. The State itself by previously granting *bumiputera* status to several minorities has set in motion a process encouraging such ethnic mobilization. In the case of non-Muslim groups a precedent was set by granting *bumiputera* status to the non-Muslim Thais, and later limited *bumiputera* recognition to the Portuguese Eurasians. These moves have also created a tension between identity as defined by the State and that perceived by communities, including those which see themselves as deserving *bumiputera* status.

However *bumiputera* status is not necessarily a long-term solution to the issues confronting acculturated minorities. Resorting to the *"bumiputera* route"*, while appearing helpful in the short run, may in the long term create obstacles to both intra-ethnic and inter-ethnic relations. Within communities it tends to confer proportionately far greater benefits to the wealthy compared to the poor, resulting in intra-ethnic inequality which may manifest itself in social chasms and political conflicts. Between

TABLE 6.1
Multiple Identities of Ethnic Minorities

Indian Muslims	Chitty	Portuguese Eurasian	Peranakan-type Chinese	Baweanese
Muslim	Chitty	Catholic	Chinese	Muslim
Malay	Hindu	Eurasian	Peranakan	Malay
Indian	Indian	Portuguese	Buddhist	Indonesian
Tamil	Tamil	"European"	"Orang Terengganu"	"Orang Boyan"
Overseas Indian	"Chinese"	*Bumiputera*	"China Kampung"	*Bumiputera*
Bumiputera	*Bumiputera*		"Overseas Chinese"	
			"Cheng Ho Chinese"	

Source: Fieldwork, 2009–11.

communities the conferment of exclusive status on some is likely to alienate others who feel left out. Furthermore, it may open the doors to claims from more groups, which could in turn generate misgivings among segments of the still economically marginalized *bumiputera* community, especially its politically significant Malays. Yielding to ethnic pressures and granting additional groups favoured status also deters and detracts from the State's primary development goal of inclusiveness and equity for all communities.

The key problem facing these acculturated ethnic minorities is not their size or their hybrid cultures, but their perceived lack of State-favoured identity and opportunity. It is a paradox that groups with rich histories and cultures deeply implanted in Malaysia's soil should seek social recognition and economic opportunity by yearning for a State-favoured indigenous identity. If accepted as they are in a system where ethnic considerations are less predominant, would they not be better able to be part of the national narrative, revel in their difference and embrace their heritage?

LIVING TOGETHER, APART: ETHNIC POLARIZATION TODAY

The experiences of these acculturated minorities underline the imperative of moving towards more inclusive politics and policies. A worrying trend in Malaysia today is that despite high economic growth rates, ethnic polarization remains an issue. Some have linked this phenomenon to Malaysia's ethnically segregated education system. While its causes are complex, in the Malaysian context polarization has its roots in the ideology of race, and the ethnic-based politics and policies it has fostered.

The British introduced the concept of "race", a term with no equivalent in the Malay language of the region, to ensure conformity and control in colonial Malaya (Farish Noor 2010, p. 61; Sumit Mandal 2004, p. 55). Highly diverse groups were compressed and categorized into three essentialized "racial" groups, leaving some hybrid minorities in a quandary. Vastly varied Nusantara peoples were labelled "Malay", immigrants from China who spoke dialects unintelligible to each other were lumped into "Chinese", while South Asians of different tongues and religions were similarly compressed into "Indians". This notion of "race" was the most powerful British bequest to us. "More than rubber and tin, the legacy of colonialism in Malaya was racial ideology," notes the scholar Charles Hirschman (Hirschman 1986, p. 357).

A key consequence of racial ideology is ethnic-based politics. Today the political party system is largely organized along ethnic lines, with Malay, Chinese and Indian political parties dominating. Given their lack of a clear-cut ethnic identity, many ethnic minorities are either ineligible or reluctant to join these larger and better organized political parties, most of which have Cabinet representation. Due to their smaller numbers most minorities also lack the voting power, economic muscle and organizational capacity to compete with larger ethnic groups in engaging the State and gaining access to opportunities and resources. These factors contribute to a perception of marginalization which makes these minorities — particularly the poor among them — anxious about their future. As the Malaysian scholar Farish Noor puts it, "I think the ones who fall through the cracks, the ones who don't neatly fit into the boxes of 'Malay', 'Chinese' or 'Indian' suffer greatly in this state of racialised politics.... And it's not just with race; it's with religion, too" (Farish A. Noor, quoted in Shah 2009).

Another factor linked to rising ethnic consciousness is State ethnic-based affirmative action policies. In Malaysia the power of the State has been enhanced by its role in providing affirmative action for indigenous groups as enshrined in Article 153 of the Malaysian Constitution. This role is fully justified for historical and economic reasons, and is balanced by clear constitutional provisions guaranteeing the rights of all other citizens. However despite outstanding progress in both ethnic and need-based affirmative action policies which have assisted large segments among all ethnic groups, perceptions of unevenness in policy implementation were still found in this study (Fieldwork 2008–11).

A recent scholarly assessment of forty years of the New Economic Policy (NEP) and affirmative action in Malaysia (1970–2010) confirms similar findings. On the one hand it found impressive poverty reduction and corporate equity growth, though with new intra-ethnic inequities (Gomez, Saravanamuttu, Mohamad, 2012, p. 9). However, it also discovered that since group membership is fluid, heterogeneous and contestable, using ethnicity as a basis for social policy "reinforces group identities", contributes to the "politics of identity", "hinders social cohesion" and "exacerbates ethnic differences". It also creates "persistent debates about rights and identities", many expressed along ethnic lines, as in the case of the Hindu Rights Action Force (Hindraf) demonstrations of 2007 (Gomez, Saravanamuttu, Mohamad, 2012, pp. 4–6, 15, 23).

In the long-term, the researchers argued, it leads to creation of "claimed identities", and perpetuates ethnic over national identity, leading to conflict.

What is required, they propose, is a "new, viable and truly inclusive policy" which considers the impact of new and evolving identities (Gomez, Saravanamuttu, Mohamad, 2012, p. 24).

A recent government-sponsored study also highlights the urgency of strengthening social cohesion through "inclusive policies" which prioritize the poor "irrespective of group membership" (Malaysia, Human Development Report, 2013). Past policies created full employment and reduced absolute poverty and inter-ethnic inequality. However today relative poverty (particularly among *bumiputera* minorities), together with wide intra-ethnic inequalities, threatens social cohesion and can fuel social tensions, it warns. The study suggests these challenges be addressed through decentralized growth involving citizen participation and "bottom-up" strategies, and reforms to tackle wage stagnation, reduce income inequality and encourage women to join the work-force. (See <mhdr.my> for full report.)

EMBRACING DIVERSITY THROUGH MORE INCLUSIVE POLICIES

While State-based affirmative action is clearly still needed to improve opportunities for all, particularly indigenous communities, the challenge is to ensure that its approach and implementation is fair, and seen to be fair. For instance, needs-based economic policies should be ethnically inclusive in both practice and perception; they should not be, or perceived to be, marginalizing Malays and Indian Muslims in Penang where the Chief Minister is Chinese, or side-lining Portuguese Eurasians and the Chitty in Malacca where the Chief Minister is Malay. Given Malaysia's complexities, such approaches demand a high degree of transparency and good governance.

In addition, State assistance should be buttressed by an economic restructuring plan involving an upgrading of investments, technology, skills, productivity and wages, coupled with systematic, targeted, annual reductions of unskilled foreign labour enforced at industry and employer level. A needs-based approach coupled with such economic restructuring can raise the wages of all citizens, including minorities, and will be far more effective in overcoming real or perceived marginalization than a mere change in their ethnic status to *bumiputera*.

Both the ruling Barisan Nasional's Tenth Malaysia Plan and "New Economic Model", and the opposition Pakatan Rakyat's alternative "New Economic Agenda" promise a needs-based approach which downplays ethnicity. In the long run however, such policies may require a shift from the ethnic-based political party system which still dominates both the ruling and opposition coalitions.

The time may be right to begin work towards such a shift. Decades of sustained growth have benefited all communities; in particular State-led educational, employment and entrepreneurial opportunities and the creation of a middle class within the once severely disadvantaged Malay-majority community has reduced a key source of ethnic discontent. Moreover seven out of ten Malaysians today are *bumiputeras*; thus ethnically-blind pro-poor policies will benefit marginalized *bumiputeras* the most.

Two recent independent surveys show that the majority of Malaysians prefer multi-ethnic parties, indicating that the current ethnic-based political party system is out of sync with their sentiments. A 2012 survey found that 70 per cent of Malaysian youths prefer multi-ethnic over ethnic or religious-based parties (Survey of Malaysian Youth Opinion, 2012, The Asia Foundation). In addition a 2015 survey by independent pollster Merdeka Centre reports that 77 per cent of Malaysian voters favour inclusive multi-ethnic parties, a preference which cuts across race, age and the political divide (Malaysian Insider, 16 March 2015).

OVERCOMING FEAR, BUILDING TRUST: INTER-ETHNIC DIALOGUE

However, much groundwork needs to be done before we can begin to transcend racial ideology and ethnic-based politics. Given the widely varying historical and social experiences of Malaysia's diverse multi-ethnic population, there is a need for public education for all groups to better understand and appreciate its Constitution, shared histories and overlapping cultures. There is also a need to initiate inter-religious dialogue to identify and practise common universal spiritual values essential for good governance, family resilience and human happiness.

Such "bridge-building" may seem paradoxical given the current institutionalized race-based politics, ethnically segmented schooling, workplaces and housing, and the sometimes deep-seated ethnic prejudices and stereotypes that still dominate aspects of Malaysian life. But meaningful inter-ethnic and inter-religious dialogue and discussion are the first essential steps in overcoming fear and building trust between communities. Non-political and non-partisan groups should take the lead in such dialogue. Cosmopolitan public intellectuals, religious organizations, citizens groups, schools, universities and the print and electronic media should be fully involved in such efforts, which could include project-based participation and experiential learning. Policy planners and the private sector can also foster interaction and acculturation by creating more culturally diverse workplaces, housing, and higher quality multi-ethnic Bahasa Malaysia-medium schools.

Despite some deficiencies, Malaysia remains in many ways a model multi-ethnic developing nation. It has, through both ethnic and need-based affirmative action, avoided the disastrous paths taken by once equally prosperous multi-ethnic, multi-religious countries such as Sri Lanka and the former Yugoslavia. However, Malaysia is today at a crossroads. While it has made great progress in reducing inter-ethnic economic divisions, it now needs to focus on bridging cultural chasms through inter-ethnic and inter-religious dialogue, in addition to strengthening social cohesion by tackling intra-ethnic inequities.

An essential first step in this direction would be to retrace our shared histories and envision a common future. Retracing our past involves exploring and appreciating our diversity, interaction and acculturation — as attempted in this book. Creating a common future requires understanding, accepting and respecting our different backgrounds and experiences with empathy and compassion, while creating strong inter-ethnic bonds through shared spiritual and cultural values.

Most importantly, we need to strive for a society based on social justice, universal values and the oneness of humankind rather than the colonial burden of race. The impetus and idealism to begin moving in this direction — towards a "*Bangsa* Malaysia" — is manifest in Malaysia's Federal Constitution, its national ideology *Rukunegara,* and the worthy goals of "1Malaysia" and "Vision 2020".

It is a monumental challenge. But with goodwill and a shared commitment, it can be done.

APPENDIX
Towards a Shared Malaysian Destiny

By Professor Shad Saleem Faruqi

This is a slightly revised version of an unpublished paper first presented at a course on Malaysian constitutional law organized by the Attorney-General's Chambers on 30 October 2014. It contains fifteen concrete proposals to improve ethnic harmony in Malayia. The author, a leading Malaysian authority on constitutional law, is Professor Emeritus at UiTM Malaysia. In 1991 he drafted the Maldives constitution. He has also been adviser to Fiji, Timor Leste, Afghanistan, Iraq and Sudan on their constitutional documents.

INTRODUCTION

Despite the obsession with race and religion in public discourse, Malaysia has made many strides towards nationhood since 1957:

- The identification of race with social and economic function has been weakened.
- The vibrant economy has united our disparate racial groups.
- Sabah and Sarawak have given to pluralism a territorial dimension.
- Malaysia has successfully used the economy to create and maintain social harmony. By encouraging entrepreneurship and allowing the minority communities to provide leadership in the economic arena, twin objectives have been achieved: the economy has developed fabulously. Every community has acquired a stake in the country.

NOT ALL IS WELL, HOWEVER

Sadly, since the nineties racial and religious polarization has reached alarming levels. We have become a "nation of strangers". In many corners of the world walls of separation are being dismantled. Sadly, in our society these walls are being fortified. Recently the U.S. Commission on International Religious Freedom, an advisory body of the U.S. Government, placed us on Tier 2 of a Watch List over concerns about limitations in Malaysia on freedom of religion. To this bleak picture two qualifications must be added.

One, some of the racial and religious discord that exists in our society is a natural process of democratic freedoms. As a transforming society opens up, pent up feelings are expressed, often in ways that are deeply hurtful to others.

Second, many of the conflicts between the Muslims and non-Muslims of this country are actually not about Islam versus non-Islamic religions but about a resurgent Eastern society seeking an alternative to the hegemony of "Western" values. For example conservative Malay-Muslim hostility towards gambling, drinking, free sex, drug-laced music concerts, same-sex marriages, homosexuality, a free-wheeling media, over-sexualization of female dressing, separation of religion and morality and extolling of a secular way of life are not reflective of a clash between Islam on the one side and Confucianism, Christianity, Buddhism, Hinduism and other religions on the other. In fact the faithful of all religions are deeply troubled by the hedonistic, sex-laced, media-driven, consumerist culture that permeates modern society. What we are all experiencing is a clash of traditional Eastern values with the moral licentiousness and moral anarchy of Western-dominated modern civilizations.

THERE IS WIDE GAP BETWEEN THE THEORY AND REALITY OF THE CONSTITUTION

If we read about the making of the Constitution, we will see that by far and large the forefathers of our Constitution were animated by a remarkable vision and optimism of a shared destiny among the various peoples of the Peninsula. Pluralism was accepted as a way of life and the unity that was sought was a unity in diversity.

The Constitution, even in its "ethnic provisions", sought to avoid extreme measures and provided for a balance between the interests of the *"Bumiputera"* and *"non-Bumiputera"* communities. Fifty-seven years ago, a pact, an understanding, a "social contract" was forged between the Malays and the non-Malays. In 1963, with the birth of Malaysia, a new pact was drawn up to safeguard the interests of Sabah and Sarawak.

Regrettably the Constitution's "social contracts" of 1957 and 1963 are not being fully observed. The public sector as well as the private sector and all sides of the racial and religious divide are culpable of causing breaches. A few examples may illustrate the point.

Article 153: This Article was about affirmative action for the weak, and not about racial exclusiveness or racial superiority or "ketuanan Melayu". In reality, however, overzealousness prevails. Affirmative action under Article 153 has metamorphosed into something else that is not easily possible to defend under constitutional jurisprudence. In some areas racism has become institutionalized.

Article 11(4): This Article permits State legislatures to enact laws to control or restrict the propogation of any religious doctrine or belief among Muslims. Ten State Assemblies have enacted such laws. Though Article 11(4) is broadly phrased, its primary purpose was to prevent conversion of Malays to Christianity due to the global reach and influence of Christian evangelists. By far and large, Article 11(4)'s restrictions have been observed. But now and then, stories of Muslim apostasy break the calm. Missionary work amongst Muslim children and critically sick Muslim patients in hospitals is not unknown. Bibles are discretely placed in hotel rooms. These proselytizing activities cause disputes now and then. For example in April 2014, the Pahang Malay and Islamic Customs Council (MUIP) barred non-Islamic materials and symbols from the guest rooms and public reading areas of all the 147 hotels in the State. The Malaysian Chinese Association questioned this ban immediately and did not take Article 11(4) into consideration.

Article 152(1)(a): This Article provides that the Malay language shall be the national language and shall be used for all official purposes. However, no person shall be prohibited from using (other than for an official purpose) or from teaching or learning any other language. The Court in *Merdeka University Bhd v Government* [1982] 2 MLJ 243 has distinguished between the right to learn a language and the right to learn *in* a language. This means that under the Constitution there is a protected right to teach and learn a language as a subject but there is no constitutional right that the language be used as a medium of instruction. Vernacular schools are permitted by the Education Act but they are not a constitutional right despite what some political parties represent.

Extremism Has Become Mainstream

In many other areas, the demagogues, the racists and extremists of all communities are preaching their own sectarian interpretation of our "document of destiny" and are fanning fears and suspicions. Extremism has become mainstream and moderation is seen as capitulation to other races and religions and as a betrayal of one's own community.

Within society, extremist race and religious organizations are mushrooming. It will not be proper to call for their ban. They have a right to exist under the Constitution. But the authorities must ensure that (i) other moderate organizations are allowed to exist and function without unfair restrictions and (ii) the law is applied fairly and equally to all and there is no selective prosecution when transgressions of the law take place.

INTER-RELIGIOUS DISPUTES ARE INTENSIFYING

- Around the world, attempts at proselytization often result in violent reactions. Malaysia has mostly been able to avoid religious riots but tensions remain high due to intense competition between Islamic *dakwah* and Christian missionary activities in regions inhabited by the *Orang Asli* and by the natives of Sabah and Sarawak.
- The use of the word "Allah" by West Malaysian Christians has aroused the anger of many Peninsular Muslims. The argument by some West Malaysian Christians that the word "Allah" is central to Christian faith and restrictions on its usage will hinder freedom of religion has not convinced Muslims, most of whom suspect that the new-found veneration for the word Allah in West Malaysian Christian dialogue is an adroit attempt to circumvent the pre-Merdeka restriction contained

in Article 11(4) on propagation of other religions to Muslims. On the other side of the fence is the equally convincing argument that sermons in private places and in books clearly marked "For Christians Only" cannot amount to proselytization of Muslims.

- Some Muslims allege that the constitutional limitation on preaching to Muslims in Article 11(4) is often adroitly evaded or ignored.
- The occassional case of Muslim apostasy causes much tension.
- There are disputes pertaining to the religious status of a deceased. Muslim authorities are known occassionally to seize dead bodies for Muslim burial.
- Recently, Jabatan Agama Islam Selangor (JAIS), in clear disregard of the Constitution and of the sensitivities of Christians, raided a Christian place of worship and seemingly served notice that non-Muslim places of worship are subject to monitoring by Islamic authorities. Earlier, it had raided a Christian place of worship because of the suspicion that proselytization was taking place.
- Recently there was the incredible allegation of a "Christian conspiracy to take over the country".
- There are unedifying and unsolvable problems of custody and conversion of infants when in a non-Muslim marriage, one party converts to Islam.
- There are seemingly irreconcilable jurisdictional disputes between syariah and civil courts (something which is quite common in countries with legal pluralism).
- Islamization of all aspects of life is proceeding at a rapid pace and this is impacting on non-Muslims. Moral policing is resulting in imposition of Islamic values on others.
- The dispute about whether Malaysia is an Islamic or secular state flares up now and then.
- The drive towards implementation of *hudud* is scaring all non-Muslims and many Muslims. Some Muslim groups like ISMA are alleging that non-Muslims have no right to comment on the gathering momentum for *hudud*.
- Many Muslims allege that non-Muslim dominated NGOs raise their voice of concern, and rightly so, in many areas of human rights concern. Regrettably they are thunderously silent when Muslims in Palestine, the Balkans, Afghanistan, Iraq, Syria, Kashmir and Iran are brutalized, demonized and de-humanized.

WHAT, THEN, IS NEEDED TO RESTORE UNITY?

1. Improve constitutional literacy

We need to improve knowledge of the Constitution's glittering generalities, especially its provisions on inter-ethnic relations. The lack of familiarity with the basic charter's provisions is glaring even within the top echelons of the civil service, the police, parliamentarians and politicians. Their constitutional literacy must be improved.

Our secondary schools and universities must have a familiarization course on the basic features of the Constitution and the reasons for the many delicate compromises contained therein. Knowledge of the Constitution is a prerequisite to good citizenship. Such knowledge will also help to moderate extremism and to give appreciation of one of the world's most unique and hitherto successful experiments in peaceful co-existence in a nation of dazzling diversity.

2. We need need to go back to the spirit of 1957

As a nation we are farther apart today than we were fifty-seven years ago. Knowledge of the Constitution's delicate provisions dealing with inter-ethnic and inter-regional relations can help to provide some understanding of the give and take that lay at the basis of our supreme law. If we have to go forward as a united nation, we need to go back to the spirit of moderation, accommodation and compassion that animated the body politic in 1957.

3. We must provide a new statutory, institutional framework for reconciling race and religious conflicts

Conflicts are unavoidable in any vibrant society. What is necessary is to reconcile them with the least friction and to provide appropriate remedies when rights are infringed.

- It is time to consider a new legislative initiative. A National Harmony Act (or a Race and Religious Relations Act or a Maintenance of Religious Harmony Act) should be drafted after wide consultation.
- The National Unity Council should be upgraded to a statutory status (much like the Race Relations Boards of the U.K.) or converted to a statutory Community Mediation Council.
- Perhaps there should also be a statutory Inter-Faith Council whose job should be to foster dialogue over all that unites us and to seek tolerance and compassion towards all that divides us.

- Race relations training should be part of the agenda.
- The Community Mediation Council as well as the Inter-Faith Council could be incorporated into a new National Harmony Act.
- All in all, the new National Harmony Act should have a triple purpose. First, to administer cautions and warnings whenever peace is poisoned by hate speech or actions. Second, to try to bring parties together through education and conciliation. To this end, a Community Mediation Council could be set up. Singapore offers such an example. Third, to impose sanctions as a matter of last resort when conciliation fails. Sanctions, when imposed, need not be custodial. Community-service, injunctions and damages may be better alternatives.

4. We must promote interfaith studies

In schools, colleges and universities, interfaith studies should be encouraged as a step towards understanding, tolerance and unity. Most prejudices are born out of ignorance. With greater knowledge and understanding we learn that it is not differences that cause disunity. It is intolerance of differences that leads to disunity and violence. We have to teach people that the primitive ethic of tribalism, racism or religious exclusiveness has no place in modern society. The circle of life has expanded. We are all brothers and sisters on this big blue marble.

In our homes, classrooms and workplaces we have to teach our wards and brethren that justice is the highest virtue. Justice is impossible unless we try to be objective. Objectivity is impossible unless we are prepared to be subjective from the other person's point of view! This entails that we must consciously try to view the world through the other person's lenses, to step into the shoes of the other, to feel his or her pain. In sum we should, as the Bible says, do unto others as we wish to be done unto us. Or as Prophet Muhammad says: "No man is a true believer unless he desireth for his brother that which he desireth for himself".

I believe that just as religion is a divisive force it can also be a great uniting force for justice. (Refer to Martin Luther King's query to his brother pastors about what Christianity says on racial discrimination). I came across a quotations from Prophet Muhammad which I wish to share with you:

Shall I not inform you of a better act than fasting, alms and prayers? Making peace between one another: enmity and malice tear up heavenly rewards by the roots.

5. Subject to the Article 153 quotas, racial discrimination must be prohibited in both public and private sectors

In both the public and private sectors, ethnicity reigns supreme. We are caught up in a vicious circle. The absence of a Civil Rights Act or a Race Relations Act prevents sanctions against ethnic discrimination that transgresses constitutional provisions. Both sides of the divide are to blame for ignoring the painstaking compromises and the gilt-edged provisions of the Constitution. Lack of legal literacy about the Constitution contributes to the eclipsing of the basic law. For example Article 136 (on non-discrimination in the public services) is obviously ignored. Under the Constitution's Article 153(5), Article 136's equality clause is not overridden by Article 153.

Likewise, non-Chinese applicants to Chinese-dominated private sector enterprises are often asked at interviews: "How good is your Mandarin?"

The prohibition of unconstitutional discrimination must be incorporated into the National Harmony Act. I do not recommend the nomenclature of an Equality Act or a Non-Discrimination Act as these will be viewed by the critics as anti-Malay.

6. Depoliticize implementation of Article 153 programmes

On another note the implementation of Article 153 policies by civil servants and politicians has not worked well. We need an impartial, professional body (like an Affirmative Action Board) to handle this aspect of our social transformation.

Specifically the limits of Article 153 protection seem not to have been complied with. A closer look at the Article reveals that affirmative action is allowed only in areas permitted by the Constitution — positions in the public service; educational scholarships and facilities; places in institutions of higher learning; and permits or licences.

The Article specifically enjoins the King to safeguard "the legitimate interests of other communities". Nothing in Article 153 permits Parliament to restrict business or trade solely to Malays and natives of Sabah and Sarawak. Article 153 does not override Article 136 which requires impartial treatment in the public services. Reading Articles 136 and 153 together, it is apparent that reservations and quotas are permitted at entry point but in the post-entry milieu there should be no ethnic preferences.

An impartial, multi-racial Commission or Board, acting under the directions of the King, can put the Article on an even keel and restore moderation and balance.

7. As fellow-citizens, we must build bridges, not walls

It is time for building ethnic bridges and dismantling walls; for healing and reconciliation; and for developing a vision of unity. I couldn't say it better than Datuk Azlina Aziz (wife of Datuk Seri Nazir Razak). "It is time for engagement, for listening, for cutting the invisible barbed wires that separate 'them' and 'us' and extending a hand over the divide to those who may disagree with your views but have as much of a stake and future in the country as you do."

8. Our educational system must be revamped

An educational system must nurture tolerance, mutual respect and intercultural dialogue. It must bring the learners together, not separate them on grounds of race, religion or language. If young people do not learn together, how will they live together? For a start, the ethnic diversity of school teachers and school principals must be restored, and we should use school sports as a uniting force.

9. The Federal-State division of powers often prevents remedial action

In the light of the recent JAIS raid, it is clear that interfaith and interracial institutions and procedures must exist not only at Federal but also State levels. Perhaps the Conference of Rulers can play a significant role in this area to build bridges of understanding.

10. Declaration on Religious & Racial Harmony

Let us put our heads together to draft such a Declaration, similar to the Rukun Negara. It will act as a polestar for executive and judicial action and will exert normative influence on citizens.

Admittedly a mere declaration will not have the status of law but its existence will provide a yardstick by which to judge executive and legislative actions that impinge on racial and religious interactions. Supplementing the declaration could be a Race and Religious Harmony Commission to provide community mediation to resolve interreligious and interracial disputes.

11. Criminalize hate speech

Hate speech polarizes communities and often leads to violence. Existing provisions in the Penal Code, Communications and Multimedia Act, Printing Presses and Publications Act and the Sedition Act need to be buttressed by a new law.

The new law, to be administered by a Race and Religious Harmony Commission, should adopt a multi-pronged approach. It should aim at community education to remove prejudices born out of ignorance. It should resort to community mediation and only on the failure of mediation should the criminal provisions be invoked.

12. Liberalize *locus standi* requirements to enable wrongdoers to be exposed and made accountable

Equality under the law refers to equal protection under the law as well as equal harassment under the law. Selective prosecution is a violation of our Constitution. There should be vigorous, impartial and speedy invoking of the law whenever race and religious harmony is intentionally breached. The statutory boards proposed above must be given statutory powers to prosecute. Citizens and citizens' groups must be given *locus standi* to raise civil proceedings or private prosecutions. This may require an amendment to Article 145(3) which gives a monopoly to the Attorney-General to raise or discontinue criminal proceedings.

13. Race and religion based political parties must open up to others

Dato' Onn Jaffar was a visionary who sacrificed his political career for this cause. In the 70s the idea of ADMO (Alliance Direct Membership Organization) was revived but didn't go anywhere. The idea of Associate Membership of race and religious parties has been put forward in some States. It is time to allow these ideas to germinate. In this day and age of humanism, it is rather odd to still have race and religious polarisation, and race and religious discrimination (other than affirmative action).

14. We need to learn from others

In many societies — including Singapore, the United Kingdom and the United States — the law is being used to socially engineer a more tolerant society. There is no shame in emulating others and building our garland with flowers from many gardens.

15. We need leadership

Political leaders, media personalities and community chiefs must condemn hate crimes and hate speech immediately, strongly, publicly, and consistently. They must send out a message of tolerance and restraint. It is not enough to ignore the ignorant and the extremists.

Finally, to the young idealists present here I wish to quote Prophet Muhammad: "Four things support the world: the learning of the wise, the justice of the great, the prayers of the good, and the valor of the brave".
Be one of these four. May Allah be with you.

BIBLIOGRAPHY

Abdul Rahman Embong. *State-Led Modernisation and the New Middle-Class in Malaysia*. Basingstoke: Palgrave, 2002.

Abdur-Razzaq, Lubis and Khoo Salma Nasution. "The Port of Penang and the Regional Haji Network". Paper presented at Shared Histories Conference organized by the Penang Heritage Trust and sponsored by Southeast Asian Studies Regional Exchange Program (SEASREP), Penang, Malaysia, 30 July – 3 August 2003.

Ackerman, Susan and Raymond L.M. Lee. *Heaven in Transition: Non-Muslim Religious Innovation and Ethnic Identity in Malaysia*. Kuala Lumpur: Forum, 1990.

Allied Telesis. "Mydin Mohamed Holdings Berhad, Malaysia". *Allied Telesis* 2007 <www.alliedtelesis.sg/media/pdf/mydin_cs.pdf> (accessed 27 February 2010).

Amrith, Sunil S. "Tamil Diasporas Across the Bay of Bengal". *American Historical Review* (2009): 547–72.

Andaya, Barbara and Leonard Andaya. *A History of Malaysia*. Macmillan Asian Histories Series. London: Macmillan, 1982.

Anderson, Benedict. *Imagined Communities: Reflections on the Origin and Spread of Nationalism*. London: Verso, 1991.

Augustine, James F. *Bygone Eurasia: The Life Story of the Eurasians of Malaya*. Kuala Lumpur: Rajiv Printers, 1981.

Azizah Kassim. "Indonesian Immigrant Settlements in Peninsular Malaysia". *Sojourn: Journal of Social Issues in Southeast Asia* 14, no. 1 (2000).

Baginda, Abdullah Malim. "Our Baweanese People". *Intisari* 11, no. 4 (1967).

Balaisegaram M. and S. Pillai. "Looking Beneath the Surface". *Sunday Star*, 29 September 1996.

Banton, Michael. *Ethnic and Racial Consciousness*, 2nd ed. Harlow: Addison Wesley Longman, 1997.

Barnard, Timothy, ed. *Contesting Malayness: Malay Identity Across Boundaries*. Singapore: Singapore University Press, 2004.

Barth, F. *Ethnic Groups and Boundaries*. London: Allen and Unwin, 1969.

"Bashah". Comment on "The Hybrid-Malay Malaysian Dilemma, Interview with Farish Noor". *The Nut Graph*, comment posted on 17 June 2009 <http://www.thenutgraph.com> (accessed 24 June 2009).

Baweanese Corner, The. "Reasons behind the similarity in culture between Baweanese and Malays", 2009 <http://endahvision.blogspot.com/> (accessed 17 July 2010).

Baxter, Alan. *A Grammar of Kristang (Malacca Creole Portuguese)*. Canberra: Pacific Linguistics, 1988.

———. "The Linguistic Reflexes of the Historical Connections between the Malay and Portuguese Language in the Malay World". In "Save Our Portuguese Heritage" conference papers, edited by Gerard Fernandis, 1995.

Beg, M.A.J. *Arabic Loan Words in Malay*. Kuala Lumpur: University of Malaya Press, 1983.

Benmayor, Rina and Andor Skotnes. *International Yearbook of Oral History and Life Stories*. Oxford: Oxford University Press, 1994.

Bernama. "Chinese in Terengganu village losing their Malayness". *The Star*, 1 May 2006.

———. "Forget the Country of Origin, We are Malaysians — Mahathir". Malaysian National News Agency, Bernama.com, 24 December 2009 <http://www.bernama.com/bernama/v5/newsindex.php?id=464233> (accessed 13 January 2010).

Bhabha, H.K. *The Location of Culture*. London: Routledge, 1994.

———. "Cultures in Between". In *Questions of Cultural Identity*, edited by S. Hall and P. Du Gay London: Sage Publications, 1996.

Carstens, Sharon A., ed. *Cultural Identity in Northern Peninsular Malaysia*. Ohio: Ohio University, 1986.

———. *Histories, Cultures, Identities: Studies in Malaysian Chinese Worlds*. Singapore: National University of Singapore Press, 2005.

Carvalho, Martin. "Brief Introduction of the Portuguese Arrival to the Far East and on the Portuguese Settlement in Ujong Pasir, Melaka". In *Festa San Pedro Souvenir Booklet*. Portuguese Settlement Regedor's Panel, 2007.

——— and Chen Pelf Yeen. "Centuries-Old Chitty Village Residents See Red Over High-Rise Project". *The Sunday Star*, 22 November 2009 <http://thestar.com.my/news/story.asp?file=/2009/11/22/nation/5162811&sec=nation> (accessed 5 May 2010).

Cempaka_s Inauguration Booklet. Association of Chetti Melaka (Peranakan Indians), Singapore, 19 January 2008.

Chandra Muzaffar. "Accommodation and Acceptance of Non-Muslim Communities". In *Rights, Religion, and Reform: Enhancing Human Dignity through Spiritual and Moral Transformation*. London and New York: Routledge-Curzon, 2002.

————. *A Plea for Empathy: The Quest for Malaysian Unity.* Kuala Lumpur: Zubedy Ideahouse Sdn Bhd, 2010.

————. *The NEP, Development and Alternative Consciousness.* Penang: Aliran, 1989.

Channel NewsAsia, "Peranakan Festival ends with Chitty Melaka Show". 11 May 2008 <http://www.channelnewsasia.com/palmnews/singaporelocalnews/view/347052/1/.html (accessed 5 May 2010).

Cheah, Bernard. "Residents Call on Govt to Intervene In Portuguese Settlement Land Reclamation Works". *The Sun*, 25 March 2015.

Chin, Grace. "Grand Ancestral Legacy". *The Star* (Section 2, Lifestyle), 10 March 1997.

Clammer, John R. *The Ambiguity of Identity: Ethnicity Maintenance and Change among the Straits Chinese Community of Malaysia and Singapore.* Occasional Paper No. 54. Singapore: Institute of Southeast Asian Studies, 1979.

Cohen, Robin and P. Kennedy. *Global Sociology.* London: Macmillan, 2000.

Columbia Electronic Encyclopaedia, 6th ed. Columbia University Press, 2007 <www.blackwellreference.com/>.

D'Cruz, Percy. "60's trio get set to croon again". *The Star*, 18 October 2002.

————. "Portuguese community keeps tradition aglow". *The Star*, 28 June 2008.

————. "Malacca's Portuguese-Eurasian Community Holds Palm Sunday Procession". *The Star*, 19 March 2008.

David, Maya Khemlani and Caesar Dealwis. "Reasons for Assimilation: Focus on the Indian-Muslims in Kuching, Malaysia". *Migration and Ethnic Themes*, No. 1–2 (2009): 35–48.

David, Maya Khemlani et al. *Ethnic Relations and Nation Building: The Way Forward.* Petaling Jaya: Strategic Information and Research Development Centre, 2010.

de Silva, Patrick. "Culture". Paper presented at the Malacca Story Seminar organised by the Malacca Museum Board, Malacca, Malaysia, 14 January 2003.

————. "Lingo-Cultural aspects of the Malaysian-Portuguese Community". In *Save the Portuguese Community,* compiled by Save Portuguese Community Committee, (Research Division). Malacca: Save Portuguese Community Committee, 19 August 1979.

Department of Statistics, Malaysia. *Yearbook of Statistics 2006.* Putrajaya: Department of Statistics, Malaysia, 2006.

————. *Population Distribution and Basic Demographic Characteristic Report, Population and Housing Census.* Department of Statistics, Malaysia, 2010.

————. Official Portal www.statistics.gov.my/ (accessed 9 May 2014).

Dhoraisingam, Samuel S. *The Peranakan Indians of Singapore and Melaka: Indian Babas and Nyonyas — Chitty Melaka.* Singapore: Institute of Southeast Asian Studies, 2006.

———. "Origin of Peranakan Indians during the Malacca Sultanate". In *Cempaka_s Inauguration Booklet*. Association of Chetti Melaka (Peranakan Indians), Singapore, 19 January 2008, pp. 12–14.

———. "The Peranakan Indians in Portuguese Malacca". In *Cempaka_s Inauguration Booklet*. Association of Chetti Melaka (Peranakan Indians), Singapore, 19 January 2008, pp. 23–25.

———. "The Peranakan Indians in Dutch Malacca". In *Cempaka_s Inauguration Booklet*. Association of Chetti Melaka (Peranakan Indians), Singapore, 19 January 2008, pp. 27–28.

———. "The Peranakan Indians under British Rule in Melaka and Their Migration to Singapore". In *Cempaka_s Inauguration Booklet*. Association of Chetti Melaka (Peranakan Indians), Singapore, 19 January 2008.

Encyclopædia Britannica Online, s.v. "assimilation", <http://www.britannica.com/EBchecked/topic/39328/assimilation> (accessed 24 November 2011).

Endon Salleh. "Wayang Kulit". Infopedia — National Library Board, Singapore, 20 January 1999 <http://infopedia.nl.sg/articles/SIP_193_2004-12-23.html> (accessed 18 June 2010).

Expressindia. "Indian-Muslims in Malaysia want to be called Malays". Expressindia. com, 3 March 2008 <http://www.expressindia.com/latest-news/Indian-Muslims-in-Malaysia-want-to-be-called-Malays/279692/> (accessed 19 June 2008).

Fadzal Mansor, Haji. "My Baweanese People". *Intisari* 11, no. 4 (1967).

Farish A. Noor. *The Other Malaysia: Writings on Malaysia's Subaltern History*. Kuala Lumpur: Silverfish Books, 2003.

———. "Munshi Abdullah bin Kadir and the Predicament of the Modern Colonial Subject". *The Other Malaysia*, 3 November 2006 <http://www.othermalaysia.org/2006/11/03/013-munshi-abdullah-part-i/> (accessed 7 November 2009).

———. *What Your Teacher Didn't Tell You*. The Annex Lectures, vol. 1. Petaling Jaya: Matahari Books, 2009.

——— and Edin Khoo. *Spirit of Wood: The Art of Malay Woodcarving*. Hong Kong: Periplus, 2003.

Fernandis, Gerard. "Save Our Portuguese Heritage". Conference papers, 1995.

———. "Terms of Reference in Determining the Bumiputera Status of the Portuguese Descendants Of Malacca". Paper presented to Select Committee in Support of Bumiputera Status (Undated) in "Save Our Portuguese Heritage" conference papers, 1995.

———. "The Catholic Church and the Portuguese Eurasian Community of Malacca". Paper presented at the Malacca Story Seminar organized by the Malacca Museum Board, Malacca, 14 January 2003.

———. "*Papia Relijand e Tradisang:* The Portuguese Eurasians in Malaysia: *Bumiquest,* A Search for Self-Identity". *Lusotopie* (2000): 261–68.

Ferzacca, Steve. "Learning How to Listen: Keroncong Music in a Javanese Neighborhood". *The Senses and Society* 1, no. 3 (November 2006): 331–58.

Found in Malaysia. Petaling Jaya: ZI Publications, 2010 (Interviews by The Nut Graph).

Fujimoto, Helen. "The South Indian-Muslim Community and the Evolution of the Jawi Peranakan in Penang up to 1948". Monograph of Master's thesis, University of Malaya, 1989.

Gabriel, Paul. "The buzz on the 12th floor". *The Star*, 6 September 2009.

Gellner, Ernest. *Nations and Nationalism*. Oxford: Blackwell, 1983.

Ghai, Yash, ed. *Autonomy and Ethnicity: Negotiating Competing Claims in Multi-Ethnic States*, Cambridge: Cambridge University Press, 2000.

Ghulam-Sarwar, Yousof. "The South Asian Cultural Impact upon Penang". Paper presented at "Indians in Penang", 2nd colloquium of "The Penang Story" organized by Penang Heritage Trust and Malaysian Indian Chamber of Commerce and Industry, Penang, Malaysia, 22 September 2001.

Gibbons, David S. "National Integration and Cultural Diversity: The Case of Malaysia". In *Development in Southeast Asia: Issues and Dilemmas*, edited by S.S. Hsueh, pp. 115–41. Hong Kong: Southeast Asian Social Science Association, 1972.

GM (pseud). "Indian-Muslims long mocked at". Malaysiakini, 23 February 2001 <http://www.malaysiakini.com/letters/7631> (accessed 27 February 2001).

Goh, Beng-Lan. *Modern Dreams: An Inquiry into Power, Cultural Production, and the Cityscape in Contemporary Urban Penang, Malaysia*. Ithaca: Cornell Southeast Asia Program Publications, 2002.

Golomb, Louis. *Brokers of Morality: Thai Ethnic Adaptation in a Rural Malaysian Setting*, Honolulu: University of Hawai'i Press, 1978.

Gomez, Edmund T. *Chinese Business in Malaysia: Accumulation, Ascendance, Accommodation*, Honolulu: University of Hawai'i Press, 1999.

―――, ed. *The State of Malaysia: Ethnicity, Equity and Reform*. London: RoutledgeCurzon, 2004.

―――, ed. *Politics in Malaysia: The Malay Dimension*. London: Routledge, 2007.

―――― and Johan Saravanamuthu, eds. *The New Economic Policy in Malaysia: Affirmative Action, Ethnic Inequalities and Social Justice*. Singapore and Kuala Lumpur: National University of Singapore, SIRD and Institute of Southeast Asian Studies, 2012.

―――, Johan Saravanamuthu and Maznah Mohamad. "Malaysia's New Economic Policy: Resolving Horizontal Inequalities, Creating Inequities?". In *The New Economic Policy in Malaysia: Affirmative Action, Ethnic Inequalities and Social Justice*, edited by Edmund Terence Gomez and Johan Saravanamuthu. Singapore and Kuala Lumpur: National University of Singapore, SIRD and Institute of Southeast Asian Studies, 2012.

Hafiz Yatim. "Project IC' whistleblower: Pakatan States at risk". Malaysiakini, 18 May 2011.

Halimah Mohd Said and Zainab Abdul Majid. *Images of the Jawi Peranakan of Penang: Assimilation of the Jawi Peranakan Community into the Malay Society.* Kuala Lumpur: Universiti Pendidikan Sultan Idris, 2004.

Haslam, Anne. "New Revelation at Bujang Valley". *The Star* (Nation section), 8 March 2010.

Hirschman, Charles. "The Making of Race in Colonial Malaya: Political Economy and Racial Ideology". *Sociological Forum* 1, Issue 2 (Spring 1986): 330–61.

Hokkien Association of Terengganu. *Terengganu Hokkien Huay Kuan: Sixtieth Anniversary (1945–2005).* Souvenir Publication, 2005.

———. "History of Ho Ann Kiong Temple". In *Terengganu Hokkien Huay Kuan Sixtieth Anniversary (1945–2005)*, pp. 30–31. Souvenir Publication, 2005.

———. "Kampung Cina, Kuala Terengganu". In *Terengganu Hokkien Huay Kuan Sixtieth Anniversary (1945–2005)*, p. 62. Souvenir Publication, 2005.

———. "Early Chinese Settlement in Terengganu". In *Terengganu Hokkien Huay Kuan Sixtieth Anniversary (1945–2005)*, p. 63. Souvenir Publication, 2005.

———. "Hokkien Dialect in Terengganu". In *Terengganu Hokkien Huay Kuan Sixtieth Anniversary (1945–2005)*, pp. 65–66. Souvenir Publication, 2005.

———. "Name and Nickname". In *Terengganu Hokkien Huay Kuan Sixtieth Anniversary (1945–2005)*, p. 66. Souvenir Publication, 2005.

———. "English-educated and Malay-educated Terengganu Hokkiens". In *Terengganu Hokkien Huay Kuan Sixtieth Anniversary (1945–2005)*, pp. 67–68. Souvenir Publication, 2005.

———. "The Hokkiens are the pioneers in Terengganu Chinese". In *Terengganu Hokkien Huay Kuan Sixtieth Anniversary (1945–2005)*, p. 68. Souvenir Publication, 2005.

Hugo, Graeme. "Indonesian Labour Migration to Malaysia: Trends and Policy Implications". *Southeast Asian Journal of Social Science* 21, no. 1 (1993).

Hussin Mutalib. *Islam and Ethnicity in Malay Politics.* Singapore: Oxford University Press, 1990.

iGeorge Town Penang. "Habib Jewels", n.d. <http://www.igeorgetownpenang. com/section-3/73-habib-jewels> (accessed 27 February 2010).

"Indian Mee". *Pulau Pinang Magazine* 1, no. 4 (n.d.), p. 46.

Jamilah Ariffin. "Foreign Migrant Labour In Malaysia: A Study of Institutions and Mechanisms at the Local Level". In *Cross-National Labour Migration in Asia and Regional Development Planning: Implications for Local-Level Management.* Nagoya: United Nations Centre for Regional Development, 1995.

Jary, David and Julia Jary. *Collins Dictionary of Sociology,* 2nd ed. Great Britain: Harper Collins Publishers, 1995.

Jeman Sulaiman. "The Rise of Malay Newspapers". Abstract. In List of Publications on the *Jawi Peranakan* newspaper (the first Malay newspaper published in Singapore in 1876), edited by Nor Aishah Binte Mohamed Rashid. 26 November 2008 <http://rpe.nl.sg/Southeast_Asia/31e1f1f8-97b6-46b6-80e6-08f0dc1857d1.aspx> (accessed 1 December 2008).

Jomo, K.S. *Beyond 1990: Considerations for a New National Development Strategy.* Kuala Lumpur: Institute of Advanced Studies, University of Malaya, 1989.

———. "Malaysia's New Economic Policy and National Unity". In *Ethnicity in World Politics,* Special issue of *Third World Quarterly* 11, no. 4 (October 1989).

——— and Wee Chong Hui. *The Political Economy of Malaysian Federalism: Economic Development, Public Policy and Conflict Containment.* Helsinki: World Institute for Development Economics Research, United National University, 2002.

JourneyMalaysia.com. "Hungry Ghost Festival, Malaysia" <http://www.journeymalaysia.com/MCUL_ghost.htm> (accessed 18 June 2010).

———. "Mooncake Festival, Malaysia" <http://www.journeymalaysia.com/MCUL_midautumn.htm> (accessed 18 June 2010).

Kahn, Joel S. *Other Malays: Nationalism and Cosmopolitanism in the Modern Malay World.* Singapore and Copenhagen: Singapore University Press and Nordic Institute of Asian Studies, 2006.

——— and Francis Loh, eds. *Fragmented Vision: Culture and Politics in Contemporary Malaysia.* Sydney: Allen and Unwin, 1992.

Kesavapany, K., A. Mani and P. Ramasamy, eds. *Rising India and Indian Communities in East Asia.* Singapore: Institute of Southeast Asian Studies, 2008.

Kessler, Clive S. *Islam and Politics in a Malay State: Kelantan, 1838–1969.* Ithaca, N.Y.: Cornell University Press, 1978.

Keyes, Charles F., ed. *Ethnic Change.* Seattle: University of Washington Press, 1981.

Khoo Salma Nasution. "Weaving a Tale of Success". *The Star* (Section 2), 27 September 2001*a*.

———. "Indians in Penang". Message in Souvenir Programme, 2nd Colloquium of 'The Penang Story" co-organized by Penang Heritage Trust and Malaysian Indian Chamber of Commerce and Industry, Penang, 22 September 2001*b*.

———. "The Tamil Muslims in Early Penang: Networks for a Global Frontier". In *Straits Muslims: Diasporas of the Northern Passage of the Straits of Malacca,* edited by Wazir Jahan Karim. Penang: Straits G.T., 2009.

Khor, Neil. "Indian-Muslim- In Defence Of Mahathir". Malaysiakini, 29 December 2009 <http://www.malaysiakini.com/news/120703> (accessed 5 January 2010).

Kumpulan Barkath. "About Us". Kumpulan Barkath, n.d. <http://www.barkath.com/about.html>.

Kupusamy, Baradan. "Racial divisions sharper after 50 years". Malaysiakini, 2007 <http://www.malaysiakini.com/opinionsfeatures/71556>.

Lee, Felix George. *The Catholic Church in Malaya.* Kuala Lumpur: Eastern University Press, 1963.

Lee Hock Guan. "Ethnic Relations in Peninsular Malaysia: The Cultural and Economic Dimensions". ISEAS Working Papers on Social and Cultural Issues, no. 1. Singapore: Institute of Southeast Asian Studies, 2000.

Lee Kam Hing and Tan Chee Beng, eds. *The Chinese in Malaysia*. Shah Alam: Oxford University Press, 2000.

Lee, Raymond L.M., ed. "Ethnicity and Ethnic Relations in Malaysia". Monograph series on Southeast Asia. Occasional Paper No. 12. Northern Illinois: Center for Southeast Asian Studies, 1986.

———. "The State, Religious Nationalism and Ethnic Rationalization in Malaysia". *Ethnic and Racial Studies* 13, no. 4 (1990): 482–502.

——— and Susan Ackerman. *Sacred Tensions: Modernity and Religious Transformation in Malaysia*. Columbia: University of Southern Carolina Press, 1997.

Lim Huck Chin and Fernando Jorge. *Malacca: Voices from the Street*. Malaysia: Lim Huck Chin, 2006.

Lim, Teck Ghee. *Peasants and Their Agricultural Economy in Colonial Malaya, 1874–1941*. Kuala Lumpur: Oxford University Press, 1977.

Loh Kok Wah, Francis. "Marginalisation of the Indians in Malaysia: Contesting Explanations and the Search for Alternatives". In *Southeast Asia Over Three Generations: Essays Presented to Benedict Anderson*, edited by James T. Siegel and Audrey R. Kahin. New York: Southeast Asia Program Publications, Cornell University, 2003.

———, ed. *Bridging Bridges, Crossing Boundaries: Everyday Forms of Inter-Ethnic Peace Building in Malaysia*. Jakarta and Kajang: The Ford Foundation, Indonesia and Malaysian Social Science Association, 2010.

Mahathir Mohamad. *The Malay Dilemma*. Kuala Lumpur: Federal Publications, 1981.

———. *The Way Forward: Vision 2020*. Kuala Lumpur: Institute of Strategic and International Studies, 1991.

———. *A Doctor in the House: The Memoirs of Tun Dr Mahathir Mohamad*. Malaysia: MPH Publishing, 2011.

Malaysia Human Development Report. "Redesigning an Inclusive Future". United Nations Development Program, 2015.

Malaysian Insider. "Race-Based Parties Growing More Irrelevant, Survey Shows", 16 March 2015.

Malaysiakini. "Road through Kg Chitty could destroy homes". 6 January 2014.

Mandal, Sumit K. "Transethnic Solidarities, Racialisation and Social Equality". In *The State of Malaysia: Ethnicity, Equity and Reform*, edited by Edmund Terence Gomez. RoutledgeCurzon, 2004.

———. "The National Culture Policy and Contestation over Malaysian Identity". In *Globalization and National Autonomy: The Experience of Malaysia*, edited by Joan M. Nelson, Jacob Meerman and Abdul Rahman Embong, pp. 273–300. *Singapore*: Institute of Southeast Asian Studies, 2008.

Marbeck, Joan Margaret. *Linggu Mai: Mother-Tongue of the Malacca-Portuguese — A Kristang Keepsake*. Portugal: Calouste Gulbenkian Foundation, 2004.

Marginalised TMIM. "Indian-Muslims 'ethnically cleansed'". *Malaysiakini*. 6 March 2008 <http://www.malaysiakini.com/letters/79274> (accessed 22 February 2009).

Mariam Ali. "Ethnic Hinterland: Contested Spaces Between Nations and Ethnicities in the Lives of Baweanese Labour Migrants". PhD thesis, Harvard University, Cambridge, Massachusetts, 1996.

————. "Islam, the Public Sphere and Social Construction of Baweanese Worker's Identity". Paper presented at the Workshop on Migrations in Contemporary Southeast Asia, Institute of Southeast Asian Studies, Singapore, 22–23 January 1998.

Masjid India. "History". Masjid India, n.d. <http://www.masjidindia.com/history.htm> (accessed 22 May 2010).

Mason, Richard and Ariffin S.M. Omar, eds. "The 'Bumiputera Policy': Dynamics and Dilemmas". Special issue of *Kajian Malaysia* 21, no. 1 & 2 (2003).

Matusky, Patricia and Tan Sooi Beng. *The Music of Malaysia: The Classical, Folk and Syncretic Traditions*. United Kingdom: Ashgate Publishing, 2005.

Mearns, David James. *Shiva's Other Children: Religion and Social Identity Amongst Overseas Indians*. New Delhi: Sage Publications, 1995.

"Mellow Yellow Canai". *Pulau Pinang Magazine* 2, no. 1 (n.d.): 38–39.

Meredith, Paul. "Hybridity in the Third Space: Rethinking Bi-cultural Politics in Aotearoa/New Zealand". Paper presented at the Te Oru Rangahau Maori Research and Development Conference, organized by Massey University, New Zealand, 7–9 July 1998.

Metropolitan Museum of Art, The. "Drum model with four frogs, Dongson culture, 300 B.C.–200 A.D.". The Metropolitan Museum of Art <http://www.metmuseum.org/toah/works-of-art/2000.284.57> (accessed 18 June 2010).

Milner, Anthony. *The Malays*. Wiley-Blackwell, 2011.

Miyazaki, Koji. "Javanese-Malay: Between Adaptation and Alienation". *Sojourn: Journal of Social Issues in Southeast Asia* 15, no. 1 (April 2000): 76–99.

Mohamed Alias. "Kuala Berang's glorious past". *Travel Times*, 10 October 2008 <http://history.nst.com.my/Current_News/TravelTimes/article/HeritageCulture/20070319140706/Article/index_html> (accessed 18 June 2010).

Morais, J.V. *Mahathir: A Profile in Courage*. Petaling Jaya: Eastern Universities Press, 1982.

Muhriz, Tunku Abidin. *Roaming Beyond The Fence*. Singapore: Editions Didier Millet, 2013.

Murali R. "Malacca CM Steps In To Solve Chitty Village Row". *The Star*, 1 January 2014.

Musicmall Productions Pte Ltd. "Folk Dance Form: Ronggeng" <http://www. musicmall-asia.com/malaysia/folk/ronggeng.html> (accessed 9 May 2010).

Muzzi, Gerardo Affonso. *The Portuguese in Malay Land*. Malaysia: Geraldo Affonso Muzzi, 2002.

My Malaysia Books. "Chinese celebrations and festivals in Malaysia and Singapore". My Malaysia Books <http://www.mymalaysiabooks.com/malaysia/chinese_ festivals.htm#Cheng_Beng> (accessed 18 June 2010).

MySinchew. "Being a true Malaysian is the greatest wish of my life". 28 September 2009 <www.mysinchew.com/node/29634>.

Nadarajan Raja. "Chitty Seek Bumi Status". *The Star*, 15 March 2011.

Nagata, Judith. "What is a Malay? Situational Selection of Ethnic Identity in a Plural Society". *American Ethnologist* 1, no. 2 (1974): 331–50.

———. *Malaysian Mosaic: Perspectives from a Poly-Ethnic Society*. Vancouver: University of British Columbia, 1979.

———. "In Defense of Ethnic Boundaries: The Changing Myths and Charters of Malay Identity". In *Ethnic Change*, edited by Charles F. Keyes. Seattle: University of Washington Press, 1981.

———. *The Reflowering of Malaysian Islam: Modern Religious Radicals and their Roots*. Vancouver: University of British Columbia Press, 1984.

———. "Religion and Ethnicity among the Indian-Muslims of Malaysia". In *Indian Communities in Southeast Asia*, edited by K.S. Sandhu and A. Mani, pp. 513–39. Singapore: Institute of Southeast Asian Studies, 2006.

Najmudeen, Kader. *Celebrating 50 years of Community Service* (Souvenir Book). Penang: Penang Muslim League, 2007.

Narayanan, Suresh. "Impact of International Migration on Malaysia: The Positive and Negative Aspects". Paper presented at the Asian Regional Conference on Industrial Relations, Japan Institute of Labour, Tokyo, Japan, 10–11 March 1992.

———. "From Malabris to Malaysians: The Untold Story of Malayalees in Penang". Paper presented at The Penang Story International Conference, organized by Penang Heritage Trust and Malaysian Indian Chamber of Commerce and Industry, Penang, Malaysia. 18–21 April 2006.

Narayanasamy, K. "The Melaka Chitty: A Unique Contribution and Addition to the Colourful Heritage of Melaka". Paper presented to Malacca Historic City Tourist Guides Association, Malacca, Malaysia, 24–25 July 2004.

Narinasamy, K. "The Melaka Chitty". In *Melaka: The Transformation of A Malay Capital 1400–1980, vol. 2*, edited by K.S. Sandhu and P. Wheatley. Kuala Lumpur: Oxford University Press, 1983.

National Archives, Malaysia. "Jawi Peranakan Newspaper, 1888", <www.arkib. gov.my/en/suratkhabarjawiperanakan> (accessed 23 April 2012).

New Straits Times. "No Compromise on Citizenship Rules". 20 February 1995.

——. "Panel has proof Cheng Ho visited Kampung Jeram". 1 December 2004.

——. "Poser over Cheng Ho's visit". 10 April 2005.

Newbold, T.J. *Political and Statistical Account of the British Settlements in the Straits of Malacca*. First printed 1839. Kuala Lumpur: Oxford University Press (Oxford in Asia Historical Reprints), 1971.

Nicholas, Colin. *The Orang Asli and the Contest for Resources: Indigenous Politics, Development and Identity in Peninsular Malaysia*. Copenhagen: International Work Group for Indigenous Affairs; and Subang Jaya: Centre for Orang Asli Concerns, 2000.

Nor-Afidah Abd Rahman and Marsita Omar. "The Baweanese (Boyanese)". 2007 <http://infopedia.nl.sg/articles/SIP_1069_2007_06_20.html> (accessed 17 July 2010).

Norani Othman. *Shari'a Law and the Modern Nation-State*. Kuala Lumpur: Sisters in Islam, 1994.

Noriah Mohamed, "The Malay Chetty Creole Language of Malacca: A Historical and Linguistic Perspective". *Journal of the Malaysian Branch of the Royal Asiatic Society (JMBRAS)* 82, pt 1, no. 296 (June 2009): 55–77.

O'Neill, Brian Juan. "Kristang Family Heritage: Preliminary Remarks". In "Save Our Portuguese Heritage" conference papers, edited by Gerard Fernandis, 1995.

Ooi, Jin-Bee. *Land, People and Economy in Malaya*. London: Longman, 1963.

Ozay, Mehmet. *Development in Malaysia: Poverty, Wealth and Trusteeship*. Kuala Lumpur: INSAN, 1986.

Pillai, Patrick. *People on the Move: An Overview of Recent Immigration and Emigration in Malaysia*. Research Paper. Kuala Lumpur: Institute of Strategic and International Studies (Malaysia), 1992.

Pillai, Patrick Noel Anthony. "Indonesian Labour Immigrants in Malaysia: A Case Study of Kampung Sungai Kayu Ara, Selangor, Malaysia". PhD thesis, Institute of Postgraduate Studies, University of Malaya, 2005.

Rahman, A. Shukor. "The Street was Full of Coffins". *New Straits Times*, 28 February 2010.

Rashid, Abdul Aziz. *Foreign Labour in the Malaysian Construction Industry*. Sectoral Activities Programme Working Paper. Geneva: International Labour Organisation, 1995.

——. "Foreign Workers and Labour Segmentation in Malaysia's Construction Industry". *Construction Management and Economics*, Issue 19 (2001): 789–98.

Ratnam, K.J. *Communalism and the Political Process in Malaya*. Kuala Lumpur: University of Malaya, 1965.

Redfield, Robert. *Peasant Society and Culture: An Anthropological Approach to Civilization*. Chicago: University of Chicago Press, 1956.

Rengayah-Knight, Veni. *Foods of my Ancestors: The Best of Peranakan Indian — Chitty Melaka Cuisine*. Singapore: Glenn J. Knight, 2007.

Roff, William R. *The Origins of Malay Nationalism*. New Haven: Yale University Press, 1967.

Sadka, Emily. *The Protected Malay States, 1874–1895*, Kuala Lumpur: University of Malaya Press, 1968.

Sakai, Minako. "Reviving Malayness: Searching for a New Dominant Ethnic Identity". *Inside Indonesia* 78 (April–June 2004) <www.insideindonesia.org/edition-78.../reviving-malayness-2607240>.

Sam Poh Kong Temple Committee. Terengganu Sam Poh Kong Temple Publication (Mandarin) n.d. (Verbal translation by Lua Yik Hor, Chairman, Terengganu Hokkien Association Education Committee).

Sandhu, Kernial Singh. *Indians in Malaya: Some Aspects of their Immigration and Settlement, 1786–1957*. Cambridge: Cambridge University Press, 1969.

Sandhu, K.S. and A. Mani, eds. *Indian Communities in Southeast Asia*. Singapore: Institute of Southeast Asian Studies, 1993.

Saravanamuttu, Johan. "Kelas Menengah dalam Politik Malaysia: Tonjolan Perkauman atau Kepentingan Kelas?" [Middle Class in Malaysian Politics: Communal Manifestation or Class Interests?]. *Journal of Malaysian Studies* 7, nos. 1 and 2 (June and December 1989): 106–26.

———. "Multiculturalisms in Crisis: Reflections from Southeast Asia". In "Malaysia: Crossroads of Diversity in Southeast Asia", *Macalester International* 12 (2003): 3–36.

Sarkissian, Margaret. "The Contribution of Portuguese Culture to Tourism in Malacca". In "Save Our Portuguese Heritage" conference papers, edited by Gerard Fernandis, 1995, pp. 31–39.

———. *Albuquerque's Children. Performing Tradition in Malaysia's Portuguese Settlement*. Chicago: University of Chicago Press, 2000.

———. "Playing Portuguese: Constructing Identity in Malaysia's Portuguese Community". In *Diaspora*, Special Issue on Portugueseness, Migrancy and Diasporicity, vol. 11, no. 2 (Fall 2002).

Sazali M. Noor. "Fire Damages 200-year-old Ho Ann Kiong Temple". *The Star Online*, 23 February 2010 <http://thestar.com.my/news/story.asp?file=/2010/2/23/nation/20100223125714&sec=nation> (accessed 18 June 2010).

Seeni Naina Mohamed. "Indian-Muslims in Penang: Role and Contributions". Paper presented at 2nd Colloquium of "The Penang Story", organized by Penang Heritage Trust and Malaysian Indian Chamber of Commerce and Industry, Penang, Malaysia, 22 September 2001.

Selvarani, P. "Historical Zone Gazetted by Malacca". *New Straits Time*, 23 August 1990.

———. "Joy in togetherness." *New Straits Times*, Life & Times, 2 December 2009.

Shah, Shanon. "The Hybrid-Malay Malaysian Dilemma". The Nut Graph,

11 June 2009 <http://www.thenutgraph.com/the-hybrid-malay-malaysian-dilemma/> (accessed 27 October 2010).

Shamsul A.B. *Debating About Identity in Malaysia: A Discourse Analysis, Two Recent Essays on Identity Formation in Malaysia*. Reprinted from *Tonan Ajia Kenkyu* (South East Asian Studies), Bangi, Universiti Kebangsaan Malaysia, 1997.

──────. "Economic Dimension of Malay Nationalism: Socio-Economic Roots of the New Economic Policy and Its Contemporary Implications". *Developing Economies* 35, no. 3 (1997): 240–61.

────── and Arunajeet Kaur, eds. *Sikhs in Southeast Asia: Negotiating an Identity*. Singapore: Institute of Southeast Asian Studies, 2011.

Shamsul Bahrin, Tunku. "The Indonesians in Malaya, A Study of the Patterns of Migration into Malaya". MA Thesis, Department of Geography, University of Sheffield, 1964.

──────. "The Growth and Distribution of the Indonesian Population in Malaya". *Bijdragen tot de Taal-, Land- en Volkenkunde* 123 (1967): 267–86.

Shankar, Ravi A. *Tamil Muslims in Tamil Nadu, Malaysia and Singapore: Historical Identity, Problems of Adjustment, and Change in the Twentieth Century*. Kuala Lumpur: A. Jayanath, 2001.

Sibert, Anthony. "The Malacca Portuguese Community: The Merdeka Period". Paper presented at the Malacca Story Seminar organized by the Malacca Museum Board. Malacca, Malaysia, 14 January 2003.

Siddique, Sharon and Leo Suryadinata. "Bumiputera and Pribumi: Economic Nationalism (Indiginism) in Malaysia and Indonesia". *Pacific Affairs* 54, no. 4 (1981): 662–87.

Sim, Rita. *Unmistakably Chinese, Genuinely Malaysian*. Kuala Lumpur: The Centre for Strategic Engagement, 2011.

Singh, Jasbir Sarjit and Hena Mukherjee. "Education and National Integration In Malaysia: Stocktaking Thirty Years After Independence". Occasional Paper 3, Institute of Advanced Studies, University of Malaya, 1990.

Singho, Michael. "Reclamation and the Portuguese Settlement". In "Save Our Portuguese Heritage" conference papers, edited by Gerard Fernandis, 1995.

──────. "Portuguese colony sidelined by Melaka Gateway project". Letters Column, *The Sun*, 26 October 2014.

──────. "Portuguese folk sidelined by Melaka Gateway project". Letter to *Malaysiakini* by President, Malacca Portuguese-Eurasian Association, 24 October 2014.

Snodgrass, Donald R. *Inequality and Economic Development in Malaysia*. Kuala Lumpur: Oxford University Press, 1980.

Spaan, Ernst. "Taikongs and Calos: The Role of Middlemen and Brokers in Javanese International Migration". *International Migration Review* 21, no. 1 (Spring 1994).

Sta Maria, Bernard. "Evolution of the Malaysian Portuguese Community". In *Save the Portuguese Community*, compiled by Save Portuguese Community Committee, (Research Division). Malacca: Save Portuguese Community Committee, 19 August 1979.

———. *My People, My Country*. Malacca: The Malacca Portuguese Development Centre Publication, 1982.

———. "The Scope and Dimension of Portuguese Consciousness in the Far East". Paper presented at the Cultural Institute of Macau, 1986. Reprinted in Festa San Juang booklet, published by Tropa de Assunta, Praya Lane, Bandar Hilir, Malacca, 23–25 June, 1990.

Sta Maria, Joseph. *Undi Nos By Di Aki? (Where do we go from here?)*. Malaysia: Sakti Bersatu Enterprises, 1994.

———. "Leadership in the Malacca Portuguese Community towards the Year 2000". Paper presented at the Save Portuguese Community Heritage International Convention, Portuguese Settlement Hall, 19 February 1995. In "Save Our Portuguese Heritage" conference papers, edited by Gerard Fernandis, 1995.

———. "Culture", p. 13, Festa San Pedro, 23–29 June 2011, Portuguese Settlement, Malacca, Programme, published by Pesta San Pedro Organizing Committee, June 2011.

Sta Maria, Rachel. "The Origin of the Portuguese Settlement". Paper, Seminar, *Save the Portuguese Community*, compiled by Save Portuguese Community Committee, (Research Division). Malacca: Save Portuguese Community Committee, 19 August 1979.

Star, The. "Rahim 'No' To Portuguese Reservation". 10 October 1987.

———. "Help for red IC holders to get citizenship". 7 April 2008,

———. "Govt to ensure stateless children get education: DPM". 20 July 2010,

———. "Kimma Becomes Umno Associate Member". 28 August 2010,

———. "Striking a Balance in Foreign Labour". 19 February 2011.

———. "Chitty Seek Bumi Status". 15 March 2011.

Stark, Jan. "Indian-Muslims in Malaysia: Images of Shifting Identities in the Multiethnic State". *Journal of Muslim Minority Affairs* 26, no. 3 (2006): 383–98.

Stenson, Michael. *Class, Race and Colonialism in West Malaysia: The Indian Case.* St. Lucia: Queensland University Press, 1980.

Strauch, Judith. "Multiple Ethnicities in Malaysia: The Shifting Relevance of Alternative Chinese Categories". *Modern Asian Studies* 15, no. 2 (1981): 235–60.

Suhaini Aznam. "What constitutes a Malay?". *Sunday Star*, 11 May 2008.

Suryadinata, Leo, ed. *Peranakan Chinese in a Globalizing Southeast Asia*. Singapore: Chinese Heritage Centre, Nanyang Technological University, and Baba House, National University of Singapore, 2010.

Syed Husin Ali, ed. *Ethnicity, Class and Development: Malaysia.* Kuala Lumpur: Persatuan Sains Sosial Malaysia, 1984.

Tan, Chee Beng. "Acculturation, Assimilation and Integration: The Case of the Chinese". In *Ethnicity, Class and Development Malaysia*, edited by S. Husin Ali, pp. 189–211. Kuala Lumpur: Persatuan Sains Sosial Malaysia, 1984.

————. "Ethnic Relations in Malaysia in Historical and Sociological Perspectives". *Kajian Malaysia* 5, no. 1 (1987): 99–119.

————. *The Baba of Melaka: Culture and Identity of a Chinese Peranakan Community in Malaysia*. Petaling Jaya: Pelanduk Publications, 1988.

————. *Chinese Minority in a Malay State: The Case of Terengganu in Malaysia*. Singapore: Eastern Universities Press, 2002.

————. "Intermarriage and the Chinese Peranakan in Southeast Asia". In *Peranakan Chinese In A Globalizing Southeast Asia*, edited by Leo Suryadinata. Singapore: Chinese Heritage Centre, Nanyang Technological University, and Baba House, National University of Singapore, 2010.

Tan, Sooi Beng, "From Folk to National Popular Music: Recreating Ronggeng in Malaysia". *Journal of Musicological Research* 24, Issue 3 & 4 (October 2005): 287–307.

Tate, Muzafar Desmond. *The Malaysian Indians: History, Problems and Future*. Kuala Lumpur: Strategic Information and Research Development Centre, 2008.

Teo, Kok Seong. *The Peranakan Chinese of Kelantan. A Study of the Culture, Language and Communication of an Assimilated Group in Malaysia*. London: ASEAN Academic Press, 2003.

Thomaz, Luís Filipe F. Reis. *Early Portuguese Malacca*. Macau: Macau Territorial Commission for the Commemorations of the Portuguese Discoveries, Polytechnic Institute of Macau, 2000.

Tugby, Donald. *Cultural Change and Identity: Mandailing Immigrants in West Malaysia*. St. Lucia: University of Queensland Press, 1977.

United Nations Statistics Division. "Demographic and Social Statistics, Indonesia". 2011 <unstats.un.org/unsd/demographic/products/.../population.htm>.

Vasil R.K. *Politics in a Plural Society: A Study of Non-Communal Political Parties in West Malaysia*. Oxford: Oxford University Press, 1971.

Vredenbregt, J. "Bawean Migrations: Some Preliminary Notes". *Anthropologica VI, Bidrajen*. Martinus Nijhoff, 1964.

Wain, Barry. *Malaysian Maverick: Mahathir Mohamad in Turbulent Times*. Basingstoke: Palgrave Macmillan, 2009.

Wake, C. Staniland. "The Asiatic Affinities of the Malay Language". Proceedings of the American Philosophical Society, Vol. 28, no. 132 (January–June 1890): 81–87. Republished in Melayu Online.com on 30 May 2008.

Wang Gungwu. *Community and Nation: China, Southeast Asia and Australia*. Asian Studies Association of Australia/Allen and Unwin, 1992.

————. *Global History and Migrations*. Colorado: Westview Press, 1997.

Wang Ma, Rosey. "Chinese Muslims in Malaysia. History and Development".

Light of Islam. <http://www.islamhk.com/eng/malaysia/ChineseMuslim_in_Malaysia.asp> (accessed 18 June 2010).

Wee, Vivienne. "Material Dependence and Symbolic Independence: The Construction of Malay Ethnicity in Island Riau, Indonesia". In *Ethnic Diversity and the Control of Natural Resources in Southeast Asia*, edited by A. Terry Rambo et al. Ann Arbor: University of Michigan, Center for South and Southeast Asian Studies, 1988.

———. "Melayu, Indigenism and the 'Civilizing Process': Claims and Entitlements in Contested Territories". Hong Kong: Southeast Asia Research Centre, City University of Hong Kong, 2005.

Wikipedia. "Baju Kurung". n.d. <http://en.wikipedia.org/wiki/Baju_Kurung> (accessed 22 February 2008).

———. "Baju Melayu". n.d. <http://en.wikipedia.org/wiki/Baju_melayu> (accessed 22 February 2008).

———. "Nasi Kandar". n.d. <http://en.wikipedia.org/wiki/Nasi_kandar> (accessed 22 February 2008).

———. "Roti Canai". August 2007 <http://en.wikipedia.org/wiki/Roti_canai> (accessed 22 February 2008).

———. "Teh Tarik". December 2009 <http://en.wikipedia.org/wiki/Teh_tarik> (accessed 22 February 2008).

Winzeler, Robert L. *Ethnic Relations in Kelantan: A Study of the Chinese and Thai as Ethnic Minorities in a Malay State*. Singapore: Oxford University Press, 1985.

Wong, Alcoh and Liew, K.B. "Kampung Cina: Chinatown of Kuala Terengganu". eTerengganu.com <http://www.eterengganu.com/chinatown/> (accessed 18 June 2010).

World Population Review. "Indonesia, Population 2014" <worldpopulation review.com>.

Yamamoto, Hiroyuki. "The Muslim Brotherhood Movement among Malay-speaking Muslims in the 1950s". In *Flows and Movements in East Asia*. Kyoto: Center for South-East-Asian Studies, 2004.

Zainah Anwar. *Islamic Revivalism in Malaysia: Dakwah among the Students*. Petaling Jaya: Pelanduk Publications, 1987.

Zarina Daud. "Indian-Muslims want 'Bin' and 'Binti' in Names". *The Star*, 5 May 1994.

Zawawi Ibrahim, ed. *Representation, Identity and Multiculturalism in Sarawak*. Dayak Cultural Foundation, Kuching, and Persatuan Sains Social Malaysia, Kajang, 2008.

GLOSSARY

achi	bride or elder sister
adat	customary sayings, practices and law
adimasam	the sowing season
akhoh	diagonal-shaped Malay cake made of egg, coconut milk and rice flour
ambilak	Portuguese-Eurasian meat or dry fish curry
anak	child/child of
attap	thatch from palm fronds
baba-nyonya	descendants of Chinese immigrants to Malay archipelago between the 15th and 17th centuries. *Baba* is the term for men and *Nyonya* for women. Also referred to as Peranakan Chinese
bahasa melayu	Malay language
baju kurung	loose tunic and sarong worn mostly by Malay girls and women
bangsa	race or people
bangsawan	eclectic urban commercial theatre, evolved from Muslim India; mostly based on royal legends, it developed indigenously in Penang and spread to the region
batik	method of producing coloured designs on textiles; parts of the fabric not intended to be dyed are covered with removable wax; the term is of Javanese origin
belacan	fermented shrimp paste
bomoh	mystic healer
boria	a once religious folk performance unique to Penang, where it arrived in the 19th century via

	the Sepoy Regiment; today it is performed for entertainment
branyo	dance related to Malay *joget*
budu	pickled fish
bumiputera	a term of Sanskrit-origin, meaning "sons of the soil"; it was introduced after the formation of Malaysia in 1963 to encompass both Malays and indigenous communities in the Peninsular, Sabah and Sarawak
cheng beng	All Souls Day, or Qing Ming, a major event in the Chinese calendar
Chitty	anglicized version of Chetti/Shetti, originally denoting trading caste (see Appendix 2.1 for details)
Cina Kampong	village Chinese, particularly Peranakan-types, living in or near Malay villages in Trengganu
cincalo	fermented shrimp relish
cucur	fritters
dabaia kurtu	short kebaya (blouse) worn by younger women
darah keturunan kling	having Indian blood
daun pandan	pandanus leaf
Deepavali	festival of lights
dikir barat	secularized version of *zikir*, involving choral singing with musical accompaniments; two opposing groups sing in call-and-respond pattern; often involves social commentary
dondang sayang	interactive love songs sung in quatrains (four-line poems)
fado	Portuguese urban-folk musical genre
gotong royong	cooperative venture
haj	pilgrimage to Mecca
halal	permissible according to Islamic law
ikan bilis	anchovies
ikan goreng kunyit	turmeric-marinated fried fish
imam	leader of a congregation at prayer in a mosque
Jawi Peranakan	locally-born Muslim with Indian blood; *Jawi* is a term of Arabic origin referring to Southeast Asian Muslims, while *Peranakan* refers to those locally born and acculturated

Jinkly Nona	popular *branyo* song, with origins in mixed-race Portuguese diasporic past
joget	popular rhythmic folk dance, with diverse cultural elements.
kain pelikat	chequered sarongs; it was once imported from Pulicat, an ancient port north of Madras (Chennai)
kain songket	traditional Malay hand-woven silk/cotton fabric, embroidered with gold/silver threads, usually worn during ceremonial occasions
kaka	a popular term referring to Indian Muslims from the Malabar coast
kampung	village; also spelled as *kampong*
kandar	balance
kasot manek-manek	handmade beaded slippers
kavadi	physical burden or offering in Hindu religious sacrifice
kayu gaharu	resin-embedded agar wood; its fragrance and essential oil had great cultural and religious significance in ancient civilizations
kebaya	traditional blouse, often fastened with buttons, pins or brooches; the term is derived from the Arabic word for clothing, and was introduced to the region via the Portuguese language
kebaya kompridu	long *kebaya* (blouse)
kedai mamak	Indian-Muslim shop
keramat	a holy place, considered miraculous; often a tomb, rock, tree
kerongsang	Peranakan-style brooches/pins, often in a set of three, for fastening *kebaya* blouse
keturunan ibu-bapa	parent's ancestry
keturunan India	of Indian descent
Kristang	Christian; also refers to Portuguese Creole
kueh kochi	glutinous rice dumpling filled with a sweet paste, shaped into a small cone, wrapped with banana leaves.
kuih lapis	steamed cake made from rice flour, coconut milk and sugar, with individual layers of various colours
kyai	respected religious teacher
lardeh	Portuguese-Eurasian pepper-based curry

lebai	in India, the British used this term to refer to a trading caste, but in Southeast Asia the term was used more loosely, often referring to a religious cleric
lengkuas	galangal
lian	traditional Chinese posters signifying luck or prosperity
loghat	dialect
loghat tanjong	Penang Malay dialect
lurah	district head or head of a *pondok*
madrasah	Islamic religious school
Maha Sivarathri	Lord Shiva devotions
Mak Yong	traditional Malay dance-drama with roots in Kelantan
mamak	thought to have originated from "mama", a respectful Tamil term for an older man; used in the case of Indian Muslims it can be neutral or negative, depending on context
mamak mee	noodle dish adapted by Indian Muslims to cater to Malays, and now enjoyed by many Malaysians; a fine example of cross-cultural culinary exchange
marakaryars	Coromandel coastal clan of seaborne traders, referred to as Mericans in Malaysia
masjid	mosque
mata kantiga	male-female song duels, akin to *dondang sayang*
mee goreng	fried noodles
mee rebus	blanched noodles
Meggammay	annual devotions to goddess Mariamman
merantau	regional/circular migration
"mereka sayang kita"	they are fond of us/they love us
nanak	term once used to refer to grooms
nasi	rice
nasi kandar	popular Penang dish comprising steamed rice, curries and side dishes
nasi kembuli	traditional rice dish for brides
navuruthri	dedications to Goddess Sakti
orang boyan	Baweanese people; *Boyan* is a British corruption of the word *Bawean*
orang darat	"hinterland" people

orang kampong	"village" people
orang pantai	"coastal" people
pantun	Malay poetry in rhyming quatrains (four-line poems)
parchu	Chitty ancestor worship
parchu buah-buahan	ancestor worship, with fruit offerings
parchu ponggal	ancestor worship the day before the harvest festival
pasembur	a Malaysian Indian Muslim version of Indonesian-Malay *rojak* or salad
perahu	small boat
Peranakan	a Malay word meaning "local-born people"; often refers to an acculturated ethnic minority living in a Malay environment.
Peranakan Indian	Indians who are locally born and acculturated (See Appendix 2.1 for details)
pesantren	Islamic boarding school
pondok	iterally "hut", a collection of huts; also refers to a communal house where newly-arrived Baweanese immigrants from the same area lived together
Ponggal	harvest festival
rantau	area of circular migration
Rawthers (Rowther)	Coromandel inland clan, descendants of horse-traders and cavalrymen, who became urban traders in Tamil Nadu
rebab	violin
rebana	hand-drum used in Malay folk music
regedor	headman (of Portuguese Settlement)
rempah giling	grounded spices
ronggeng	dance where couples exchange verses to music
roti canai	pan-fried flatbread served with curry or dhal
saias	long skirts worn by Portuguese-Eurasian women
sambal	sauce made from chilli and secondary ingredients such as shrimp paste, fish sauce, garlic, ginger or lime
sambal belacan	paste of chillies, sugar and toasted *belacan*
sambal tumis	chilli fried with belacan shrimp paste, onions, garlic and tamarind juice; *tumis* means to sauté (fry lightly/quickly)
sanggul nyonya	tight hair bun with protruding pins

santri	students at a *pesantren,* an Islamic boarding school
sarong	long piece of cloth worn wrapped around the body and tucked at waist or under armpits, traditionally worn in Southeast Asia
sarong kebaya	short blouse over long Malay-style sarong
semutar	head-cloth, often made of batik, common among Malay rural dwellers in the Peninsula's east coast
serai	citronella grass
Serani/Nesrani	Christians/people of Nazareth
sheikh	religious teacher
songkok	local Islamic headgear worn by men
sungai/sg	river
surau	Muslim prayer-house
susu bandung	a concoction of rose syrup, milk and crushed ice
syair	poetry
tabla	hand drum used in traditional South Asian music
taikong	illegal Indonesian labour brokers
tarikat	spiritual path
tau kwa	fried bean curd
teh tarik	"pulled" or "poured" tea
tenawak	gong
tongkangs	small wooden boats
tudung	headscarf
ulama	Islamic scholar, usually engaged in religious instruction
ustaz	Islamic teacher
Varusa Pirapu	Tamil Hindu new year
vibhuti	sacred ash used in religious worship by Hindus
wakaf	religious endowment
wayang kulit	puppet show, derived from Javanese Hindu-Buddhist tradition, performed in the Malay archipelago
zikir	Islamic religious chanting/litanies, involving body language and music

INDEX

Note: Page numbers followed by "n" refer to notes.

ABOUT THE AUTHOR

Patrick Pillai, a sociologist, began his career as a journalist with the *New Straits Times* and was later a researcher at Malaysia's Institute of Strategic and International Studies (ISIS). He studied at University Sains Malaysia, Penang, was a British Council scholar at the London School of Economics and Political Science, and gained his doctorate in Migration Studies from the University of Malaya in 2006. His interests include migration, ethnic studies and the sociology of development.

The 1887 Sivan Temple (*Kuil Baru*) (right), and decorative arch (left) at the entrance of the five-acre Chitty Village in Gajah Berang, outside Malacca town.
Source: All photographs are from the author's collection.

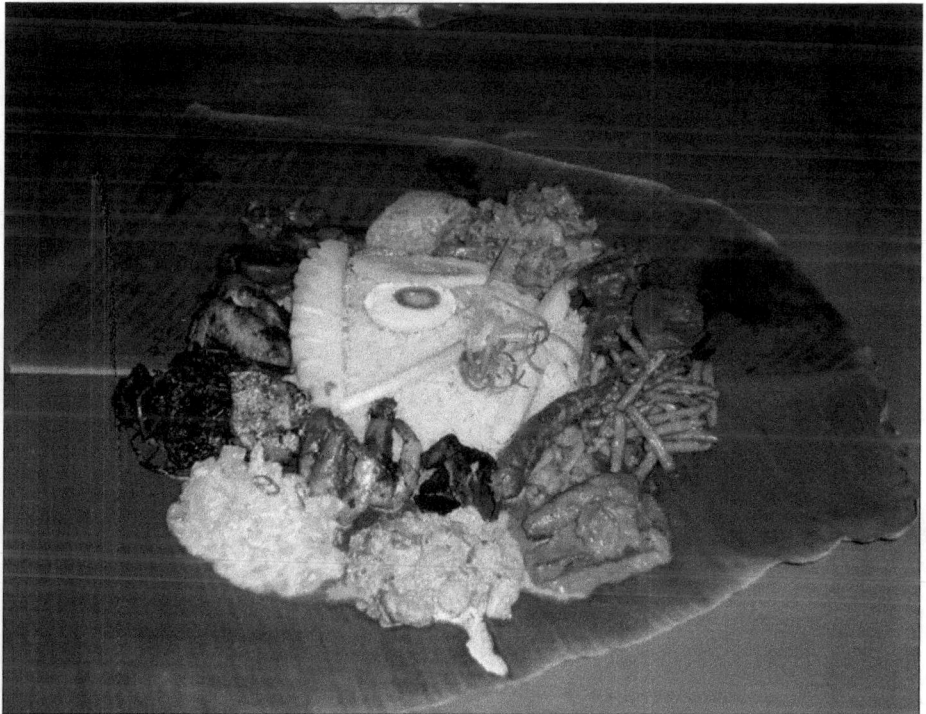

A lavish homemade banana-leaf rice meal in honour of ancestors served during the Parchu Ceremony. It has thirteen side-dishes, including fried and curried chicken, mutton, fish, prawns, vegetables, pineapple and salted egg.

Teaching rituals to the new generation; S.K. Pillay with his son (left) and daughter (right). In the foreground are two red candles, similar to those used by the Hokkien Chinese during prayers.

Traditional cakes, mostly of Peranakan Chinese and Malay origin, offered during Parchu.

The 1781 Sri Poyyatha Vinayagar Moorthi Temple (left, beige and blue) and the 1748 Kampung Kling mosque (right, white) have been harmonious neighbours on Goldsmith Street for over 200 years.

A young Chitty outside the Sri Poyyatha Temple (1781) prepares a brass pot to carry a milk offering (*pal kavadi*) to the village Mariamman Temple (1822) during May devotions to the Goddess Mariamman. This event, called "Meggammay" by the Chitty, has been celebrated for over 200 years.

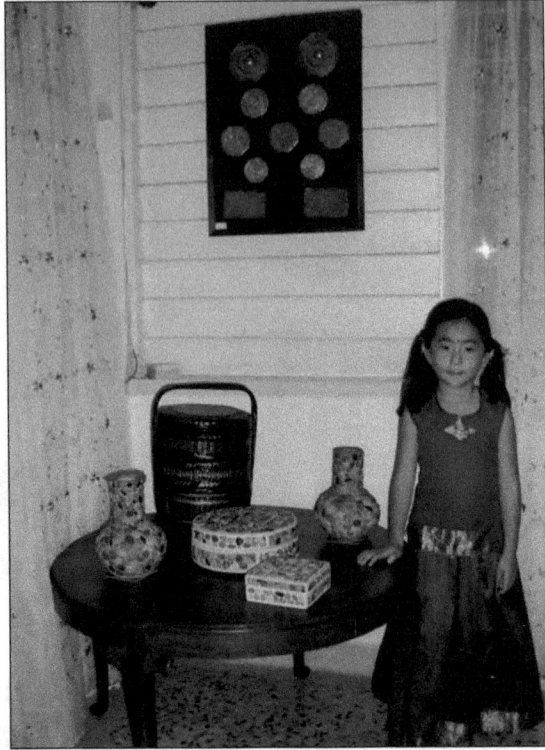

A Chitty girl in traditional Indian clothes at home in the Chitty Village during the Meggammay celebrations. Notice the Peranakan Chinese wedding basket on the table and the wall display of Peranakan Indian jewellery and coins.

A group of Chinese women devotees leaving the Sri Poyyatha Temple (1781) in procession.

An old Chitty woman watches the Meggammay procession. She wears a Malay-style *sarong kebaya*, has Chinese features, but is a Hindu, as indicated by the *vibuti* (sacred ash) on her forehead. The white-washed wall behind her belongs to the 1748 Kampung Kling mosque, which is architecturally eclectic, having Indian, Chinese, Sumatran and European influences. It is located next to the 1781 Sri Poyyatha Temple.

A Chitty man braces himself for the *kavadi* spikes as he prepares for the Meggammay procession.

The chariot bearing the deity of the Goddess Mariamman leaves the 1781 Sri Poyyatha Vinayagar Moorthi Temple, and is seen here juxtaposed against the minaret of the neighbouring 1748 Kampung Kling Mosque.

The chariot bearing the deity of the Goddess Mariamman halts as a mark of respect to the deities of the 1645 Cheng Hoon Teng Temple, located just down the street from the 1781 Sri Poyyatha Vinayagar Moorthi Temple and the 1748 Kampung Kling Mosque.

A Chinese man in prayer as the chariot bearing the deity of the Goddess Mariamman passes by.

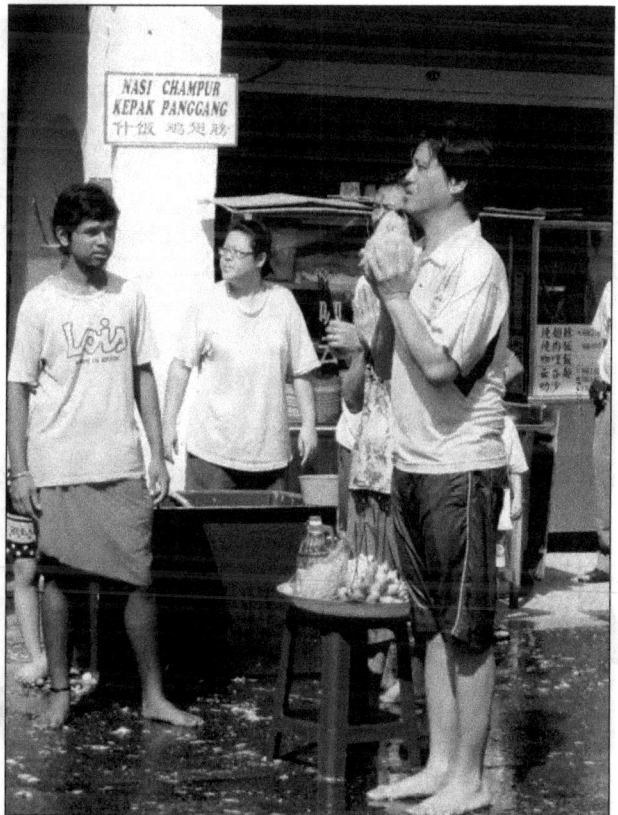

NASI CHAMPUR
KEPAK PANGGANG
什饭 鸡翅膀

A Chinese man with coconut in hand awaits the chariot bearing the deity of the Goddess Mariamman. A Chitty boy watches.

An attentive elderly Chinese man minds the chariot bearing the deity of the Goddess Mariamman. People outside the community not only participate in prayers, but sometimes also assist in the organization of Peranakan Indian festivals.

Thousands, including non-Peranakan Indians, greet the chariot as it arrives in the Mariamman Temple (1822), in the Chitty Village.

A Chitty bridal party arrives. The bride's *kebaya labuh*, which is traditional Peranakan Indian wedding attire, reflects Malay-Indonesian influences.

The groom's relatives in traditional Peranakan Indian attire.

Decorated fishing boats during St Peter's Feast in 2009. Portuguese settlement residents were traditionally fishermen, and St Peter is considered their patron saint. In the background is the state-run Lisbon Hotel, built on reclaimed land.

Members of the Irmoes da igreja, in procession with St Peter's statue. In the background is the Portuguese Square, Dr Mahathir Mohamad's pet project.

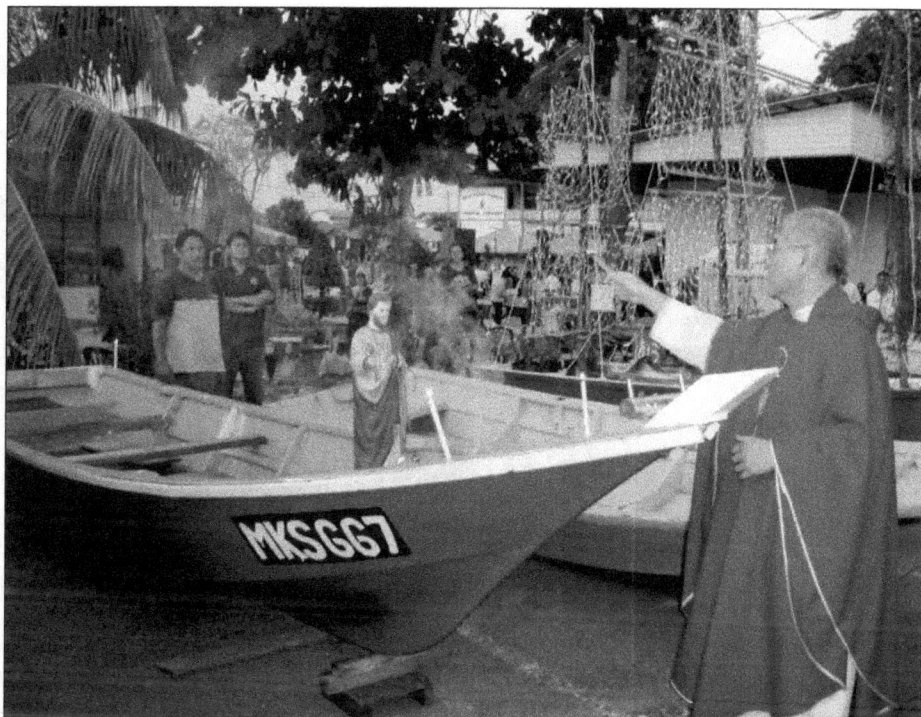

A priest blessing a boat and a statue of St Peter, the patron saint of fishermen.

Mr Noel Felix singing a Portuguese song at the evening cultural show at St Peter's Feast at the Portuguese settlement.

A Portuguese traditional dance performed by girls from the settlement.

Home-made cakes for sale in the settlement. On the left is a Malay speciality, *ketupat palas*, glutinous rice cake wrapped in palm fronds. On the right, curry puffs, an Anglo-Indian influence.

Fishing boats next to the State-run Lisbon Hotel, which was built on reclaimed land at the settlement's seafront.

Former teacher Horace Sta Maria, 90: "Many (Portuguese Eurasian) fishermen just couldn't afford to keep their kids in school; they needed their help at home or with fishing."

Fisherman Napolean Fernandez, 58, repairing his boat: "Even if some of us cannot afford to invest (in ASN), our relatives and friends can, and the community benefits."

A view of the Straits of Malacca from the Portuguese Settlement.

Mr Koo Ong Jin, the head of the Peranakan Chinese in Kampung Tirok, Terengganu. He speaks fluent Malay and enjoys Malay food.

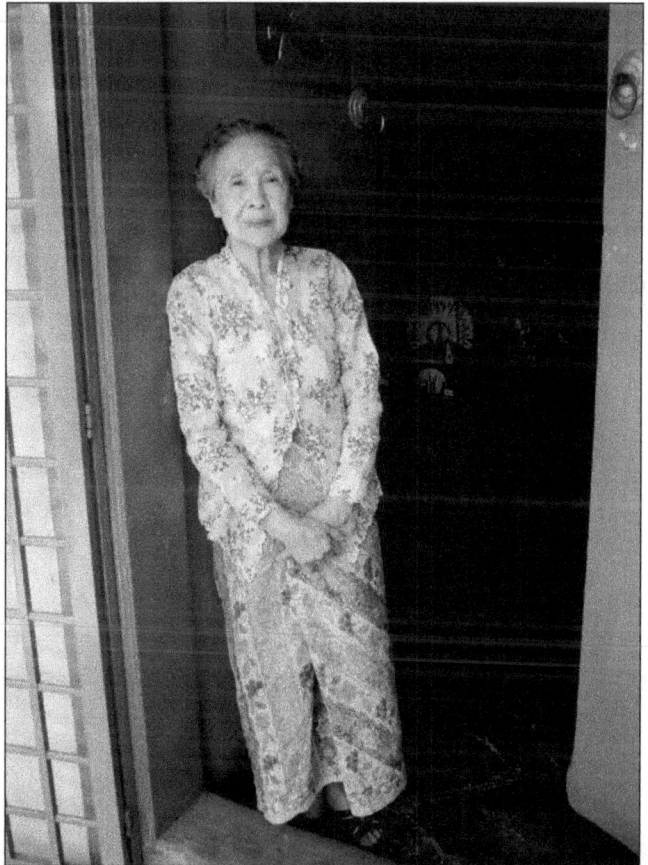

Mrs Wee Kwee Siew, 87, at the entrance of her Peranakan-style house in Kuala Terengganu. On the door is a *Lian* poster with words signifying luck or prosperity, a traditional practice still maintained by the Peranakan Chinese. Her great-grandmother was from Kampung Tirok. It was then a drop-off point for Chinese immigrants and was larger than Kuala Terengganu.

Kampung Tirok villager Chia Ban Hock and wife (top, centre), with daughters and grandchildren at the entrance of their Malay-style wooden home. Note the *Lian* poster on the door. Peranakan Chinese still practise putting up the poster. It acts as a social boundary marker to distinguish Chinese houses in Malay-dominated neighbourhoods.

Another view of Chia Ban Hock's house.

Singapore-educated Mr Tan, 61, at Kampung Tirok during *cheng beng*, when villagers pay respects at the graves of ancestors. He wears a *semutar*, a head-dress made of batik sarong cloth common among Malay peasants in Terengganu and Kelantan.

Three generations — grandparent, parent and child — pay respects to their ancestors during *cheng beng* at Kampong Tirok. Many older folk are Malay-educated, while their grandchildren are Chinese-educated. The three generations communicated with each other in Malay during the ceremony.

A Chinese man enjoys a home-made rolled cigarette after *cheng beng* prayers. Called *rokok daun* (leaf cigarette), it is made from *nipah* leaves and is popular among rural Malays.

A Peranakan-type Chinese woman poses for a photograph after the *cheng beng* ceremonies at Kampung Tirok.

Dumplings (*chang*), cakes and fruits offered during *cheng beng*.

A Peranakan-type Chinese woman in *sarong kebaya* and *semutar* at *cheng beng* prayers.

Tan Eng Hong, a *kain songket* material trader, still operates at the refurbished shop-house of Syarikat Tan Eng Leong (above), which belonged to his "great-great-great grandfather". It is located in the Chinatown area of Kuala Terengganu.

A beautifully preserved old Chinese heritage shop-house in Kuala Terengganu's Chinatown.